GW00643722

Pax Christi was founded in Europe in 1945 as a reconciliation movement bringing together French and Germans after World War II. Today, the movement has 120 Member Organisations active in more than 50 countries worldwide. Pax Christi is a member organisation led movement, comprised of national sections and local groups, all carrying the Pax Christi name, and also of affiliated organisations that work under their own names.

The Catholic Nonviolence Initiative is a project of Pax Christi International, initiated in 2016 to affirm the vision and practice of active nonviolence at the heart of the Catholic Church.

Pax Christi operates as an autonomous Catholic entity in which laypeople, bishops, and other religious members work as equals in pursuit of peace and reconciliation. To learn more about Pax Christi International, please visit our website at paxchristi.net.

Copyright © 2020 Pax Christi International

The content contained herein represents contributions from more than 100 contributors who have given permission for their experiences and ideas to be included.

Published by Pax Christi International, Office of the International Secretariat, Rue du Progrès, 323, B-1030 Brussels, Belgium.

Queries regarding rights and permissions should be addressed to: Catholic Nonviolence Initiative at nonviolence@paxchristi.net

To order individual or bulk copies, visit paxchristi.net

Printed by PODWW, 9 Culley Court, Orton Southgate, Peterborough, PE2 6XD

Manuscript typesetting and design by Olivier Willems.

ISBN:
Subjects: Peace — Religious Aspects — Catholic Church. Nonviolence — Religious Aspects — Catholic Church. International Security — Religious Aspects — Nonviolence, Peacekeeping, Asymmetrical Power. Theology — Biblical Studies — Peace, Nonviolence, Just Peace.

ADVANCING NONVIOLENCE AND JUST PEACE
IN THE CHURCH AND THE WORLD

Biblical, Theological, Ethical, Pastoral and
Strategic Dimensions of Nonviolence

The Catholic Nonviolence Initiative,
a project of Pax Christi International

CONTENTS

PREFACE: WHY "NONVIOLENCE"?

"Advancing Nonviolence and Just Peace in the Church and the World" is the fruit of a global, participatory process facilitated by the Catholic Nonviolence Initiative, a project of Pax Christi International, to deepen Catholic understanding of and commitment to Gospel nonviolence.

As part of these ongoing global conversations, urgent attention has been paid to two critical "signs of the times:" the global crisis of violence with the unspeakable suffering it unleashes and, by the grace of God, the spread of active and powerful nonviolence. Violence is not in accord with human dignity. Rejecting the legitimation, reasoning and actualization of violence, we need a new path – a paradigm shift to full-spectrum nonviolence – to take us into the future.

Nonviolence is critical to the life of the Catholic Church and essential to the work of fostering a culture of peace, disarmament and development. A sustainable culture of peace can only be established by nonviolence that absolutely respects human dignity. Rooted in the interconnectedness of God's creation, it also opens the way to an "integral ecology," as expressed by Pope Francis in *Laudato Si'*. Violence undermines this interconnectedness. Nonviolence sustains it. Nonviolence teaches us to say "no" to an inhuman social order and "yes" to the fullness of life.

This book includes biblical, theological, ethical, pastoral and strategic resources that might serve as a contribution to Catholic thought on nonviolence. It details how:

- Nonviolence is a core Gospel value, constitutive of the life of faith
- Nonviolence is essential to transforming violence and injustice
- Nonviolence is a universal ethic, and
- Nonviolence is a necessary foundation for a culture of peace

1. Nonviolence is a core Gospel value, constitutive of the life of faith

The modern term "nonviolence" names a central dimension of the vision and mission of Jesus: the thorough rejection of violence combined with the power of unconditional love in action.

We know that Jesus consistently practiced nonviolence in a context that was extremely violent, but "nonviolence was not just a response to particular situations in the life of Jesus — it was the whole life of Jesus," as Cardinal Peter Turkson remarked in 2017.[1] Jesus called his disciples to abstain from violence and killing, return good for evil, prophetically stand against injustice, respond to the cry of the poor, foster unity and put sacrificial love into action. The word "nonviolence" comprehensively captures and integrates these and many other dimensions of what being a Christian means. Like justice, peace, mercy and reconciliation, nonviolence is at the core of our identity as Christians and constitutive to our life of faith.

The early Church practiced the nonviolence that Jesus taught and lived. The spirit of Gospel nonviolence has been maintained by particular individuals, communities and movements within the Church, even when the institution itself has wavered in its commitment. Over the past century this tradition of nonviolent Christianity has increasingly re-emerged in Church documents, scripture scholarship, theology, Catholic social teaching and the lived experience of Catholics around the world. Facing the immense violence of our era, we are called to recommit to this core Gospel value, bring it more clearly into the heart of the Church, and invite the Church to spread the power of nonviolence to promote just and sustainable peace globally.

---

1 Cardinal Peter Turkson, University of San Diego, October 7, 2017.

2. Nonviolence is essential to transforming violence and injustice

Nonviolence is vital to dealing with violence and injustice in a meaningful way. In its struggle with violence and injustice, nonviolence typically rejects three traditional strategies: avoidance, accommodation or counter-violence. These approaches generally do not resolve the issue at hand. Instead, they often exacerbate conflict, leading to escalating retaliation or to the domination of one party over the other. In neither case is the root cause of the conflict dealt with and resolved.

Nonviolence engages violence and injustice, not by retreat, accommodation or more violence, but by the power of love in action. It seeks to create the conditions for revealing the truths at stake in the conflict and to foster the possibility for resolution and reconciliation. Violence clouds such a process; abstaining from violence clarifies it. This is rooted in the spiritual power of nonviolence. Love in action seeks to overcome the fear, deception, greed, hatred or the propensity to dominate or destroy that fuel violence and injustice. Nonviolence resolutely but lovingly challenges and resists the violence and injustice of the perpetrator while, at the same time, maintaining steadfast regard for the opponent as a human being. This often requires courage, creativity, community, mercy and relentless persistence.

Jesus revealed this nonviolent dynamic throughout his life in many ways, including when he peacefully intervened as men threatened a woman accused of adultery (John 8: 1-11); defied a Sabbath law to heal a man with a withered hand (Mark 3: 1-6); confronted the powerful at the Temple and purified it (John 2: 13-22); and commanded Peter to put down his sword in the Garden of Gethsemani (Matthew 26: 52). This commitment to nonviolence is formed of compassion and nourished by the Eucharist, enabling a nonviolent encounter with the broken heart of God. Through God we discover and apply concrete ways to embrace nonviolence as a core teaching of our faith; to resist violence without violence; to put the power of love into action; and to develop the virtue of nonviolent peacemaking.

3. Nonviolence is a universal ethic

Our God of unconditional, self-giving love calls all humanity to the way of primordial nonviolence. In addition to being a practical method for confronting violence and fostering justice without violence, nonviolence is a paradigm of the fullness of life that reaches into all the dimensions of the Church and the world. As Bishop Robert McElroy stated, "We need to mainstream nonviolence in the Church. We need to move it from the margins of Catholic thought to the center. Nonviolence is a spirituality, a lifestyle, a program of societal action and a universal ethic."[2]

As a universal ethic, nonviolence offers the Church a theological, pastoral and strategic foundation for addressing innumerable forms of violence and injustice. Nonviolence is personal, interpersonal and social-structural. It includes nonviolent strategies, nonviolent resistance and nonviolent action for social change — but also everyday techniques and practices, including nonviolent communication, compassionate listening, restorative justice, peace circles, peaceful parenting, trauma healing, anti-racism training and nonviolent community-building for personal and interpersonal transformation.

4. Nonviolence is a necessary foundation for a culture of peace

The universal ethic of nonviolence provides a clear lens for confronting a culture of violence and an essential grounding for a culture of peace, disarmament

---

2 Bishop Robert McElroy, comments at "Path of Nonviolence: Toward a Culture of Peace," Vatican seminar, Dicastery for Promoting Integral Human Development, April 5, 2019.

and development. Nonviolence can make a genuine culture of peace possible by rooting it in a principled stand against violence and in the creativity and transformative power of love. Concretely, this includes spreading the tools for nonviolent change and engaging in struggles for justice.

Nonviolence strengthens a culture of peace by helping it to resist the temptation to establish peace through violence. The peace of the Roman Empire and its many descendants, established and maintained through violence, is not the peace of Jesus.[3] Peace is a core Christian value, found in many places in the Gospel and throughout the Christian tradition, and the goal of nonviolence is peace in its fullest sense. The principles, methods and universal ethic of nonviolence, with its clear stance against violence, is essential to creating a true culture of peace.

A culture of peace will be most authentic when it integrates the vision, principles, formation, strategies and tactics of nonviolence at its heart. This nonviolent core will encourage the residents of a culture of peace to acknowledge their own violence; to let go of their belief in violence; to join movements resisting injustice and fostering nonviolent change; and to build nonviolent structures and options.

A sustainable culture of peace, disarmament and development cannot be established or maintained by violence. Nor by passivity. Nonviolence is broader than pacifism or only the refusal to do harm. It is, instead, a courageous way of life actively challenging violence with love. Nonviolence — a core value of the Gospel; our calling as Christians; a toolbox for change; and a universal ethic — is foundational to the long-term work of struggling for and building a true culture of peace in the world.

Nonviolence is a paradigm of the fullness of life with which we are called to respond to monumental contemporary challenges, from the destruction of the Amazon to

---

3 Cardinal Peter Turkson, "Christian Nonviolence and Just Peace," keynote address, University of San Diego (USA), October 7, 2017.

the threat of nuclear weapons; from the systemic oppression of migrants to the unspeakable suffering caused by human trafficking; from the violence of rampant poverty to the catastrophe of war. Nonviolence is a theological and practical framework that cuts across these and many other forms of violence.

We seek to live nonviolently because that is the way God calls us to live, no matter the outcome. At the same time, the way of nonviolence can often create possibilities for ending violence and for nurturing the seeds of a culture of peace. Nonviolent engagement in contexts of enormous violence and injustice throughout the world has revealed the practical power of active nonviolence.

The Church can become a global leader and model of nonviolence, helping the world to shift from a paradigm of perpetual violence to a paradigm rooted in active nonviolence. In its first three centuries, the Church publicly practised the nonviolence that Jesus taught and lived, but too often as time went on, the Church itself perpetrated or failed to prevent egregious violence. Now, the Church can renew the roots of Gospel nonviolence in its institutional life and mission and in Catholic communities everywhere.

This text explores key dimensions of nonviolence, inviting the Church to:

- *Illuminate and embrace anew the biblical foundations of nonviolence in the Hebrew Bible and the Christian scriptures;*

- *Recover and elucidate the contribution of nonviolence to classical themes of Christian theology, including creation, anthropology, Christology, pneumatology, and ecclesiology;*

- *Highlight the development of Church teaching on nonviolence as evidenced in Church documents and papal and episcopal statements over the past half-century;*

- *Articulate a new moral framework based on active nonviolence and just peace that will enable the language of the institutional Church as a moral authority to be more consistent with the nonviolent creativity of the Gospel and its transformative initiatives which break the vicious cycles of violence;*

- *Encourage Catholics worldwide to study nonviolence and to engage energetically in the development of more effective nonviolent practices for protecting vulnerable communities, preventing violent conflict, transforming structures of violence, and promoting cultures of integral peace inside and outside the Church;*

- *Integrate Gospel nonviolence explicitly throughout the life and work of the Church, including in its preaching, education, formation and ministries at every level of the institution: its dioceses, parishes, agencies, schools, universities, seminaries, religious orders, and voluntary associations;*

- *Call on the world to develop comprehensive nonviolent approaches to the monumental challenges of our time, including war, nuclear weapons, the arms trade, poverty, economic inequality, racism, sexism, climate change and environmental destruction; and*

- *Learn from and partner with the world's religions to spread and activate nonviolence for peace and justice between religious communities and throughout the world.*

For the Church, alleviating human suffering is not a pretext, but a moral duty. As Christians we must not "stand idly by the blood of a neighbor" (Leviticus 19:16). We have a duty to protect the life of our neighbor with every tool of nonviolence available to us. In the same way, we have a duty to prevent violence, preserve just peace, and promote reconciliation.

Pope Francis has placed special value on the spiritual and practical power of active nonviolence to promote integral human development and cultures of peace, including through the 2017 World Day of Peace message on "Nonviolence: A Style of Politics for Peace," where he proclaimed: "To be true followers of Jesus today... includes embracing his teaching about nonviolence."

In a violent world, nonviolence nurtures hope. Actively embracing the way of nonviolence can renew the Church and invite the entire world to discover the powerful hope of creative nonviolent solutions to the monumental challenges of our time.[4]

---

4 Adapted from a statement from the "Path of Nonviolence: Towards a culture of peace" workshop, sponsored by Pax Christi International and held at Dicastery for Promoting Integral Human Development in Rome (4-5 April 2019).

Acknowledgements

The Catholic Nonviolence Initiative (CNI), a project of Pax Christi International, is grateful for all the ways the Catholic Church is increasingly reaffirming Gospel nonviolence. This nonviolence initiative is at the service of the Church in supporting this powerful and timely process and has produced the present document as a resource for Catholic social teaching on nonviolence. This is not the last word on this subject, but a contribution to a global process of advancing nonviolence in the Church and the world.

In addition, the editorial team wishes to thank Cardinal Peter Turkson and his colleagues at the Dicastery for Promoting Integral Human Development. We are indebted to Muriel Gella, Aurélie Marrane, Anne Marsaleix, Xavière Quillien, Rocío Peñaranda Llanos and Fr. Joe Nangle, OFM, for their facility with translations; to Michael Duggan for the gift of his proofreading; and to Olivier Willems for layout and design. We particularly are grateful to Sr. Teresia Wamuyu Wachira, IBVM, and Bishop Marc Stenger, co-presidents of Pax Christi International, and Greet Vanaerschot, secretary-general of Pax Christi International.

Rose Marie Berger, *Sojourners* magazine
Ken Butigan, DePaul University and Pace e Bene Nonviolence Service
Judy Coode, project coordinator, Catholic Nonviolence Initiative
Marie Dennis, senior advisor, Pax Christi International

PART I: RETURNING TO NONVIOLENCE

"I grew up under the brutal dictatorship of Idi Amin. After my high school seminary education, I decided to join the 'liberation war' to fight Idi Amin. It was only by God's grace that I was saved from this lie of liberation through violence. The 'liberation war' ended, but then the liberators soon became dictators and we needed another 'liberation war' to get rid of the 'liberators'. This is a story that is repeated all over Africa. It is a lie. Violence does not end violence - it only creates endless cycles of violence. Nonviolence is a calling, not simply because it 'works' but because it is the way of God. That is the way that God creates, governs and redeems the universe. As Munzihirwa reminded the people of Bukavu before he was assassinated, every Christian is invited to 'enter' the way of Christ — 'God's self-sacrificing love.' Or as Kataliko, his successor, reminded the Christians about the logic of Gospel, 'the only response to evil (violence) is an excess of love.'"

Fr. Emmanuel Katongole, Uganda

"Nonviolence is the solution to the protracted conflicts which have resulted in the loss of meaning to the preciousness of life and subjected many people to live in dehumanising conditions. However, many people working for peace do not have a deeper knowledge of the practice of nonviolence. The Catholic Church is connected with people all over the world. Therefore, the Church can be a good channel of active nonviolence. Jesus is an icon of nonviolence. If active nonviolence is taught at all levels, then it will become a language that can overcome the violence experienced in many parts of the world."

Ms. Elizabeth Kanini Kimau, Kenya

"War is the mother of ignorance, isolation and poverty. Please tell the world there is no such thing as a just war. I say this as a daughter of war. We can't respond to violence with worse violence ... It's like a dragon with seven heads. You cut one and two others come up. ... We women don't speak a lot about violence and nonviolence in Iraq but we try to create an environment of nonviolence."

Sr. Nazik Matty, Iraq

"In my Catholic country, our nuns and priests joined the guerrillas because of the just war paradigm. The Catholic paramilitaries pray to the Virgin before slaughtering people because of the just war paradigm ... We faced radical opposition when we were working in the Magdalena region for 14 years. Our purpose was to accompany the regional communities in a programme of development and peace in the middle of the conflict. I am certain that because of the generosity of my companions, women and men, and due to the way they devoted themselves to protect life and dignity in extreme difficulties, the Magdalena process became a reference [point] in the construction of structural peace."

Fr. Francisco De Roux, Colombia

"We need a clear message from the Church — from the pope to the grassroots — that the Church stands for nonviolence. We want an encyclical ... The weapon of the Church is love. The Church is a mother and has a strong weapon: Love for everybody. In South Sudan, the Church has been with all the people but never ever advocated for weapons. ... The Church has to be a place where there are no guns, and no fear. Whenever I am asked to turn over my weapons [at a checkpoint], I say: 'My Lord has already come and taken them all away.'"

Bishop Paride Taban, South Sudan

1. Introduction

Jesus lived and proclaimed the universal ethic of nonviolence: a paradigm of the fullness of life rejecting violence and killing, returning good for evil, healing divisions, and putting sacrificial love into action for a just, peaceful, sustainable and reconciled world. Increasingly, the Church is re-affirming the centrality of nonviolence to its life and mission — and to the life of all peoples.

Nonviolence is an orientation and a set of practices for clearly standing against all forms of violence. As a comprehensive ethic, as a foundational principle of the spiritual journey, and as a means of healing and transforming the world, nonviolence provides a powerful direction for the life and work of the Church.

Returning to Gospel Nonviolence

A growing number of papal and episcopal statements have illuminated how nonviolence is a core value of the Gospel. An expanding body of theological research and biblical exegesis over the past half century has also made this point. Nonviolence education, formation and pastoral practices have begun to take root in the Church. Perhaps most significant of all, Catholics throughout the world — alongside many others from a wide range of religious, social and cultural contexts — have been consciously living the nonviolent life as a spiritual journey and as a courageous witness for justice, peace and reconciliation, often in environments of extreme violence.

This growing leadership of the magisterium, theological and scriptural research, ecclesial programming and prophetic faithfulness point to the rediscovery of the central place of nonviolence in the life and mission of Jesus and, thus, in the life and mission of the Church.

Nonviolence is a way of life, a spirituality, and a method for preventing or stopping violence without using violence, while also fostering just and peaceful alternatives.[5] It is broader than pacifism or only the refusal to do harm. It is an active force for peace, justice and reconciliation. It calls us to acknowledge our own violence and to grapple with it; to grow beyond a belief in violence; to stand against violence and to risk the consequences for doing so; to break the cycles of retaliatory violence; to pursue nonviolent options and justice for all with humility, compassion, determination and vulnerability; and to put nonviolent power and potential into practice in our lives and our world.

We live nonviolently because that is the way God wants us to live. The results are in God's hands. At the same time, the way of nonviolence — in our lives, our Church and our world — can open powerful and creative opportunities for ending violence and for nurturing the seeds of a culture of peace — not a peace based on weapons, like the peace of the Roman Empire, but the nonviolent peace of Jesus.[6] A sustainable culture of peace cannot be established or maintained by violence. As Pope Francis says in *Laudato Si'*, a true culture of peace is rooted

---

5 The word "nonviolence", while it has a long history in other traditions, is a relatively new term in Christianity. Increasingly, however, theologians, Church leadership, and Christians in many parts of the world have come to see that this word most effectively characterises Jesus's way — a way that combines both an unmistakable rejection of violence and the power of love and truth in action for justice, peace and integrity of creation. Nonviolence is a paradigm of the fullness of life, which its etymological roots shine light on. Nonviolence is the English translation of the Sanskrit term "ahimsa" (literally "non-violence"). Gandhi drew on this ancient term to convey his powerful, active, and deeply grounded approach. As nonviolence scholar Michael Nagler writes, "In Sanskrit abstract nouns often name a fundamental positive quality indirectly, by negating its opposite. Thus courage is conveyed by 'abhaya', which literally means 'non-fear'; or we encounter 'akrodha', 'non-anger', for 'kindness', and the Buddha's 'avera', 'non-hatred', meaning 'love'. The reason ancient India's great thinkers expressed themselves in this apparently oblique way is that phenomena such as love, absolute courage, and compassion are primordial things that cannot be fully expressed in fallible, conditioned human language…. 'Ahimsa' is not really a negative term … 'Ahimsa' suggests something profoundly positive, which would not be possible to name directly. 'Ahimsa', a kind of double negative, actually stands for something so original that we cannot quite capture it with our weak words." (Michael Nagler, *The Search for a Nonviolent Future* [Inner Ocean Publishing, 2004]). "Nonviolence" can be further illuminated by reflecting on an analogous word: "non-dualism". "Non-dualism" means absolute unity. At the same time, it clearly highlights that which undermines this unity: dualism, binaries, the division of reality into opposites. Non-dualism is thus not a negative term. It is a positive word that helps us conceptualise what "unity" means. So, too, with nonviolence. Nonviolence is a kind of double negative that signifies the comprehensiveness of love in action but also clearly names the reality that undermines that fullness: violence.

6 October 7, 2017. Cardinal Peter Turkson, "Christian Nonviolence and Just Peace, " keynote address, University of San Diego (USA), October 7, 2017.

in the interconnectedness of God's creation, what the pope calls an "integral ecology".[7] Violence undermines this interconnectedness. Nonviolence sustains it.

To affirm nonviolence as a foundation of our tradition is a path of spiritual faithfulness but also a crucial gift to our planet besieged by intractable violence. The world is awash in violence and the unspeakable suffering it unleashes in the lives of people everywhere. Violence is not only specific acts of cruelty but also the global systems of domination that destroy and diminish humans and non-humans alike. Violence is personal and interpersonal; it is also structural and systemic, including the violence of poverty, racism, gender violence, war and preparations for war, systems of oppression, and the relentless destruction of our common home, planet Earth. Our very humanity hinges on responding to the reality of violence in its almost unfathomable comprehensiveness. Nonviolence offers us a powerful way to do this. It opens the space for life-giving alternatives; trains us for active love and healing rather than for fear and killing; and becomes a sign and channel of God's nonviolent love for the Church and the world. With nonviolence, transformation and healing are possible and creative options can appear.

To deepen and expand the Church's vision and practical commitment to nonviolence could encourage a world mired in violence to consider more seriously the potential for nonviolent action to address the tremendous challenges that confront our planet. By explicitly embracing nonviolence, the Church could also take a powerful step towards challenging the moral legitimacy by which all forms of violence are excused and encouraged.

---

7 Ibid.

Growing Momentum for Nonviolence in the Church

The Vatican has co-sponsored two important gatherings advancing nonviolence. From 11-13 April 2016, the Holy See's Pontifical Council for Justice and Peace (now the Dicastery for Promoting Integral Human Development) and Pax Christi International co-led a landmark conference at the Vatican entitled "Nonviolence and Just Peace". From 4-5 April 2019, the Dicastery for Promoting Integral Human Development and Pax Christi International's Catholic Nonviolence Initiative co-sponsored a follow-up gathering entitled "Path of Nonviolence: Towards a Culture of Peace."

The 2016 conference brought together participants from around the world who represented a broad spectrum of Church experience in creative nonviolence and peacebuilding to contribute to a renewed Catholic understanding of nonviolence. Central to the conversation were voices of people living in the midst of horrific violence. Together, they wrote *An Appeal to the Catholic Church to Recommit to the Centrality of Gospel Nonviolence*, which called on Pope Francis to consider writing an encyclical on nonviolence and just peace, and made a series of recommendations for integrating nonviolence throughout the Church.

In the wake of this gathering, Pax Christi International launched the global Catholic Nonviolence Initiative, which has played an important role in moving these possibilities forward and has seen many developments over its first three years. Pope Francis's 2017 World Day of Peace message was the first ever on nonviolence ("Nonviolence: A Style of Politics for Peace"), a theme that was proposed by conference participants. Many regional and local conferences on nonviolence have been held around the world, including at a series of Catholic universities. Curricula and publications promoting the way and methods of nonviolence have been produced. And since the 2016 conference, Pope Francis has energetically called for nonviolence throughout the world in many statements and interviews.

Beginning in 2017 the Catholic Nonviolence Initiative organised an international popular process of discussion, discernment and research on key themes related to nonviolence and just peace, involving theologians, academics, peacemakers and some Church leadership. The purpose of this process, encouraged by Vatican officials, was to gather and produce material that could be a resource to support an expansion of Church teaching on Gospel nonviolence. The present volume is the result of this collaborative project.

In this three-year effort, the Catholic Nonviolence Initiative explored a systematic theology and a careful scriptural exegesis of nonviolence. It began to articulate a new moral framework for a theology of nonviolence and just peace in a violent world. It reflected on women and nonviolence, ecology and nonviolence, and nonviolence in other faith traditions. It gathered powerful examples of nonviolent action and experience in different circumstances around the world and it developed proposals for how the institutional Church could integrate nonviolence into its very fabric.

In April 2019 these findings were shared at the "Path of Nonviolence: Towards a Culture of Peace" gathering in Rome. People from nations around the world travelled to Rome for this meeting, including Brazil, Canada, Colombia, Costa Rica, Ethiopia, Fiji, France, Honduras, Italy, Kenya, Mexico, Nigeria, Pakistan, Palestine, the Philippines, South Sudan, Sri Lanka, Uganda, the United Kingdom, the United States and Venezuela. Peacemakers, theologians, archbishops, bishops, educators and those in pastoral ministry attended this historic assembly. In addition, the Dicastery's Prefect, Cardinal Peter Turkson, was present, as was Cardinal Joseph Tobin.

At this important consultation, each of the foundational elements of the Catholic Nonviolence Initiative's popular process and global study of nonviolence was presented. Participants from around the world also shared powerful accounts of the extreme violence they have faced in their contexts and the role that faith-based nonviolence had played in responding to it.

This Vatican consultation urged the Church to bring nonviolence from the periphery of Catholic thought to the centre — to mainstream nonviolence as a spirituality, a style of life, a programme for societal action and a universal ethic. It also proposed a series of concrete steps for integrating nonviolence at every level of the Church.

These two Vatican gatherings, and the research they prompted and disseminated, have been important steps towards inviting the larger Church to affirm the centrality of nonviolence to the faith and to bring nonviolence concretely alive in the global community.

Reaffirming the Nonviolent Way of Jesus

This growing shift toward nonviolence is rooted in the call and mission of Jesus. Jesus was nonviolent. He taught his followers to put down the sword, to offer no violent resistance to the one who does evil and to not kill. He consistently practised nonviolence in a violent and unjust time and context, calling his disciples to love their enemies and to expect the nonviolent Reign of God. The paschal mystery of Jesus's cross and resurrection lay at the heart of Gospel nonviolence.

Jesus made visible the nonviolence of God — the God who created the universe, not out of violence but out of love. Creation is good, as the Book of Genesis tells us, and human beings are made in the image of the God who declares this goodness. Nonviolence is the nature of creation and points us toward the "new creation", where all will be reconciled.

God's vision for humanity is the nonviolent life. The Church is thus called to practise, teach and be a sign of this Gospel nonviolence, inviting people of faith and all people everywhere to live this way of light and truth.

Gospel nonviolence says "no" to violence and "yes" to the humanity of the other, even enemies. It seeks reconciliation and restorative justice through active engagement and conflict transformation. It is prayer and action mobilising tenderness, mercy and empathy, even as it relentlessly resists injustice and courageously challenges the destructive power of violence. Gospel nonviolence is a paradigm of the fullness of life and the basis for the present initiative for renewing the centrality of nonviolence in the life of the Church.

Fostering a Culture of Peace through Nonviolence

People inside and outside the Church have increasingly discovered how nonviolence is a powerful way to foster justice, peace and reconciliation, even in the midst of acute violence. Empirical research has demonstrated that nonviolent approaches are twice as effective as violent ones.[8] While the Church's commitment to nonviolence is rooted in faithfulness to the way of Jesus rather than in specific results — grounded in a Gospel stand against violence, no matter the outcome — it nonetheless can often have real-world consequences for challenging violence and creating peace. Indeed, were the Church to embrace nonviolence in a robust and thoroughgoing way, it would likely contribute powerfully to a global shift mobilizing many nonviolent solutions to the monumental challenges of our time. This present volume explores these possibilities in detail.

Such a call to the world would be strengthened if the Church took concrete steps to integrate nonviolence throughout its global community, including by humbly grappling with its own historical and contemporary violence. Bringing the spirit of

---

8 Erica Chenoweth and Maria Stephan, *Why Civil Resistance Works: The Strategic Logic of Nonviolent Conflict* (Columbia University Press, 2011). In addition, their study concluded that nonviolent campaigns are more likely to foster democratic and peaceful societies. Nonviolent campaigns succeeding in terms of their political objectives have led to "durable democracies" at least ten times more often than "successful" violent revolutions. Armed rebel victories almost never produce democratic societies (less than four percent resulted in democracy) and more importantly there is little evidence they produce sustainable peace; worse, they are often followed by political corruption and/ or relapses into civil war. The data clearly show that the means by which peoples challenge injustices and oppression strongly influence the character of the societies that follow. For a Catholic faith community that places a premium on the avoidance of war and the protection of human life as the moral foundation of society, these are significant findings.

the nonviolent Christ to every level of the Church would include reckoning with clergy sexual violence and other patterns of violence and injustice by confessing this violence, acknowledging the harm, engaging in restorative justice, opening to metanoia and seeking reconciliation. It is Gospel nonviolence that calls us to this process of conversion, new life and restored community.

Furthermore, this call invites us to honour, learn from and spread all the ways the power of nonviolence is at work in our world. For example, in northern Kenya and South Sudan, Elizabeth Kanini Kimau — one of the contributors to this volume — uses nonviolence in her peace mission amid armed conflict among pastoralist communities. She has lived with the people in the Leyai IDP (Internally Displaced Persons) camp. She teaches, trains and mobilises nonviolent practices. Kanini worked with the Catholic diocese to establish a Peace and Trauma Healing museum. She says, "The language of nonviolence helped me transform myself and empowered me to be able to live and work in these hostile environments and among people who are violent as the result of protracted conflicts. Nonviolence has also been key in transforming the conflict in northern Kenya." Kanini has quickened the work of the Catholic Nonviolence Initiative with this insight: "Nonviolence is a crop that can feed the whole world, but the farmer must know her own soil."

Nonviolence is a life-giving crop — critical to nourishing the processes of justice, peace, security, mercy, and constructive change — but it must be planted, watered, cared for, harvested, shared and planted again.

The Present Volume

This text provides research and reflection on biblical, theological, ethical, pastoral and practical dimensions of nonviolence as a resource for advancing it in the Church and the world.

Part One: Returning to Nonviolence highlights the voices of those committed to nonviolence in violent contexts and the "signs of the times" that ground this initiative: the growing spread of active and powerful nonviolence in the Church and around the world and the global crisis of violence.

Part Two: Foundations of Nonviolence presents an overview of papal statements and church documents on nonviolence, acknowledging the Church's growing articulation of the fundamental importance of nonviolence to its life and mission; biblical foundations of nonviolence in the Hebrew Bible and the Christian scriptures, based on ground-breaking scriptural exegesis over the past half-century; and a profile of contemporary theological research on nonviolence in the light of classical themes of Christian theology, including creation, anthropology, Christology, pneumatology and ecclesiology.

Part Three: The Practice and Power of Nonviolence illuminates the history, dynamics, methods and transformational impact of nonviolence, with a special focus on the experience of faith-based agents of peace, justice and reconciliation. Reflection on contemporary first-person accounts, shared in Part One, of nonviolence as it is creatively and courageously experienced today at the local level provides fresh insight into the types of violence pertinent today and the effective nonviolent practices Catholics are using in response.

Part Four: Embracing Nonviolence demonstrates how the Church can integrate Gospel nonviolence throughout its life and work. A new moral framework is articulated based on active nonviolence and just peace that will enable the institutional Church as a moral authority to be more consistent with the nonviolent creativity of the Gospel. Catholics worldwide are encouraged to study nonviolence and to engage in the development of more effective nonviolent practices for protecting vulnerable communities, preventing violent conflict, transforming structures of violence and promoting cultures of integral peace inside and outside the Church. The Church is invited to learn from and partner with the world's religions to spread and activate nonviolence throughout the world.

In all of this, we acknowledge Pope Francis, whose leadership and example reinvigorates our Catholic faith. In his 2017 World Day of Peace message on "Nonviolence: A Style of Politics for Peace", Pope Francis proclaimed: "In the most local and ordinary situations and in the international order, may nonviolence become the hallmark of our decisions, our relationships and our actions, and indeed of political life in all its forms." Pope Francis has relentlessly combined the vision and practice of the nonviolent option in countless statements, including when he wrote, "A culture of nonviolence is not an unattainable dream, but a path that has produced decisive results. The consistent practice of nonviolence has broken barriers, bound wounds, healed nations."[9]

Pope Francis has illuminated the path of nonviolence by taking nonviolent action himself, from gestures of unity and solidarity (washing the feet of non-Christians, detained immigrants and the incarcerated during Holy Thursday services), to making a surprise visit to a refugee camp in Greece (where he arranged to bring three Muslim families to Rome), to a call for global prayer and action to prevent an aerial bombing campaign and to a plea for peace in South Sudan, in which he kissed the shoes of the warring parties as a heartfelt gesture of humility and a deep hope that reconciliation could be established and the war end. His sacrificial acts are transforming the world.

---

9 Letter from Pope Francis to Cardinal Blase Cupich, April 4, 2017.

2. The Signs of the Times

The Second Vatican Council taught us to see and respond to "the signs of the times." [10] Today we discern two critical "signs": the global crisis of violence with the unspeakable suffering it unleashes and, by the grace of God, the spread of active and powerful nonviolence.

We live in a time of unprecedented violence that disproportionately impacts non-combatants and severely limits quality of life and the ability to flourish, which is the God-given right of all whom God created. Violence forces migration, increases poverty, disrupts families, despoils the earth and generates hatred.

Yet, this global crisis of violence has called forth a resilience, courage, creativity and willingness to sacrifice for others. This powerful force that has spread around the world is called active nonviolence. As we look clearly at the violence in the world and in the Church, [11] we must match and surpass global, pernicious violence by proclaiming and practising the power of active nonviolence that is given to us through Jesus Christ.

In the context of brutal repression in El Salvador in the late 1970s, for example, Saint Oscar Romero condemned structural and institutionalised violence, the arbitrary and repressive violence of the state, violence of the extreme right and terrorist violence perpetrated against innocent persons. At the same time, he consistently sought nonviolent means to achieve a just peace. In his third pastoral letter (August 6, 1978), he wrote: "We are living in explosive times and there is a great need for wisdom and serenity. We extend a fraternal invitation to all, but especially those organisations that are committed to the struggle for justice, to move forward courageously and honourably, always to maintain just

---

10 Second Vatican Council, *Gaudium et Spes*, No. 4.

11 "Failure of War and Its Weapons" by Paul Rogers, 2018 www.nonviolencejustpeace.net

objectives and to make use of nonviolent means of persuasion rather than put all their trust in violence."

As violence escalated and civil war became more likely, he urged the pursuit of a third way - a genuine and just national dialogue that was inclusive of all social sectors and would pursue the deep structural changes that could rid the country of the root causes of violence.

The world is more aware of the devastating consequences of violence and war - physical, economic, psychological, environmental, moral. We have witnessed how war begets violence begets war and the long-term self-perpetuating destructive impact of violence, even where it appeared to achieve some limited short-term success. For example, people in recently liberated African nations, while not repudiating their liberation struggles, are asking questions about the methods used, and even whether the end result is really the "liberation" for which they made such enormous sacrifices; is it a just peace?

In times of enormous crisis, violence will not resolve our most urgent problems. It will not answer the climate crisis, global poverty, racism, gender violence or the many forms of injustice that people everywhere face. Nor will violence end war and terrorism.[12]

Pope Francis has said, "Many things have to change course, but it is we human beings above all who need to change ... A great cultural, spiritual and educational challenge stands before us, and it will demand that we set out on the long path of renewal."[13] This renewal invites all to cultivate the virtue of nonviolence, study and teach, pray with and make holy, live into and pass on the nonviolent way in order to bind up the wounds of violence and injustice, protect and love

---

12 Ibid.

13 Pope Francis, *Laudato Si'* 202, 2015

our vulnerable "Sister, Mother Earth,"[14] build vibrant cultures of nonviolence and just peace and establish a transformative spirituality for present and future generations.

A Sign of the Times: The Spread of Nonviolence

Nonviolence in Action: Contemporary Catholic Experience

We begin our exploration of the nonviolent way forward by examining the lived experience of nonviolence in action today.

The Catholic Nonviolence Initiative spent more than two years exploring contemporary Catholic practices of nonviolence and just peace in violent settings across the globe. While there is a rich history of Catholic nonviolence, we wanted to know what kinds of violence Catholics face today and what nonviolent practices they are employing. Over the course of this work, it became clear that Catholics have a vibrant, if under-nurtured, spirituality of nonviolence deeply rooted in their relationship with Jesus, their closeness to scripture and in the intimacy of liturgy and personal or communal devotional practices.

Deep Catholic faith has driven out indifference, educated for effective obstructive and constructive nonviolent practices and approaches, and provided communities experiencing conflict with transformational processes that keep conflict generative. Perhaps most important, those who engage in nonviolent practices generate by their actions a profound and contagious theological hope in those around them. "Nonviolent action is a modern way of witnessing to faith, a modern way of evangelising in a secular, pluralistic society," said Croatian theologian Ana Raffai.

---

14 Canticle of the Creatures, in Francis of Assisi: Early Documents, vol. 1, New York-London-Manila, 1999, 113-114.

Many Catholic responses to conflict seek to establish a dynamic and responsive just peace,[15] using constructive nonviolent methods and practices such as peacebuilding, diplomacy, encounter, education. How can listening to and learning from Catholic practices of nonviolence in contemporary contexts of violence meaningfully contribute to the next evolution of Catholic Social Teaching on just peace? In 2017-2018, the Catholic Nonviolence Initiative facilitated an in-depth global listening project with Christian nonviolence practitioners working in 21 countries.

As a basis for these conversations we sought to:

• Focus on comprehensive violence, not only on war;
• Explore both grassroots and global experiences;
• Examine pastoral and theoretical perspectives;
• Reflect on ways of living, organising and being in relationship in the world; and
• Understand the effectiveness of nonviolent action.

"Nonviolence is happening at the front lines. The faithful must get themselves to the front lines," said Christian Peacemaker Teams member and nonviolence trainer Sarah Thompson Nahar.[16]

---

15 "No Longer Legitimating War: Christians and Just Peace" by Rose Marie Berger, 2016. "Just peace is a Christian school of thought and set of practices for building sustainable peace, including at all stages of acute conflict – before, during, and after. Just Peace norms draw on three key approaches – principles and moral criteria, practical norms, and virtue ethics – for building a positive peace and constructing a more 'widely known paradigm with agreed practices that make peace and prevent war'. These three aspects form a 'head, body, heart' approach. Just peace is not merely the absence of violence but the presence of social, economic and political conditions that sustain peace and human flourishing and prevent conflicts from turning violent or returning to violence. Just peace can help Christians move beyond war."
<https://nonviolencejustpeacedotnet.files.wordpress.com/2016/05/no_longer_legitimating_war.pdf>

16 Case studies, interviews and comments from reviewers are drawn from the unpublished "Nonviolence Is a Crop that Can Feed the Whole World": A Listening Project on Catholic Nonviolence, Catholic Nonviolence Initiative (Roundtable 5), 2017-2018.

The Catholic Church proclaims that human life is sacred and that the dignity of the human person is the foundation of a moral vision for society. This belief is the foundation of all the principles of Catholic social teaching. Pope Francis reminds us that "human life is grounded in three fundamental and closely intertwined relationships: with God, with our neighbour and with the earth itself."[17] Catholic climate leader Gill Burrows pushed Francis's statement one step further: "Centring nonviolent methodology and practice in the Vatican and through the Catholic Church and its organisations is vital to face the enormous challenges the Earth is facing."[18]

Pope Francis says, "Conflict cannot be ignored or concealed."[19] It can only be transformed through a culture of encounter, which enables people to understand the opposition rather than conquering or ignoring them. This applies both within and outside the Church. Conflict is inevitable and may be creative and generative in promoting dignity and life. Violence is a choice that always brings death — of spirit, if not body.

Seven Stories: Contemporary Examples of Catholic Nonviolent Responses to Violence

Although Catholics around the world experience violence in all its subtle and brutal varieties, listening to Catholic nonviolence practitioners revealed three categories of violence they experience today: non-militarised structural violence, militarised violence, and militarised commerce (which is exponentially increasing in our era). Nonviolent responses fell naturally along patterns first articulated

---

17 Pope Francis, *Laudato Si'* (2:66), 2015

18 Case studies, interviews, and comments from reviewers are drawn from the unpublished "Nonviolence Is a Crop that Can Feed the Whole World": A Listening Project on Active Nonviolence, Catholic Nonviolence Initiative (Roundtable 5), 2017-2018.

19 *Gaudium Evangelium* (3:226)

by Gandhi: "obstructive nonviolent practices" and "constructive nonviolent practices."[20]

Seven stories[21] follow of Catholic nonviolent practices drawn from very different settings. These are small windows into the daily practices that are the predominant expression of nonviolence over time. These practices are happening before, during and after situations of acute violence.

Kenya

In Northern Kenya, Elizabeth Kanini Kimau works in the context of armed conflicts among pastoralist communities. She began her ministry in nonviolence in Sudan in 2009 when she taught at the Reconcile (Resource Centre for Civil Leadership) Peace Institute.[22] Reconcile International was established in 2003 by the New Sudan Council of Churches. The Peace Institute offers courses in peace studies and conflict transformation and community-based trauma healing and increases the impact of religious and community leaders engaged in nonviolence, economic development and trauma recovery. They acquire tools for initiating peace and mobilising communities to develop in sustainable ways.

---

20 Michael Nagler, "Six Principles of Nonviolence," OpenDemocracy, July 27, 2017: https://www.opendemocracy.net/en/transformation/six-principles-of-nonviolence: Gandhi initiated 18 projects that enabled Indians to take charge of their own society, making it much easier to "dismiss" British rule and lay the groundwork for their own democracy. Constructive work has many advantages: It enables people to break their dependency on a regime by creating their own goods and services. You cannot get rid of oppressors when you depend on them for essentials. You are not just reacting to offenses but taking charge. Being proactive helps you shed passivity, fear and helplessness. It gives a movement continuity, as it can continue when direct resistance is not advisable. Studies have shown that working together is the most effective way to unite people. It builds community and reassures the general public that your movement is not a danger to the social order. Most importantly, it establishes the infrastructure that will be needed when the oppressive regime falls. Many an insurrection has succeeded in dislodging a hated regime only to find a new set of oppressors rush into the vacuum. A good rule of thumb to follow is: be constructive wherever possible, and obstructive wherever necessary.

21 Case studies, interviews and comments from reviewers are drawn from the unpublished "Nonviolence Is a Crop that Can Feed the Whole World": A Listening Project on Active Nonviolence, Catholic Nonviolence Initiative (Roundtable 5), 2017-2018.

22 Resource Centre for Civil Leadership <www.reconcile-int.org/drupal/about>

Kanini moved to northern Kenya to live at the Internally Displaced Persons camp at Leyai with women and children displaced by violence between Rendille and Borana pastoralist communities. The roads around the camp were stalked by men with guns. Between 2009-2012, more than 14 people were killed on the road, including schoolchildren. Leyai was a farming settlement until 2008 when inter-communal conflicts caused its disintegration. There was a police patrol base in Leyai to protect locals from attacks but there were only two officers. Civilian defenders were ill-equipped to support the police. These are typical dynamics in many rural areas with violent conflicts.[23] Kanini said, "For the last five years I have met participants who were born, lived, married and are now ageing in war. Most of them have been in and out of refugee camps ... I observed that the Rendille and Borana communities were deeply divided and never interacted. They perceived each other as an enemy and whoever killed an enemy was praised and termed as a hero. I witnessed situations where people were killed and cattle were raided. The pain of loss, bitterness, anger, was temporarily 'relieved' after revenge."

In this context, Kanini used several types of obstructive nonviolent practices to break cycles and habits of violence. These were "obstructive" because she inserted herself and disrupted behaviour that had become normalised. She worked with the Catholic Justice and Peace Commission and a local priest to build trust between her and the conflicted communities. She trained both the Borana and Rendille communities in nonviolent communication. She focused on community elders by removing them from the conflict zone, where they could reflect on their situation without fear. The elders became leaders whom the people could trust. With the elders, she focused on reaching the young warrior men within both Borana and Rendille communities who were the biggest threats to building peace. The youth leaders took responsibility for promoting interaction between Rendille and Boran youth through sports and parties, which promoted good relationships among the young people.

---

23 "Violence stalks little known refugees living in the camps for last seven years" (Daily Nation, 12/04/12)
<https://pastoralistskenya.wordpress.com/2012/04/12/violence-stalks-little-known-refugees-living-in-the-camps-for-last-seven-years-5/>

She also implemented constructive nonviolent approaches. They are constructive because they improve and strengthen local institutions and strengthen existing systems. The justice system in the region was influenced by bias for or against the communities. Kanini said, "We worked to reform the justice system so that criminals were now punished with no regard, rather than a bias, to which group they were from, creating a deeper sense of justice."

Over the course of 8-10 years, Kanini has seen a remarkable transformation. She said, "The elders have become instruments of peace. They walked with me from village to village encouraging that each community begin their own peacebuilding process. The elders, who are key decision makers, have started holding dialogues and resolving disputes before they escalate to violence. Incidents of killing raids have reduced. People have gone back to their farms and resumed agricultural activities."

Not only has the violence been greatly reduced and a conflict transformation process been adopted by the community, but the community contributed 5,000 kilograms of maize to nearby areas affected by drought. The communities have also developed an enhanced communication system to alert other communities when they sense danger. The elders developed a programme to trace raided cattle and return them to their owners, thus removing a violence ignition point in a culturally appropriate way. Kanini reports, "The Rendille and Borana have now lived in a peaceful environment for the last three years after many years of bloody conflict."

Kanini operates in the context of disorganised, armed, communal violence, a situation vulnerable to political manipulation by armed militias. The militarised violence is amplified by structural violence, which disproportionately impacts women and girls and disrupts healthy land stewardship. But through Kanini's practice of nonviolence, killing raids are reduced, security is re-established, communities stabilise, restorative ecological land practices resume and local self-reliance is re-established.

Croatia

In post-war Croatia, theologian Ana Raffai is practising nonviolence in the context of violent nationalism, xenophobia and anti-women political and religious structural violence. During the time of Yugoslavia, her father, a Croatian nationalist, spent a short time in prison. The 1971 Croatian Spring was a turning point for her family. From 1991 to 1993, during the war in Croatia, Ana took refuge in Switzerland where she became involved with a peace movement. After returning to Croatia, together with her husband Otto Raffai, she continued her engagement with the peace movement and was one of the first to spread the idea of anti-war action and nonviolence. Today, Ana and Otto Raffai run Regional Address for Nonviolent Action (RAND) organisation, through which they educate and promote the values of nonviolent action combining spirituality, social engagement and study.

"Nationalism is often linked to religious identity," Ana said. "I deal with the problem of nationalism as structural and cultural violence, which unfortunately has its support in some representatives of Church structures. In Croatia, it is the Catholic Church. In Serbia, the Orthodox Church."

As far-right movements rise again in Croatia, the Catholic Church is closely and publicly associated with nationalist movements. In 2008, a Croatian military vicar-bishop, positively quoted a neo-Nazi nationalist slogan equivalent to "Heil Hitler" during a sermon in the political tinder-box of Vukovar.

Ana said, "The problem with this is that it connects Christianity with nationalism, so that original and fundamental Christian values such as reconciliation, forgiveness, and love for the enemy are concealed beneath national interest. Nationalist values are presented as *primary* Christian values. As a result, we have parallels in which the homeland becomes an idol."

Nationalist movements thrive on social inequality and social distance. Nonviolent action is more effective when there is a shorter social distance between the "oppressed" and the "oppressor". When the social distance is great, nonviolent action becomes more difficult because nonviolent resisters may be seen as foreign or sub-human. Social distance can result from any number of factors including racism, exclusive nationalism, ethnic polarisation, dehumanisation and propaganda that vilifies the other. Nonviolent action can still be effective in cases of great social distance if there are human "links", or intermediaries, that can communicate the grievances of the oppressed group in a meaningful way to the opponent.[24]

Ana developed practices to decrease social distance in post-war Croatia, Bosnia-Herzegovina and Serbia. "Encounter," she said. "Getting to know each other and creating one's own image of the 'other' as a form of resisting the media image/propaganda that is created of the other. This breaks down the fear and builds trust." She created educational programmes where participants develop arguments about why their religion is incompatible with nationalism, which leads to knowing their own as well as the other in a non-nationalistic way. She works in the communities to organise public actions to show unity among those that nationalism separates, demonstrating this visibly in the streets. She works across Hrvatska/Croatia, Bosnia-Herzegovina and Macedonia to foster these conversations so communities can learn from one another. Ana also uses the print, online, radio and TV media to spread a different message from the nationalist rhetoric and to model conversations between "enemies". She presents true Christian values separate from nationalist values, which sadly sets her against many Catholic leaders. She models nonviolent communication in public.

Ana is beginning to see transformation through her work: "There are more and more votes, offered in the name of the faithful, against nationalism. More and more co-operation between believers and unbelievers on the theme of resistance to nationalism. 'Good Faith' and 'Not in my name' initiatives have been launched.

---

24 Nonviolent Struggle by Maria J. Stephan, Stephen Zunes, Hardy Merriman. The International Studies Encyclopedia. Denmark, Robert A. Blackwell Publishing, 2010 <http://www.isacompendium.com/subscriber/tocnode.html?i-d=g9781444336597_yr2015_chunk_g9781 44433659714_ss1-7>

There is great value in Catholic/Orthodox/Muslim religious representatives publicly modelling reconciliation and peace. We are now able to identify our differences, but we are able to live our differences when each one has space to describe their own beliefs and can explain themselves in their own words."

Colombia

Around the world, violence in the context of militarised commerce is on the rise and a predominant and poorly understood experience in many Catholic communities. Militarised commerce[25] refers to the acquisition by companies/corporations of military services from military or paramilitary forces to provide security for company operations and includes assistance granted these troops in return for protection. In practice, these forces are drawn from two different sources: national militaries or police of the country in which the firm operates; or incorporated mercenary armies or "private military companies". Violence associated with "Militarised commerce" includes one or more of the following: 1) the acquisition by companies operating in regions with grave human security and human rights concerns of security services from military or paramilitary forces, groups often implicated in serious human rights abuses; 2) the provision by companies of financial, logistical, material or infrastructural assistance to human-rights-abusing troops or their governments, usually in return for protection or access to resources; 3) the use of violent force by human-rights-abusing regimes or militaries to supply resources to a company by, for example, clearing people off oil-rich lands; 4) the generation of revenues which are used by human-rights-abusing regimes or militaries to wage war against civilian populations.

These security forces ("men with guns") are often not directly accountable to any government oversight. These clashes between civilians and private security forces often happen far from the public eye, in remote regions where extractive industries are at work.

---

25 Forcese, Craig, Deterring 'Militarized Commerce': The Prospect of Liability for 'Privatized' Human Rights Abuses (2000). Ottawa Law Review, Vol. 31, No. 2, 2000. Available at SSRN:<https://ssrn.com/abstract=2717271>

Catholics identify a variety of types of violence present in situations of militarised commerce, including: encounters with private security and extractive industry, violent conflict over basic resources such as water and arable land, human rights abuses (including human trafficking, forced prostitution, forced labour, forced conscription, and terrorising local population to suppress dissent or opposition). This type of violence is increasing with the rapid expansion of extractive industry worldwide and the increasing pressures brought on by rapid climate destabilisation and collapse.

In the highlands of central Colombia, Sarah Thompson Nahar, former director of Christian Peacemaker Teams (CPT), described land theft by a foreign palm oil corporation in Las Pavas, Magdalena de Medio, Colombia. Christian Peacemaker Teams has about 30 active team members and 200 reservists working in five locations around the world. CPT currently operates violence reduction and accompaniment teams in Iraqi Kurdistan, Palestine/Israel, Indigenous lands in Canada, US-Mexico border and Colombia. CPT places teams at the invitation of local peacemaking communities that are confronting situations of lethal conflict. These teams support and amplify the voices of local peacemakers who risk injury and death by waging nonviolent direct action to confront systems of violence and oppression.

As a result of the US-backed "war on drugs" in Colombia, Afro-Colombian and Indigenous communities were disproportionately impacted by violence. Colombia has the largest internally displaced population of any country in the world except Syria. The government offered an incentive to encourage Afro-Colombians and Indigenous communities to return to their regions: if people cultivated their land for seven years, then they could take possession of the land and receive legal ownership. But in the region of Las Pavas, when the community completed their seven years of cultivation, the government schemed to sell the land out from under them to a large Colombia-based oil palm corporation. The Indigenous community at Las Pavas came to their fields and found bulldozers guarded by armed private security (in this case, demobilised paramilitary forces). The community's fields were destroyed, crops ripped up, all replaced with a monoculture oil palm. Not only did the state not intervene, but the state prioritised strengthening large business interests over the interests of the vulnerable populations with traditional land claims, who struggled to remain on the land and develop their life projects in that region.

Sarah said, "As the state becomes one of the many purveyors of violence (and not just the only one) we need Christian nonviolence principles that articulate our stance vis-à-vis corporations. All corporations, but especially those that are hiring security guards/hitmen/thugs/harassers to reduce and/or pacify the populace. Those guards are protecting Earth's capital and the profit for a few — and not Earth's people and ecosystems."

Sarah described nonviolent obstructive programmes and practices that Christian Peacemaker Teams helped implement at the invitation of the local community in Las Pavas: "CPT was in Las Pavas as a partner/ally to the community. CPT trains in spiritual practices, as well as models, tools and strategies to train for peace as hard as soldiers train for war."

The Las Pavas community also called in lawyers, land-rights advocates and related Colombian government bodies. CPT members are trained to provide some protective space for a local community to do its work. CPT absorbs some of the harm that is targeted at a local community.

In the case of Las Pavas, CPT assisted in leading a campaign of nonviolent direct action against The Body Shop, an international corporation that was a major purchaser of palm oil from Daabon, a Colombia-based corporation. The goal of the campaign was to ask The Body Shop to cut the contract with Daabon because what Daabon was doing was illegal, immoral and unjust. The campaign included tracking the economic trail from the frontlines in the fields of Las Pavas to consumers in the Global North. CPT initiated direct conversations with all the stakeholders, launched a letter-writing campaign, documented the human-rights abuses in Las Pavas and took them directly to The Body Shop's main store in London. CPT assisted the Las Pavas community with joining an international campaign and economic boycott against The Body Shop for unjust business practices, including participating in civil disobedience at the London store. Some protesters were arrested and went to jail. As Sarah said, "People do not like it when you mess up their shopping experience." CPT was intentional about keeping the community of Las Pavas front and centre in the campaign. The Body Shop finally ended its subcontract with the Colombian palm oil company.

Sarah also described how nonviolent constructive practices emerged with CPT and the local community in Las Pavas. "Music brought people together in Las Pavas," said Sarah. "It helped pass the time. And helped record the history of what the community was doing." CPT wanted to bring to Las Pavas the solidarity of the international community to give the local community encouragement, strength and skill to persevere in their unarmed pursuit of justice. CPT created avenues of communication, wrote songs with the community, documented the communities' ordeal and provided unarmed civilian accompaniment with the Las Pavas farmers so that they could cultivate their fields regardless of threats of violence. Sarah said, "CPT members study social movement history and strategy to guide us — including religious traditions, which often contain long histories of social movements."

In the end, the Indigenous farmers of Las Pavas were able to return to their land. The international campaign by the Las Pavas community provided a successful transformation of the violence. The community was given the National Colombia Peace Prize and went on to become trainers and teachers for other communities. The Body Shop admitted in a public statement that the international pressure led them to cut their contract with the Colombian-based palm oil corporation, forcing it to pull out of the Las Pavas region. The Las Pavas nonviolent campaign set legal and social precedents for other communities in similar situations.

One major personal transformation that Sarah experienced was learning about the power of local and international collaboration to sustain and enhance an effort for nonviolent social change. "It was amazing how we could call in lots of reinforcement in the Global North, making a front line with the store; and also keep in touch regularly with the front line facing the bulldozers filled with small palm oil trees to monocrop," she said.

Political scientist Erica Chenoweth, co-author of *Why Civil Resistance Works*, commented on the Las Pavas struggle and Christian Peacemaker Teams' work with the community. "Sarah Thompson Nahar's work in Colombia speaks to the importance of transnational advocacy networks, which can often leverage change through multilateral organisations (e.g. East Timorese independence, brokered through the UN and IMF)," said Chenoweth.

Philippines

In Central Mindanao, Philippines, Myla Leguro told us about her 30 years of work with Catholic Relief Services (CRS). Most of her work has involved supporting and accompanying efforts of local communities to address, resolve, or transform political, economic, land-related, identity-based conflicts, which have at times become violent. These local conflicts involve communal issues which are often connected with the broader conflict in the context of Mindanao. The broader issues include Indigenous communities asserting their rights to traditionally govern and manage their ancestral region. For the Bangsamoro communities (ethnic Moro with Muslim identity), their struggle for recognition of their right to self-determination encompasses their call to address historical injustice, legitimate grievances, human rights violations and land dispossession.

Myla said, "I was born here, I studied here, this is home. My work as a peacebuilder began with an awareness that I needed to participate fully in changing the situation."

Land conflicts are among the primary causes of violence in Mindanao, both at the community level and at a larger level that draws in the involvement of armed groups. Questions of ancestral domain and tenure are important not only for individual claimants, but for the success of the national peace process between the government and Muslim Moro rebels fighting for an autonomous state on the island. Land conflicts often represent a collision between modern property laws and customary/traditional/Indigenous laws governing land ownership and tenure. Much of the violence in Central Mindanao is a result of competing claims over land, not militarised organised violence. However, with any kind of violence comes internal displacement.

A study funded under the World Bank's Global Program on Forced Displacement in central Mindanao underlined forced internal displacement as "a means to control strategic territory (land and natural resources) by influencing the movement and loyalties of the local population. The internally displaced persons (IDPs) or local population are pulled and pushed in multiple directions as the primary means of asserting territorial control and political influence."[26] The extraction of mineral resources also involves questions of land tenure and access. As with logging, the exploitation of mineral wealth has had major impacts on many Indigenous communities and forestry areas. In 2010, the Catholic bishops of the Philippines addressed mining issues: "Weighing down the benefits and costs of mining whether it is economic, social or environmental; judging on the lessons of the past and prospects of future generations; and, reflecting on our role as Stewards of God's creation, we, the bishops of Eastern Visayas, call on to [SIC] our responsible leaders in government, in the private sector and all those who harbour intentions of mining our region to listen to the voices of our people, 'Bring back the Beautiful Land we had once; Stop mining in our region'."[27]

---

26 N. Colletta, "The Search for Durable Solutions: Armed conflict and forced displacement in Mindanao, Philippines," 2011.

27 Statement by the Catholic bishops of Eastern Visayas in the Philippines urging that large-scale destructive mining in their region be halted (22 October 2010) <https://www.indcatholicnews.com/news.php?viewStory=16994> and What Is Happening to Our Beautiful Land? (1988) by Catholic Bishops Conference of the Philippines <https://cbcpwebsite.com/1980s/1987-89/1988whatis.html>

Resolving land conflicts in a judicial setting, where one side may win and another lose, may worsen tensions among conflicting groups and erode tenuous social cohesion, according to Leguro. During past decades of violence, distrust and tension have arisen both between and within religious and ethnic groups in Mindanao. Stakeholders include local traditional religious leaders from Muslim, Christian and Indigenous communities; conflicting parties in a land dispute; local government officials and government agencies responsible for land tenure management; local civil society and faith-based non-governmental organisations; and local power holders.

Myla identified that many areas had overlapping claims — ancestral domain concerns, lack of deeds, etc., and that the legal process often disadvantages minority communities. An alternative, community-level dispute resolution process, using sanctioned conflict-resolution structures mandated by the government, offered viable solutions for resolving the intertwined land, social and conflict-related issues. Myla and the CRS team decided on an innovative "land-plot-by-land-plot" solution. In this initiative, they used a conflict transformation paradigm espoused by Mennonite peace scholar John Paul Lederach.

With her colleagues, Myla developed a three-step approach for land conflict transformation, known as the 3Bs ("Binding, Bonding and Bridging"). This highly effective model has been adopted and adapted in a number of conflict situations around the world, particularly in countries in central Africa, where they have added the 4Ds ("Discover-Dream-Design-Deliver").

Inter-group dialogue was aimed at shifting focus to land as a concrete issue, undertaken through joint problem analysis using participatory conflict analysis techniques. Dialogue aimed at working towards negotiated resolution of the land conflict. The outcome was envisioned to be a list of workable and mutually agreed upon options, endorsed among conflicting groups, and supported by government stakeholders at the municipal level.

Myla said, "This local model demonstrates how a creative process can be done to address very complex land issues. Now the Transitional Justice Commission is looking at this model that we developed for possible use at a larger level."

Jamila Raqib, executive director of the Albert Einstein Institution, founded by Gene Sharp and which promotes the study and deliberate use of nonviolent action worldwide, reviewed the Mindanao case study. Jamila said, "Church/faith communities are embedded in the local community and bring local connections and knowledge. They are also themselves stakeholders, and therefore motivated from personal interest in a just resolution. Also, they have the benefit of bringing outside knowledge and community-based structure for reflection, with self-awareness and accountability to voluntarily withdraw as facilitators if they are parties to the conflict."

Syria/Lebanon

In contexts of organised militarised violence, implementing nonviolent practices and approaches that harness "people power" is very difficult and requires careful strategy. In a number of situations around the world, Catholics are facing armed state repression (state military, domestic police, national guard); civil unrest (armed civilian patrols, militias, gangs, paramilitaries, other armed non-state actors); civil war (armed organised separatist groups with political goal); rape as weapon of war; internal population displacement and refugees as a weapon of war; "organised crime" (defined as armed, multilevel, organised, criminal violence with economic motivation); and "vendetta culture". Organised crime includes as part of its "gang" a vertical hierarchy with street-level violent enforcers, public authorities, political parties, police and militaries, businesses and parts of civil society who create the infrastructure for an organised crime syndicate.

Sara Ianovitz told us about nonviolent practices and approaches that the Community of Sant'Egidio and Operazione Colomba (known as the "nonviolent peace corps of the Pope John XXIII Community") since 2013 have implemented with Syrian refugees in temporary camps in Lebanon, particularly in Tel Abbas in northern Lebanon, five kilometres from the Syrian border. In the context of violence associated with a conventional war fought internally in Syria and with international alliances, Syrians face expulsion from their home, armed attacks, torture and death. In the refugee camps, Syrians also become vulnerable to organised crime.

The refugees explicitly requested the presence of Operazione Colomba in the camp after suffering threats, physical assaults, evictions and having their tents burnt. Operazione Colomba (OC) provides an effective deterrent for violence. The OC volunteers live in a wood and plastic tent, sharing the hard daily life with Syrians. Moreover, they build bridges of dialogue between the local Lebanese host population, who are scared and sometimes hostile, and the Syrians themselves. Sara said, "Our starting and core point is the nonviolence as rooted in life sharing."

Operazione Colomba is an important and efficient model of the nonviolent peace corps who intervene in acute armed and social conflicts. They work alongside similar organisations such as Civil Intervention Peace teams in Italy and the Association of Social Promotion Research Institute for Peace and Civil Corps of Peace (IPRI-CCP) as well as Peace Brigades International, Nonviolent Peaceforce, Fellowship of Reconciliation and Christian Peacemaker Teams (as well as numerous local models of unarmed civilian accompaniment) to introduce effective and credible options other than military means to intervene in international, inter-state and intra-state conflicts.

Sara identified a variety of obstructive nonviolent methods tested with Syrian war refugees — particularly focused on building a model of popular democratic diplomacy, an effective approach in situations where various cultures have to quickly learn how to make decisions together. First, the OC team implemented a listening project among those living in the camp, then explained the work Operazione Colomba was doing in other parts of the world. After establishing some relationship and trust, OC members moved into the refugee camp. In the daily life of the refugee camp, OC volunteers accompanied their neighbours in medical and legal matters, particularly to the hospitals throughout northern Lebanon, paying particular attention to women, the elderly and children. The presence of OC volunteers provides pressure on those institutions to ensure that people living as refugees were treated.

As relationships strengthened, OC worked with the refugees to open humanitarian corridors throughout Europe to provide a safe route for refugees from the war zone to various safe havens in Europe. The corridors consisted of a series of linked aid and civil society organisations, much like "sanctuary routes" in the United States moving asylum seekers from Central America to safety zones in Canada. These efforts disrupt dangerous travel and push back against human traffickers.

As the Syrian war shifted, refugees began to tell OC that they wanted to go back to Syria. They wanted to rebuild their communities. Sara said, "Our Syrian friends decided to think big and they have written an amazing international appeal for peace in Syria, titled "We The Syrians",[28] claiming "the right to let the world hear our voice". They propose the creation of safe zones in Syria, into which no army or armed group would be allowed entry, and asking for a peace where responsibilities are clear and that creates a new Syria for those who don't want violence. The basis of the idea is simple, said Sara: "Why are the representatives of the forces destroying our country the only ones at the negotiating table? Why do we only have the possibility to escape and we are not allowed to put our lives, our ideas, our strength and our hopes for the creation of a peace proposal?" In 2016 and 2017, OC members and Syrians presented the peace proposal to the highest levels of European Union governance. Sara said, "We needed schemes of listening that were outside the frames we already knew. Mediation is made by dialogue, starting from the ground to the top, to governments. Operazione Colomba is just the microphone: we go to the Italian government, which possibly talks to the Lebanese or German government or institutions. It's a popular democratic diplomacy."

Also, through videoconferencing, the OC volunteers paired the Syrian refugees

---

28 "We the Syrians" international peace appeal <https://www.operazionecolomba.it/wethesyrians>

who wrote the peace appeal with members of the Peace Community of San José in Colombia, where OC also has a team. Thanks to translation services provided by OC members, participants were able to discuss how the "peace zones" in Colombia were initiated and what the differences and similarities there were with the Syrian situation. This was particularly helpful in giving Syrians the idea that they could return and build their own "peace zones", creating humanitarian areas in Syria under civil administration with various types of protection mechanisms. All these are examples of building independent social institutions under community control that meet the needs of the community.

Sara sees nonviolent transformation consistent with her Catholic vocation and effective in the community: "Following the Annunciation, God became human and came to live among us. We also try to live in the conflict, choosing to be inside, close, not far away. To face death, expulsion and refugee camps, a force is needed that responds by creating relationships, links, among faiths, human relationships. There is great personal transformation when one perceives that I have a fundamental role because I'm directly and personally involved in making change. On the one hand, you feel a huge responsibility. On the other hand, you understand that it's your involvement which creates a new reality. If you do not do something, nobody will do it. At the same time, you have to leave some space to others. You can't do everything by yourself. Other people need this empty space to take actions. To transform these principles into a process depends on the credibility given us through the years we've spent in the field. It's a daily process. It's life-sharing with the victims of violence. We need to replace the word 'solidarity' with 'sociality': Living together is different. It's sharing life."

Central African Republic
Jean Baptiste Talla told us about his work with Catholic Relief Services (CRS) since 2013, rebuilding social cohesion and implementing anti-genocide measures in the Central African Republic (CAR) amid several years of civil war. Talla gave examples of nonviolent obstructive programmes in the context of organised militarised violence. This violent conflict continues in some regions of the CAR.

Based on the work done by CRS in the Philippines and enhanced by CRS in the Central African Republic during a period of unprecedented violence and brutality between the Seleka (Alliance) and the Anti-Balaka (Anti-Machete) militias in 2013 to 2015, Talla has helped develop and implement a robust 3Bs ("Binding, Bonding and Bridging") /4Ds ("Discover-Dream-Design-Deliver") programme.[29]

In 2012, CRS began implementing the USAID-funded Secure, Empowered, Connected Communities (SECC) project to "enable cohesive, self-directed and connected communities to avoid or reduce their exposure to threats associated with the presence of armed groups and ongoing conflict in areas most vulnerable to attack. The project also addresses ongoing interreligious/inter-communal tensions in CAR."

In 2014, violence resulted in revenge attacks and the destruction of both Muslim and Christian houses as well as the main communal gathering areas of towns. Muslims were often confined to an enclave within one town, but tensions remain between Christian and Muslim communities. In surrounding rural areas, almost all citizens were targeted by or witnessed the violence. Many lost their homes and other property as well as their livelihoods. Those most impacted lost family and friends. While the attacks subsided, the trauma faced by the majority of Central Africans remains.

CRS worked with Catholic sisters and lay women who were particular targets of violence to promote trauma-healing for these community leaders.

Talla wrote: "Initially conceived as a counter to the Lord's Resistance Army and community-based protection programme in southeastern CAR, SECC responded to the crisis by adding an objective in 2014 to support communities' ability to maintain and promote social cohesion and address inter-religious and intra-community conflicts. Working in close collaboration with the Plateforme des

---

29 The Ties That Bind: Building Social Cohesion in Divided Communities (Catholic Relief Services, 2017). <https://www.crs.org/our-work-overseas/research-publications/ties-bind>

Confessions Religieuses de Centrafrique (PCRC), a collaborative reconciliation council involving the Catholic Church, the Islamic Council and the Evangelical Alliance, the Catholic Relief Services teams have trained more than 1,300 religious and community leaders as ambassadors of social cohesion. In Bangui, more than 600 religious, civil society and government leaders have been trained in social cohesion principles, many of whom have proceeded to lead neighborhood-level mobilisation activities."

In January 2016, CRS, in an interfaith partnership with World Vision, Aegis Trust and Islamic Relief, began a new project entitled the Central African Republic Interfaith Peacebuilding Partnership (CIPP) designed to support Central African institutions to promote social cohesion, increase the scale and scope of ongoing trauma-healing programming and support early economic recovery efforts.

A conflict analysis was commissioned by Catholic Relief Services in CAR. They chose the USAID conflict assessment framework because it provides a "rigorous framework for collecting and analysing data in an objective manner that can be applied uniformly across conflict settings" in order to evaluate the risks of violent conflict and simultaneously assist development and humanitarian actors to support local efforts to manage conflict and build peace. The CRS conflict analysis identified the following key conflict dynamics: fragmented security and conflict between armed groups; state services failure; competition over resources; agro-pastoral conflict; and refugee and IDP return.

At the invitation of Muslim, Catholic and evangelical religious representatives, CRS trained thousands of government, civil society and private sector leaders in social cohesion principles and techniques and equipped them with tools they could use in their workplaces and communities. This guide, titled "The Ties That Bind: Building Social Cohesion in Divided Communities," innovatively combines the 4Ds of Appreciative Inquiry ("Discover-Dream-Design-Deliver") developed in Central African Republic with CRS's 3Bs peacebuilding methodology ("Binding, Bonding and Bridging"), developed in the Philippines.

The result is a powerful nonviolent approach for use within a people-to-people peacebuilding framework. It combines both obstructive programmes of intervening in conflict or post-conflict situations on the part of the trainers and laying the groundwork for community buy-in with a nonviolent constructive programme known from peacebuilding models and well-suited for situations where Catholic institutions are present and the state is fragile.

By the end of 2015, Talla said, more than 3,000 people in the CAR had participated in CRS' social cohesion workshops. Of those participants, 35 were trained as trainers. Talla was struck by the resourcefulness and ingenuity of the trainers. For example, trainers translated the guide's accompanying tools into the language of Sango and adapted the exercises to their local environments. Talla said, "In one instance, the trainer had asked villagers to gather sticks and branches to build a fire so that the community could clearly grasp the different stages and dynamics of a conflict — gathering fuel, initiating a spark, conflagration, coals and dying out."

"My work has been to provide technical support to communities and to an interreligious platform for peace led by Cardinal Dieudonné Nzapalainga, Imam Kobine and Rev. Nicolas," Talla said. "These religious representatives have become symbols and great advocates for nonviolence in CAR, going beyond their religious identity to call for love, reconciliation, justice and peaceful cohabitation."

Working with the institutional Catholic Church, said Talla, provided opportunities to reach out to key actors in CAR, including politicians, parliamentarians, civil society leaders and even armed groups members. Those who went through the 3B/4D approach made a significant behaviour change and there are a few cases where former trainees adopted a nonviolent approach to conflict and even engaged in crossing conflict lines to rebuild the destroyed infrastructure of the "enemy".

Over two and a half years, Talla saw that a great majority of those trained were committed to actively rebuilding social cohesion. For example, a former Anti-

Balaka chief, in collaboration with the local imam, initiated a connector project to rebuild the neighbourhood mosque that his fighters had damaged, defaced and looted during the crisis.

During critical moments between 2013 to 2015, Catholic, Protestant and Muslim women, relying on the learning they had derived from social cohesion training sessions, jointly organised awareness-raising sessions to instil calm and order in their segregated communities. They did so at considerable risk to their lives.

In reviewing Talla's case study, Jamila Raqib commented on the 3B/4D process, one previously unknown to her. Jamila said, "Binding addresses negative impact through counselling, educational work to clarify harmful perceptions and prepare people to develop a vision of tomorrow that includes a more inclusive future. Bonding articulates that inclusive vision of tomorrow. Bridging brings opposing sides to the negotiating table, where the hope is that they will together identify a mutually acceptable vision of tomorrow and projects of common interest that they can work on to implement that vision. Discovery offers a self-assessment of existing resources and assets, strengths that can be brought in to build resilience and respond to the conflict. Dreaming builds out a communal vision of tomorrow with long-term objectives to guide their activities and keep people on track. Design creates a plan to achieve shared objectives while reinforcing trust and harmony. Delivery is the implementation of the communal plan."

This case study in the Central African Republic also raises some critical questions about nonviolent practices in situations of severe violence. Jamila asked, "What if maintaining harmony with perceived enemies is undesirable or impossible? What happens if grievances cannot be addressed while maintaining trust and harmony? If trust and harmony are prioritised over other objectives, can this lead to unsustainable agreements? Are there mechanisms to hold parties accountable?"

Mexico

Gandhian scholar and community organizer Pietro Ameglio was a strategist behind the Movement for Peace and Justice with Dignity (MPJD), a mass civil resistance movement in Mexico in response to killings and disappearances during the "war on drugs". This violence involves responses to killings by organised crime (multilevel organised criminal violence including state) in the drug war in Mexico. The MPJD movement is made up of thousands of relatives of the murdered and disappeared who were killed from 2006 to the present. Pietro said, "It is the greatest drama in Mexican society today, with no less than 35,000 missing and 150,000 dead according to figures from the UN and family organisations. MPJD was a massive, national movement, today followed by dozens of victims' organisations across the country. It allowed for the first time in many years to speak explicitly on nonviolence in public."

An obstructive programme of a nonviolent movement for justice in the context of organised militarised violence is very difficult and requires very careful strategy. Pietro told us that in Mexico, "we struggle with building a 'nonviolent' population because people are not just afraid, they are terrified. And they are terrified because they are being terrorised. It is hard to work in a terrorised society." In this context, the practices of "nonviolent non-co-operation" are explored more and teaching about the "moral duty to non-comply".

But, says Pietro, the relatives of victims began losing the terror of acting and denouncing in public. They became social subjects of nonviolent struggle and in the main actions of the "just peace" that continues to build today. "They have a huge faith, most religious, in their struggle; in love to their children or relatives or friends; in truth; in the strength of being united 'to give their life' for their struggle."

Pietro demonstrates the dynamics of mass civil resistance in describing how through a "series of great social mobilisations on a national scale we were able to exhibit the horror and the magnitude of the war in this country; we also dignified the victims in their social identity and individual histories, organised and consoled them, converted them into social subjects with the human rights to peace, truth and justice; we also broke the normalisation of all that which is inhuman, and the terror of this 'armed peace' model, exhibiting it as an aggravating factor of the violence, a great business deal, in which organised crime and sectors of government at all levels play a direct part, as well as businessmen and sectors of civilian society; we also questioned the neoliberal capitalist economic model, which is forced upon us, as a great multiplier of poverty and vulnerability in all social sectors, especially children and young people."

In 2011, poet Javier Sicilia began organising after his son Francisco was brutally murdered along with six other people in Cuernavaca, Morelos. Sicilia, speaking publicly, emboldened a large number of individual victims from all over Mexico and civil society organisations to join together in a great national victims movement (MJPD). One obstructive mass resistance strategy was launching the Caravan of Solace, that travelled both to the north and south of the country and then into the United States, functioning in ways similar to Gandhi's salt march. It organised, galvanised commitment, and produced effective results at the local level along the way, thus building a large mobilisation.

In 2012, Mexican youth launched the #YoSoy132 ("I Am 132") movement using social media, aimed at fair elections, fair media and a transparent electoral process. It activated youth in opposition to electoral manipulation and was a nonviolent form of facing down state power.

In 2013 there arose an example of civilian-based defence, which eventually and reluctantly decided to arm itself. The Michoacan Community Self-Defence forces were formed and supported by community victims — especially the middle class and the impoverished — of the war. This response grew out of a sector of rural-urban society that had learned through its own painful experiences that the tactic of nonviolently and symbolically pressuring authorities for justice was not working. They decided to take on directly, autonomously from the government or police, their own armed community self-defence. Their goal was to install a parallel power in order to guarantee their security in their own territory, "without asking permission".

Pietro said, "The community self-defence groups understood that Mexico was not a 'failed state' or a state that was 'at war against drugs' as the government proclaimed. They identified it as a 'criminal state' deeply involved in the wars between gangs to control an illegal commodity, territories and bodies." The decision to take on armed self-defence to "stay the murderous hand" that operated with complete impunity can be seen, said Pietro, as an intention to exercise "moral power", as well as a move made in desperation. But how effective was this and how wise was this decision?

It opens up many questions about mixing violence with nonviolent struggle, as well as the ability of nonviolent struggle to respond in situations that involve a high number of direct armed attacks in the midst of total impunity and social terror.

In September 2014, in response to the genocidal action of the government and organised crime against 43 rural normal school students, mass civil resistance again filled the streets under the slogan "It was the government" (in response to the question of who attacked, disappeared, and killed the students). This time the mass movement raised the ante of their nonviolent weapons to a proportional level of the violence by engaging in direct actions of non-co-operation (strikes, parallel municipal authorities etc) and civil disobedience.

Pietro also identified three areas for a constructive nonviolence programme: 1) a legislative process to put in place a National Victims law; 2) an attempt to build a civil society organisation with national reach; 3) and the flourishing of local victims' organisations.

Pietro believes "that the ecclesial hierarchy as part of the national moral reserve should 'put its body' into public actions, in the street, much more clearly to demand justice from the authorities and accompany the families of the victims." Church properties could be converted into "zones of peace", where all parishioners would know of the cases of violence there and create networks, supporting action at many levels: human, spiritual, economic, psychosocial, legal. "In each parish there are people with many talents who could put them at the service of those affected," said Pietro.

Pietro added, "Considering the methods of the MPJD, especially during its first two years, it certainly organised many mass mobilisations (caravans, marches) and it achieved a direct dialogue with the powers that be which, however, was mostly simulation and impunity on the governmental part, rather than real accomplishment. The mobilised moral reserve (well-known personalities and key social actors, like Zapatismo) and the moral leadership of Javier Sicilia and the victims' relatives (their courageous, direct testimonies against criminal government connivance; having 'the truth' on their side; and the great support from national and international media) were important 'nonviolent weapons'. In a certain sense, they compensated for the lack of greater intensity and radicalisation in our nonviolent actions in proportion with the level of violence and impunity we were up against."

But, says Pietro, in the long run this was not enough, because for various reasons they were not able to mobilise well enough to proceed to the next phase that the history of nonviolent civil resistance prescribes: non-cooperation and civil disobedience. When there is such a high level of violence, impunity and state complicity, if greater degrees of moral and material radicalisation are not activated, the pressure of mass mobilisation and public dialogue with authorities is not sufficient, because it allows the government a margin for simulation, "gatopardism" (a strategy of advocating for revolutionary changes, but in practice only superficially modifying existing power structures) and the creation of "virtual institutions" — such as the Victims Law and Provictima — which do not operate in practice towards the objectives for which they were created. In the words of Dr. Juan Carlos Marin,[30] the eminent Argentinian epistemologist, whose work is fundamental for the understanding and research

---

30 Marín, J.C. (1995).Conversaciones sobre el poder. (Una experiencia colectiva). (Conversations about power. A collective experience). Buenos Aires University, "Gino Germani" Institute. Buenos Aires.

of social processes: "The logical empiricism of power won the day, making us believe that discourse is reality."[31]

Nonviolence: A Force More Powerful than Violence

Just as Catholic practitioners have increasingly been turning toward nonviolence, so too has the institutional Church, beginning with Vatican II. The process of the Second Vatican Council forced forth fresh buds on the ancient tree of the Church — a flowering that still unfolds 50 years later.

The Council took up the conversation about whether it is ever theologically permissible to justify war. The final Council document, *Gaudium et Spes*, like Pope John XXIII's encyclical *Pacem in Terris* written just a few years earlier, repudiated war, especially since the development of atomic weapons of mass destruction. These documents advocated a more comprehensive peace than was provided by the policy of "mutual assured destruction".

Italian Bishop Luigi Bettazzi was one of the youngest bishops present at the Second Vatican Council. In 2016, Bettazzi said, "It was suggested during the Council that every war should be condemned. That is what Pope John XXIII did when he claimed that thinking that wars can bring justice and peace was silly (*alienum est a ratione*, or "alien to reason"). It was only with the arrival of the Council that total war — that in which the civil population is affected — was condemned."

Bishop Bettazzi added, "Now, every war is a total war, because they all affect the civil population, and therefore is against God and against humanity."[32] Every Catholic, every Christian, he said, must be a conscientious objector to total war.

---

31 In addition to these seven examples, the Catholic Nonviolence Initiative developed case studies with nonviolence practitioners in Afghanistan, Australia, Palestine, South Korea, South Sudan, Uganda, United Kingdom and the United States.

32 "What if 1.2 billion Catholics embraced Gospel nonviolence?" by Rose Marie Berger, Sojourners (December 2016).

Following the Council, Catholics rose to embrace Pope Paul VI's resounding call on the World Day of Peace in 1972: "If you want peace, work for justice!" Thousands of priests, religious and lay people threw themselves into work for social justice, economic development and the promotion of peace as an expression of their Catholic faith. These same Catholics watched as a broad school of Christian thought developed — predominantly in Protestant and Anabaptist traditions — that judged just war to be obsolete and embraced the theology, principles and practices of what has become known as "just peace". This culminated in 2013 when the World Council of Churches, a body that represents more than 560 million Christians in Protestant, Orthodox and other Christian denominations, announced that "by its calling and vocation the Christian Church is to be a peace Church".

Beginning with the Indian civil resistance movements against colonialism in the early 20th century, and growing exponentially since the Second Vatican Council, solidarity at the base has been strengthened through popular movements. Almost all these movements were nonviolent. They engaged the conflict of injustice through unarmed resistance. They prosecuted the conflict without directly harming or threatening to harm an opponent.

This form of nonviolent political action is now a mainstay around the world. While some in these campaigns also chose armed resistance for a variety of reasons, research indicates that taking up arms is much less effective at achieving a movement's stated goals.[33] This is true whether violence is carried out as part of organised military action or disorganised cadres who act spontaneously.

Nonviolence is a force that resists injustice and violence, a spiritual discipline and a powerful strategy that challenges violence without using violence, transforms conflict, fosters just, peaceful, effective and sustainable resolutions to conflict and seeks the well-being of creation and community. It promotes human dignity; teaches self-respect and healthy communication; initiates processes of restorative

---

33 Erica Chenoweth and Maria Stephan, Why Civil Resistance Works: The Strategic Logic of Nonviolent Conflict (Columbia University Press, 2011).

justice to address interpersonal, communal and systemic injustices; and facilitates trauma healing. Its byproducts are creativity, joy, virtue, deeply held relationships and a shared hope for the future.

Nonviolence can be both obstructive and constructive. The obstructive programme of non-cooperation includes a range of practices such as boycotts, strikes, civil disobedience, and refusal to pay taxes. The constructive programme of co-operation with the good includes a range of practices such as education, broad-based coalition building, meeting basic needs, environmental justice and building just institutions.

Catholic nonviolence is a way of life and a positive force rooted in the love of God, who longs for the well-being of all. It is a spiritual journey that invites each one to collaborate in fashioning a world where everyone is recognised. And it is a means for building a more just, peaceful and sustainable world, where each being flourishes.

Nonviolence is a powerful "third way" beyond fight (action-reaction) or flight (silent submission) when confronting violence and injustice. As Joan Morera Perich SJ writes, "This third way is a path that requires great lucidity, creativity, faith and constancy."[34] Qualitatively different from violent conflict, nonviolence combines active non-co-operation with any violence and steadfast regard for the opponent as a human being.[35]

---

34 Joan Morera Perich, SJ, Dismantling the Hells. Practicing the Nonviolence of Jesus Today, (Christianity and Justice Study Center, booklet 169, October 2018).

35 Nonviolence is not reduced to pacifism, especially when pacifism carries connotations of passivity or of choosing not to actively engage conflict or resist violence. According to ethicist Lisa Sowle Cahill, pacifism is not easy to define in relation to ethics, "in that it does not begin so much as an ethical reply to the violence question (as it is often interpreted to do, especially by just war theorists) but as a practical embodiment of a religious conversion experience — as a way of life rather than a theory. Christian pacifism is essentially a commitment to embody communally and historically the kingdom of God so fully that mercy, forgiveness, and compassion preclude the very contemplation of causing physical harm to another person. Pacifists generally are opposed not only to war, but to any form of direct physical violence, although they may make exceptions to this bias by permitting police action. The moral rule that absolutely excludes resort to arms is a secondary consequence of the pacifist conviction, not its focus or zenith. One reason for the Christian tradition's continuing fascination with just war-pacifist dialectic is that it embodies the ancient and profound problem of reconciling Christian discipleship with public responsibility." Love Your Enemies: Discipleship, Pacifism, and Just War Theory by Lisa Sowle Cahill (Augsburg Fortress, 1994), p 2.

People in every part of the world who have persistently practised active nonviolence in pursuit of social transformation and just peace teach that not only is nonviolence the more faithful path, it is often a more powerful and effective one — especially when properly supported and resourced. In the Philippines, for example, Catholics have implemented restorative, rather than retributive, justice practices to address discipline issues in Catholic schools and antisocial or criminal behaviour among juveniles. A review of various Catholic social documents shows that the principles advocated by the Church encourage the practice of justice anchored in grace, love, human dignity and the common good. These practices are in tune with the restorative approach to discipline, where the goal is to restore people as opposed to punishment.[36] In the Philippines, the most evident application of restorative justice is the Juvenile Justice Act of 2006, which includes an effective process of encounter, amends, re-integration and inclusion. Restorative justice as an effective nonviolent practice is a recognised, but vastly underutilised, resource.

Gandhi declared that nonviolence was "as old as the hills" But in our own time, the force of nonviolence is being rediscovered, retrieved, spread, taught and activated in response to pernicious violence.

In recent years, a greater global understanding of the perennial wisdom of nonviolence has emerged. Concepts such as *ubuntu* in Africa ("I am because we are"; "a person is a person through other persons"; the primacy of relationships), *solidaridad* from the Christian base communities in Latin America, and *minjung* (the wisdom of the oppressed) from Korea, are providing new insights into human interconnectedness.

These join traditional Catholic teaching on the absolute dignity of every person; the common good; the "pure relationality" of the Trinity as a "divine model" of human solidarity (Benedict XVI, *Caritas in veritate*, 54); and a theology of oneness with its cosmic implications in grounding and projecting a sublime mode of peaceful coexistence, communion, and the fullness of unity.

---

36 "Examining Justice Practices in Philippine Catholic Business Universities: A Review of Student Discipline Programs" by Catherine Deen and Neil Pariñas (University of St. Thomas, 2015)

Together these form an active Gospel nonviolence that effectively breaks cycles of violence — not through avoidance, accommodation or counter-violence, but through creative action in the spirit of love and truth for justice, peace and reconciliation. Nonviolence captures the dynamics of Jesus's way of life and throws into sharp relief our call to reject violence and to overcome evil with practices of love.

Looking Pernicious, Multidimensional Violence in the Eye

Human beings are endowed with the gift of and capacity for unconditional love. Called into being through the power of God's love, each of us is also called to experience and live this love in our lives, in all our encounters and in our life-long relationship with the earth and its inhabitants. At the same time, we each have destructive tendencies that, when we choose to act on them, undermine our call to love in its fullness. Fear, hatred, greed and the "will to power" over others fuel estrangement and spawn every form of violence.

Propelled by this fear, hatred, greed and will-to-power, violence dehumanises and destroys.

As individuals we commit acts of violence and share responsibility for this violence. Violence, according to the World Health Organisation, is "the intentional use of physical force or power, threatened or actual, against oneself, another person, or against a group or community, that either results in or has a high likelihood of resulting in injury, death, psychological harm, mal-development or deprivation."[37]

Over and over again, Pope Francis has pointed to this culture of violence: "While

---

37 There are many types of violence: Physical violence (when someone uses a part of their body or an object to control a person's actions); sexual violence (when a person is forced to unwillingly take part in sexual activity); psychological violence (when someone uses threats and causes fear in an individual to gain control); emotional violence (when someone says or does something to humiliate or degrade another, to make a person feel stupid or worthless);

the last century knew the devastation of two deadly World Wars, the threat of nuclear war and a great number of other conflicts, today, sadly, we find ourselves engaged in a horrifying world war fought piecemeal … we know that this 'piecemeal' violence, of different kinds and levels, causes great suffering: wars in different countries and continents; terrorism, organised crime, and unforeseen acts of violence; the abuses suffered by migrants and victims of human trafficking; and the devastation of the environment."[38]

As Pope Francis suggests, the culture of violence is not only widespread but systemic. Not simply a particular incident or pattern, it is a comprehensive reality with many interlocking facets, including physical, verbal, psychological, institutional or structural behaviour, attitudes, policies or conditions that threaten, coerce, dominate, disrespect, diminish, destroy or negatively control ourselves, our fellow beings, or our world.[39]

Through social media, we see every day the full spectrum of violence across social locations: self-directed; interpersonal; communal; social, political and economic; and collective violence. War is only one form of collective violence.

This normalised, systemic and state-sanctioned violence threatens the very existence of life on earth and causes paralysing anguish and destruction in the daily lives of the human family and creation.

---

spiritual or religious violence (when someone uses an individual's spiritual beliefs to manipulate, dominate or control that person. Not allowing the person to follow her or his preferred spiritual or religious tradition; forcing a spiritual or religious path or practice on another person; belittling or making fun of a person's spiritual or religious tradition, beliefs or practices; and using one's spiritual or religious position, rituals or practices to manipulate, dominate or control a person); cultural violence (when an individual is harmed as a result of practices that are part of her or his culture, religion, or tradition); verbal abuse (when someone uses language, whether spoken or written, to cause harm to an individual); financial abuse (when someone controls an individual's financial resources without the person's consent or misuses those resources); deprivation and neglect (when someone has the responsibility of providing care or assistance for an individual but does not). Sources: World report on violence and health (2000) by World Health Organization (Geneva); Global Conflict Tracker by the Center for Preventive Action (New York).

38 Pope Francis, World Day of Peace Message 2017

39 Ibid.

After World War II

The decades since 1945, following the most devastating war in history, have been marked not by a more peaceful world but by numerous conflicts, the development of weapons of mass destruction, a deepening socio-economic divide and severe environmental constraints. Over the last seven decades the global experience has been of multiple conflicts feeding into a military complex that has cost trillions of dollars and tremendous intellectual capacity — appalling diversions from the proper task of responding fairly to human needs and aspirations.

The threat of a nuclear apocalypse and the rise of civilians as the main victims of war, with gross violations of human rights and dignity in war zones, massive forced migrations, human trafficking and the victimisation of children fleeing conflict areas, have led the Church to be deeply sceptical of the ability of modern war to meet just war criteria. In addition, the idea that a war might be justified too often leads to structural violence in the form of massive preparations for war, a highly profitable weapons industry and an arms race for the latest destructive technology. The training of individuals to kill, the cultivation of political support for war and the development of a culture of violence are themselves making violence more likely.

The nature of the warfare that still plagues the world makes overcoming it with alternatives especially pressing.

Since the mid-20th century, the popes have not justified any specific use of military force, and instead have put focus on and moral weight behind nonviolent approaches to transform conflict and bring just peace. In the past 25 years, individual bishops and some bishops' conferences have also emphasised the need to focus on nonviolent practices.

Pope Francis wrote: "Countering violence with violence leads at best to forced migrations and enormous suffering, because vast amounts of resources are diverted to military ends and away from the everyday needs of young people, families experiencing hardship, the elderly, the infirm and the great majority of people in our world. At worst, it can lead to the death, physical and spiritual, of many people, if not of all."[40] Even more, "War always does grave harm to the environment."[41]

During the course of the 45-year Cold War, repeated efforts were made to bring the nuclear confrontation under control, including some useful bilateral and multilateral agreements. Multilateral treaties included the Limited Test Ban Treaty and the Non-Proliferation Treaty, the latter allowing five then-existing nuclear-weapon states — US, UK, France, China and the Soviet Union — to retain their forces while non-nuclear-weapon states eschewed the right to build their own arsenals. Currently, nuclear-weapon countries maintain arsenals and have programmes or plans to modernise their systems.

Over the entire period from 1945 to 2001, arms industries worked hard to ensure buoyant arms sales, ranging from small arms and light weapons to tanks, aircraft, long-range missiles and warships. One effect of the widespread availability of light weapons in regions where outright war developed was that in the chaos of war and post-war disorder, light weapons would "cascade" down to individuals and small communities without any central control. This proved a particular problem in the 1990s, a period that also coincided with a brief decline in world military spending, which was largely due to the collapse of most of the Soviet bloc economies and ended with the start of the "War on Terror" in 2001.

As military technology develops, the potential destructiveness of war and the ease with which the world moves towards war continue to grow. Unmanned aerial vehicles (UAVs) and robotics, for example, have the potential to make state killing more likely and widespread, as risk to the lives of soldiers ("force protection") is reduced. The use of chemical weapons in Syria reminds us again of the terrible shadow that weapons of mass destruction cast over humanity,

---

40 Pope Francis, World Day of Peace Message 2017

41 Pope Francis, *Laudato Si'*, 2015

despite long-standing opposition by the Church and much of the international community. The arms trade in conventional weapons continues to flood conflict zones and beyond with the tools of war, leading Pope Francis to ask, "Do we really want peace? Then let's ban all weapons so we don't have to live in fear of war."[42]

Fewer wars, greater violence

While wars between sovereign nation states are increasingly rare, many parts of the world are still plagued by internal conflicts that result in "men with guns" coming to people's doorsteps. These conflicts often last for generations. They destroy social trust and the infrastructure and economy that are outward manifestations of that trust. They lead to multi-generational suffering. These wars frequently involve non-state actors, interventions by outside powers, and terror tactics used by all sides, while lines between civilians and soldiers are disappearing. In many places not officially "at war", gangs, organised crime and militarised police and private security have made wars at a neighbourhood level painfully real. The spread of drone technology is likely to exacerbate this trend.

Not only do we now need to address the core issues of a failing economic system and potentially catastrophic climate disruption but we have to do so in the context of a military outlook best described as the "control paradigm", rooted in the idea of pre-emptively suppressing threats of violence with violence, rather than understanding their causes.[43]

Societies and indeed people's very souls are becoming militarised; even humanitarian issues such as refugees are redefined as "security" concerns and addressed by militarised means. The manipulation of social media for particular gain often exacerbates hatred and violence.

---

42 Pontifex tweet, 29 April 2018

43 "Failure of War and Its Weapons" by Paul Rogers, 2018 www.nonviolencejustpeace.net (excerpts)

Two Particular Concerns: Women and Creation

Violence against women and girls[44]

In the contemporary world, violence affects women in particularly acute ways. First, no longer is war a regulated exercise fought between soldiers on battlefields removed from population centres. Modern warfare manifests in irregular and effuse ways. Insurgencies target civilians and battlefields expand with chemical and biological warfare or increased use of automated weapons such as drones. As a result, women, children and the elderly — those often not targeted for conscription into military forces or armed groups — have become the overwhelming majority of modern war casualties.

Women are particularly affected by the pervasive use of sexual violence - rape and forced sexual enslavement - as both a tactic and consequence of war. In fact, evidence shows that even as wars end in defeat or negotiated settlement, domestic violence against women often increases as the violence of war is absorbed into the home.

Even in contexts of apparent sustained peace, a silent and often unseen war plays out on women's and girls' bodies as multiple forms of violence and exploitation, including sex trafficking and femicide, are driven by a rape culture rooted in women's perceived expendability, impurity or unworthiness. Religious and cultural belief systems are often complicit in shaping and legitimating a culture of violence against women, and these systems may be marshalled to stigmatise female survivors of violence, shunning them from communities of faith at a time when they most need spiritual and emotional support.

Finally, subtle and overt perceptions of women's inferiority and gendered norms that proscribe the limits of their authority often no further than the household,

---

44 "Following Her Lead" by Rev. Susan Hayward, 2018 www.nonviolencejustpeace.net (excerpts)

result in structural forms of injustice that harm women. Marginalised from political and social leadership, their priorities and needs are often not addressed, so perpetuating cultures of gendered violence.

The cry of the earth [45]

"We have come to see ourselves as her lords and masters, entitled to plunder her at will. The violence present in our hearts, wounded by sin, is also reflected in the symptoms of sickness evident in the soil, in the water, in the air and in all forms of life. This is why the earth herself, burdened and laid waste, is among the most abandoned and maltreated of our poor" (LS, 2).

Pope Francis urges us to hear the cry of the earth and the cry of those who are poor as one integral voice. In order to do this, we must make the linkages. There are many examples of how the earth is crying out for justice, healing and reconciliation. Some examples include the climate crisis, access to and conflict over water, extractivism, the loss of biodiversity, an increase in ecological martyrs. Each of these cries demonstrates the failure of violence to bring promised peace. Moreover, not only is violence a failed response it serves only to deepen and sharpen wounds to communities and all of creation.

War and ecological habitat

Violence done to the Earth itself is a part of war whether through habitat destruction or extraction of the Earth's resources for materials to produce weapons and technology used in war. For example, we see how extraction of natural materials in places such as Chile, Peru and the Amazon are used for military purposes in Asia, such as the construction of the US-backed military base on Jeju Island, South Korea. The construction of this military base also has its own negative impacts on the environment, such as destruction of sea-life and water contamination.

---

45 "Nonviolence and Creation Care/Climate Justice" by Amy Echeverria, Global Catholic Climate Movement 2018 www. nonviolencejustpeace.net (excerpts)

Increasingly, countries and communities are in conflict as a result of competing for access to natural resources. The global demand for fossil fuels is a good example of how military policies are driven by access to natural resources. Diminished access to basic human rights such as clean water, viable food sources and suitable living conditions and reduced access to land because of large-scale mining, are all conditions that exacerbate the vulnerability of countless communities around the world. The environmentally driven conflicts often cross boundaries of ethnic and religious divides which can lead to even more intense violence and war.

When we think of the casualties of war, we usually think of the loss of human life first, and perhaps the destruction of infrastructure such as homes, roads, schools, hospitals and in some cases entire villages, towns or cities. Rarely do we call to mind the landscape, the air, the water, the animal life that is also frequently damaged, plundered and at times irrevocably destroyed by guns, bombs, chemical warfare and other weapons. Taking into account this non-human loss of life is yet another reason to redefine Church teaching on war to recognise that no war is just against the environment.

Climate collapse

For decades scientists have been warning the world of the catastrophic and irreversible impacts of climate change. Some voices in the Church have also sounded the clarion call from a moral perspective. The denial of human-induced climate change is a kind of violence. It is the violence of ignorance and the violence of isolation, when we fail to see our interconnectedness, that perpetuates policies and lifestyles that keep the world imbalanced and diseased.

All of creation is under threat as a result of human-induced climate change created largely by an over-consumption of the environment and dependence on fossil fuels, which in turn are driven by an economic model that places profits over the common good. There are countless examples of climate-change-related natural disasters throughout the world. Typhoon Haiyan in the Philippines in 2013, Cyclone Winston in Fiji in 2016, Hurricane Maria in Puerto

Rico in 2017, heat records that soar each year higher than the last, extreme flooding in Pakistan and droughts in Africa and Australia well beyond cyclical norms all point to catastrophic suffering and loss of human and non-human life.

Water

Water holds a special place in Christian imagination and sacramental expression. We know from science of the essential nature of water to life. Our relationship with water is both spiritual and physiological and therefore demands a level of care that mirrors a sacredness for life.

The privatisation, commodification, trade and export of water can be seen as violations of both Catholic principles of universal destination of goods and care for creation. The privatisation of water often disregards the rights and needs of humans and all living things because the environment is not factored into the commercial equation. Water privatisation has had consequences such as: violent conflict between communities over access to water which results in less access to water for people who are poor, extremely high tariffs and poor water quality. We see conflicts arising throughout the world over issues of scarcity, access, privatisation and contamination. These include ongoing conflict over the Belo Monte dam project in Brazil; an 2015 attack in southern Philippines attributed to the militant Islamist sparatist group, Abu Sayyaf, that left one town without municipal water; and the situation in Flint, Michigan in the United where lead contamination in the water has been a source of strife since 2014. We see in these and many other crises that water can be the root of the conflict, a "weapon" in a conflict, or the cause of a conflict. In all cases, water is particularly vulnerable to violence.

Biodiversity

The violence of overconsumption and the extinction of plants, animals and water are real wounds for which humans bear significant responsibility. The creative and generative processes that result from diversity are threatened with the rapid loss of species and sickening of ecosystems. In *Laudato Si'* Pope Francis boldly proclaims, "Because of us, thousands of species will no longer give glory to God by their very existence, nor convey their message to us. We have no such right." (LS, 33).

'Extractivism'

We see the growing threat of a massive depletion of natural resources, loss of biodiversity and destruction of the environment caused by extractivism, which is the model of development promoted by many multinational corporations, governments and international financial institutions. It is based on the intensive exploitation of natural resources, most of which are non-renewable, and creates conditions of dependency for countries from which the resources are extracted. This model of development commodifies the natural world, which violates the relationship of balance and harmony intended for all of God's creation and often generates social conflicts, violates human rights and dignity and endangers biodiversity.

Renewing the Church's Commitment to Gospel Nonviolence

Violence desecrates the sacred gift of the human person and creation. It fails to recognise that every human being is made in the image and likeness of God and that all of creation is endowed with immense dignity. We are called to honour this "deeper dignity"[46] and the holy calling of humanity by making active nonviolence our common way forward.

With gratitude we recognise the important role of Catholics and the Vatican in opposing the death penalty and making an "unambiguous political commitment" to achieve and maintain a nuclear-weapons-free world. Pope Francis has said, "International relations cannot be held captive to military force, mutual

---

46 Pope Francis, World Day of Peace, 2017

intimidation and the parading of stockpiles of arms." Peace and security among nations must instead be "inspired by an ethics of solidarity".[47]

From the highest political levels to the streets and neighbourhoods, we must move beyond "fight" (action-reaction) or "flight" (submission or acquiescence) to Jesus's third way. While the first two are always possibilities, they do not effectively constrain or transform violence. The first engages the fallacy of "redemptive violence" and the second risks erring toward individualism, false personal piety, or selfishness. Jesus's third way requires teaching and training in strategic and effective practices of active nonviolence, support and commitment of the Church, moral conviction and courage, sacrifice, faith in God and a spirit willing to follow Jesus into the fray.

In Chicago "violence interrupters" successfully decrease gun deaths.[48] In London, a parish placed a large banner in front of their church with the message "Choose Life. Drop the Knife"[49] as part of a parish-wide organising effort to give all young people a positive sense of identity and belonging, so that they are not drawn into the destructive belonging that gangs represent and promote a knife- and gun-collecting scheme. In Central African Republic, trauma-healing teams stabilise communities in situations of extreme violence. The United Nations is advancing Unarmed Civilian Protection[50] to interrupt and break cycles of violent conflict by utilising diverse nonviolent interventions to mitigate and divert threats of harm. Modelling nonviolent behaviour stimulates nonviolent behaviour in others.

---

47 "Pope asks leaders to imagine a world without nuclear weapons" (AP, November 11, 2017) https://apnews.com/716f-909db5a141599614bcf9253895d9

48 The Effect of Intensive Cease Fire Intervention on Crime in Four Chicago Police Beats: Quantitative Assessment:https://cvg.org/wp-content/uploads/2019/09/McCormick_CreaseFire_Quantitative_Report_091114.pdf

49 See Valerie Flessati's case study of St. Mellitus in London, UK. Case studies, interviews and comments from reviewers are drawn from the unpublished "Nonviolence Is a Crop that Can Feed the Whole World": A Listening Project on Active Nonviolence, Catholic Nonviolence Initiative (Roundtable 5), 2017-2018.

50 "The Growth in Unarmed Civilian Protection" by Mel Duncan, Rolf Carriere, and Huibert Oldenhuis (International Peace Institute, Global Observatory, 29 April 2015)

In the Philippines, civilian land courts are decreasing violent property disputes through a restorative justice process. Practising active nonviolence boosts the sustainability of peace over time.

PART II: FOUNDATIONS OF NONVIOLENCE

1. The Voice of the Church on Nonviolence

Papal statements and Church documents

"I ask God to help all of us to cultivate nonviolence in our most personal thoughts and values. May charity and nonviolence govern how we treat each other as individuals, within society and in international life. When victims of violence are able to resist the temptation to retaliate, they become the most credible promoters of nonviolent peacemaking. In the most local and ordinary situations and in the international order, may nonviolence become the hallmark of our decisions, our relationships and our actions, and indeed of political life in all its forms."[51] — Pope Francis, January 2017

In his 2017 World Day of Peace message, Pope Francis shared with all Christians and with all people on earth a landmark call to learn, practise and mobilise the humanising power of active nonviolence in responding resolutely to the global crisis of violence. This message built on the accelerating articulation by the leadership of the Church over the past half century of the critical need for humanity to turn to nonviolence in our lives, our societies and our world. This papal message — "Nonviolence: A Style of Politics for Peace" — was the clearest

---

51 World Day of Peace message, 1 January 2017

statement yet by the Vatican on the centrality of nonviolence to the life and mission of Jesus, and thus to the life and mission of the Church.

Should a major teaching document on nonviolence be shared with the world, it will be built on the accelerating series of papal and Church statements and teachings on nonviolence and peace that have been promulgated over the past 50 years.[52] The following is an overview of these documents.

Gospel nonviolence has been an essential characteristic of Christianity since the first century. To be a disciple of Jesus is to live within the reign of God, as embodied in his command to "love your enemies and do good to those who persecute you ... so that you may be children of our God in heaven" (Matthew 5: 44, 45). The example and teaching of Jesus embody love, inclusion, forgiveness, willingness and sacrifice. The early Church excluded the shedding of blood for all his followers.

In the intervening centuries, the institutional Church often lost sight of the centrality of active nonviolence. In the 20th century, however, this core Gospel commitment began to come to the fore again theologically and pastorally. For example, the Second Vatican Council made a key shift, calling not merely religious but also laity to holiness. Thus the modelling of Jesus's nonviolent love was no longer simply for clergy or religious but now the way of life — the practices and virtues of Jesus were more clearly a way for all of us to try and live.

---

52 This section draws on the scholarship of Dr. Lisa Sowle Cahill, Boston College, USA (see "Official Catholic Social Thought on Gospel Nonviolence" https://nonviolencejustpeacedotnet.files.wordpress.com/2016/05/official_cst_on_gospel_nonviolence.pdf) and other sources.

From Vatican II Onward

Since the 1960s official Catholic teaching has uniformly deplored the destruction and disaster of war, pressing the point that it always represents a moral failure. Although the idea and theory of a just war has not officially been repudiated, no pope since the Second Vatican Council has approved a war, or even mounted a defence of the justice of war in principle. The use of violent force for humanitarian purposes — in cases of horrific threats to human life, human security and social order — is still acknowledged by Catholic teaching. Yet the focus of recent official statements has been certainly on nonviolence, and on the incompatibility of violence with transformational justice. Popes John XXIII, Paul VI, John Paul II, Benedict XVI and Francis have repeatedly denounced the savagery of war. John Paul, Benedict and Francis have all echoed Paul VI's cry, "No more war, war never again!"

Popes, other Catholic leaders and official Catholic organisations have made the nonviolent transformation of conflict a moral and practical priority through their teachings, symbolic actions and work to end violent conflicts and build peace. The Catholic Church urges the transformation of conflicts by peaceful, nonviolent and democratic means, insisting that the way to genuine peace lies in the creation of just and participatory social, economic and political relations and institutions.[53] One important Catholic contribution to the Christian tradition of Gospel nonviolence is to put the emphasis on constructive and practical efforts to build the conditions of peace nonviolently, in co-operation with other social entities, rather than simply to repudiate violence and refuse political participation as a countercultural act of witness. In the words of Paul VI, "If you want peace, work for justice" (1972 World Day of Peace message).

Both the Council document *Gaudium et Spes* (1965) and John XXIII's *Pacem in Terris* (1963) were written at the height of the Cold War and in the light of the

---

53 See Archbishop Renato Martino's strong endorsement of the UN's Decade for a Culture of Peace and Nonviolence, November 2000, page 25: http://www.un.org/documents/ga/docs/55/pv/a55pv49.pdf

advent of nuclear weapons, so terrifyingly balanced by the superpowers' policy of "mutual assured destruction" at the edge of planetary disaster. Both documents pose the question whether just war criteria need to be thoroughly reconsidered, and contemplate a possibility that John XXIII explicitly puts forth: "It is contrary to reason to hold that war is now a suitable way to restore rights which have been violated" (*Pacem in Terris*, 127; cf. *Gaudium et Spes*, 79-80).

Gaudium et Spes still legitimates defensive wars, and John XXIII does not definitively exclude them. Yet they agree that modern war threatens unimaginable destruction, and see the arms race as a clear and present cause of global injustice. War and preparation for war are placed under ever more stringent moral scrutiny and targeted by mounting moral disapproval (*Pacem in Terris*, 112-13; *Gaudium et Spes*, 80-81).

The foundation and heart of these two documents, however, is not the consideration of war. It is the proclamation of a Gospel-inspired and nonviolent peace, capable of engendering lasting trust among nations. Pope John appeals both to the Christian faithful and to "all men of good will", praying that Christ will banish "whatever might endanger peace" and "transform all men into witnesses of truth, justice, and brotherly love". "Besides caring for the proper material welfare of their peoples," rulers should "also guarantee them the fairest gift of peace" (171). *Gaudium et Spes* captures the practical and social meaning of Gospel nonviolence in very similar terms. Praising all who "renounce the use of violence in the vindication of their right", it calls Christians "to 'practise the truth in love' (Eph. 4:15) and to join with all true peacemakers in pleading for peace and bringing it about" (78). In accord with nonviolence as an authentically Christian and human mandate and practice, the Council for the first time recognises a right of individual conscientious objection to bearing arms (79). The Council also strongly states, "It is our clear duty, therefore, to strain every muscle in working for the time when war can be completely outlawed" (81). What if as a Church our faith formation, vocational discernment, moral framework all reflected, were consistent with, did not obstruct and were all aimed at including this goal?

Paul VI, John Paul II, Benedict and Francis all advance this trajectory, accentuating the tension latent in a tradition that has historically justified war, while holding up peace as its guiding social ideal. New developments include: language that more strongly contrasts war and nonviolent peace, even to the point of excluding violence entirely; the marginalisation and even abandonment of explicit validation of defensive war as just; the introduction by John Paul II of a duty to disarm in situations of humanitarian crises; a strengthening and elaboration of the connection between practical work for justice ("development"), nonviolence and peace; incorporation of environmental reasons to avoid war; the need for broad social conversion; and, with Francis, an explicit turn to interreligious as well as intercultural and international partners.

Paul VI emphasises that "reconciliation is the way to peace" (1975 World Day of Peace message), declaring, "No more war, war never again! Peace, it is peace which must guide the destinies of people and of all mankind" (1965 Address to the United Nations General Assembly). Not only does he hope (with *Gaudium et Spes*) that war will eventually be prohibited by international law (1975 World Day of Peace message). He states in no uncertain terms that "the Church cannot accept violence, especially the force of arms" (*Evangelii Nuntiani*, 37, 1975), and holds up Gandhi's example to urge that nonviolence can become a national and international principle of action (1976 World Day of Peace message). Nevertheless, in the context of naming the horrible consequences of armed revolution, and challenging communities to avoid it, he does not object in very rare circumstances to the potential of armed revolution to resist "long-standing tyranny" that causes grave offences to human dignity and the common good (*Populorum progressio*, 31). This pope's greatest contribution is his insistence that the only true way to peace is to engage social partners constructively to end injustice, and actualise equal dignity, economic justice and stable, participatory social and political institutions. The more privileged nations and peoples have a special responsibility. Most famously, "the new name for peace is development" — though not a neoliberal or unrestrained market model of development (*Populorum progressio*, 87).

John Paul II announces just as clearly that "Violence is evil," "a lie" and "the enemy of justice". He says: "Violence destroys what it claims to defend: the dignity, the life, and the freedom of human beings. Violence is a crime against humanity." He calls on us not to follow any leaders who "train you in the way of inflicting death … Give yourself to the service of life, not the work of death. Do not think that courage and strength are proved by killing and destruction. True strength lies … building up … the ways of peace." (Homily at Drogheda, Ireland, 18-20, 1979; partially quoted in the 2006 *Compendium of the Social Doctrine of the Church*, no. 496). Raising deeper questions about the idea of a "just war", John Paul II de-links the notion of justice from war, calling us "to reject definitively the idea that justice can be sought through recourse to war".[54]

Like previous popes, John Paul sees violence as leading to more injustice, and deplores the scale of modern warfare. Combining Paul VI's distinctive contribution with his own call for solidarity as an active commitment to the common good of all, he titles his 1987 World Day of Peace message "Development and Solidarity: Two Keys to Peace". Yet the 1990s saw humanitarian disasters in the face of international apathy or ineffectiveness in the former Yugoslavia, Rwanda and Somalia. Hence this pope acknowledges the new concept of "humanitarian intervention" (2000 World Day of Peace message, 11). In the context of Bosnia he said that when "populations are succumbing to the attacks of an unjust aggressor, States no longer have a 'right to indifference'. It seems clear that their duty is to disarm this aggressor, if all other means have proved ineffective" (Address to the Diplomatic Corps, 16 January 1993). But how we disarm remains an open and challenging question.

Along the same lines, and responding again to recent events, John Paul II allows for a nation's right of defence against terrorism (2002 World Day of Peace message, 5), even while holding up forgiveness and interreligious co-operation

---

54 Centesimus Annus (1991) in the Compendium of the Social Doctrine of the Church, no. 438

as by far the better path. Yet when confronted in advance with specific military interventions such as the Gulf War and a US invasion of Iraq, John Paul rejects the possibility of war as "a decline for humanity" (Address to the Diplomatic Corps, no. 7, 1991) and "a defeat for humanity" (Address to the Diplomatic Corps, no. 4, 2003). He says, "A peace obtained by arms could only prepare new acts of violence."[55] Rejecting the inevitability of war in both cases, he urges dialogue and diplomacy in accord with international law.

Benedict XVI returns to the basic question of whether a just war can even exist today (wondering "whether it is still licit to admit the very existence of just war"), agrees that the war against Iraq was unjust, and notes that modern weapons inevitably violate noncombatants ("Cardinal Ratzinger on the Abridged Version of Catechism", Zenit, 2003). "Violence never comes from God" (Angelus Address, 2007). Specifically rejecting violence and embracing Gospel nonviolence, Benedict calls "love your enemies" its "magna carta". Nonviolence is for Christians not merely a behavioural approach, much less a form of obedience to a heteronomous norm. It is "a person's way of being, the attitude of one who is convinced of God's love and power, who is not afraid to confront evil with the weapons of love and truth alone" (Angelus Address, 2007; see also Good Friday message, 2011). "The truth is that it is impossible to interpret Jesus as violent. Violence is contrary to the Kingdom of God. It is an instrument of the Antichrist. Violence never serves man, but dehumanises him" (Angelus Address, 2012). On a visit to Cameroon, Benedict asserted that all genuine religion rejects violence in any form ("The Saving Message of the Gospel Needs to be Proclaimed", 2009).

Nevertheless, Benedict acknowledges the emerging international principle of the responsibility to protect. He says, "Recognition of the unity of the human family, and attention to the innate dignity of every man and woman, today find renewed emphasis in the principle of the responsibility to protect". Yet in the

---

55 Pope John Paul II, "War, a Decline for Humanity." Origins 20 n. 33 (January 24, 1991)," 527, 530.

same address he focuses on how this principle gives priority to prevention and juridical, diplomatic and other nonviolent means of intervention (Address to the General Assembly of the United Nations, New York, 2008). Like John Paul II, Benedict does not explicitly reject the possibility of armed force. Yet, perhaps reflecting scepticism about whether violence can actually end violence, Benedict adds in *Caritas in veritate* that the responsibility to protect must be implemented "in innovative ways" (7). While the Church in the global south has raised concerns about "responsibility to protect" the Holy See has also become increasingly critical of the principle. For example, in September 2008 Msgr. Celestino Migliore stated to the 63rd Session of the General Assembly of the United Nations, "In the past, the language of 'protection' was too often a pretext for expansion and aggression ... [T]his same understanding and practice tragically continues today. This principle is still being invoked as a pretext for the arbitrary use of military might. The use of violence to resolve disagreements is always a failure of vision and a failure of humanity". In 2014, Pope Francis continued to express this concern: "We need to remember how many times, using this excuse of stopping an unjust aggressor, the powerful nations have dominated other peoples and made a real war of conquest".[56]

Benedict follows both Paul VI and John Paul II in urging economic and political "development" as a necessary part of the solution to social problems, and the best way to prevent and remedy injustices. He repeatedly confirms this aspect of Catholic social teaching in his World Day of Peace messages (2008, 2009, 2010), and makes it the centrepiece of *Caritas in veritate*, an encyclical written to commemorate *Populorum progressio*.

It will come as no surprise that Pope Francis reaffirms these same themes, often in the very same phrases. He calls on international parties in conflict to seek peace by dialogue, reconciliation, negotiation and compromise. He appeals repeatedly

---

56 See recent critiques of R2Protect and promotion of "responsibility to prevent" https://www.transcend.org/tms/2018/09/mass-atrocities-and-western-imperialism-evaluating-responsibility-to-protect/

for nonproliferation and disarmament, especially but not only of nuclear arms. Praying for peace in Egypt, Francis reiterates that "the true force of the Christian is the force of truth and love, which means rejecting all violence. Faith and violence are incompatible!" The way of Jesus is the way of peace, reconciliation, "living for God and for others". The strength of the Christian is "the force of meekness, the force of love" (Angelus Address, 19 August 2013). When, like John Paul and Benedict, Francis is confronted by the prospect of a military intervention in Syria by US and French "superpower", he is insistent that "war brings on war! Violence brings on violence" (Angelus address, 31 August 2013). In 2014, he declares that "war is never a necessity".[57] In 2016, he clearly states, "The commandment, 'Thou shalt not kill' has absolute value, and concerns both the innocent and the guilty, and even criminals maintain the inviolable right to life, the gift of God."[58]

Expanding on these themes, Francis adds, "My Christian faith urges me to look to the Cross ... *violence is not answered with violence*, death is not answered with the language of death. In the silence of the Cross, the uproar of weapons ceases and the language of reconciliation, forgiveness, dialogue and peace is spoken. This evening, I ask the Lord that we Christians, and our brothers and sisters of other religions, and every man and woman of good will, cry out forcefully: *violence and war are never the way to peace!* .... War always marks the failure of peace, it is always a defeat for humanity. Let the words of Pope Paul VI resound again: 'No more one against the other, no more, never! ... war never again, never again war!'. 'Peace expresses itself only in peace, a peace which is not separate from the demands of justice but which is fostered by personal sacrifice, clemency, mercy and love'. Forgiveness, dialogue, reconciliation – these are the words of peace, in beloved Syria, in the Middle East, in all the world!"[59]

57 Message to Sant' Egidio, 8 Sept. 2014.

58 http://www.catholicherald.co.uk/news/2016/02/22/pope-calls-on-international-leaders-to-abolish-death-penalty/

59 Pope Francis, Vigil of Prayer for Peace [in Syria], 7 September 2013.

After the publication of *Laudato Si'*, in which he connected war and ecological destruction (no. 56), Pope Francis urged the United Nations in New York to support sustainable development while protecting the environment. He decried the hypocrisy of talking about peace while manufacturing arms; and rebuked international leaders for failing to find peaceful solutions to global conflicts, especially in the Middle East.[60]

Some ambiguity in Pope Francis's position on violent force has been introduced regarding the dilemma of how to defeat the international terrorist organisation known as Islamic State (IS or ISIS). In November 2014, the pope remarked informally to reporters that dialogue even with ISIS should not be considered a "lost cause".[61] Yet, "I can only say that it is licit to stop the unjust aggressor. I underscore the verb 'stop'; I don't say bomb, make war — stop him. The means by which he may be stopped should be evaluated."[62] Perhaps going beyond John Paul and Benedict, Francis explicitly adds that he is not endorsing bombs and war.[63]

A new or at least more visible dimension of the endorsement of Gospel nonviolence by recent popes is their awareness that ethical analyses, Church teachings and publicly accepted ideals and norms are one thing; commitment, solidarity, and the political will to live up to ideals and abide by norms are another. Therefore condemning violence is not enough; a huge task remains to convert hearts and minds, and to show that another way is truly possible. A similar awareness is manifest in *Laudato Si's* use of prayer and poetry, its invocation of saints and heroes, its multiple references to local bishops' conferences, its appeal to

---

60 Pope Francis, Address to the General Assembly of the UN, 28 September 2015.

61 "Dialogue with terrorists is almost impossible, but the door must always remain open" (La Stampa, Pubblicato il 25/11/2014) https://www.lastampa.it/2014/11/25/vaticaninsider/dialogue-with-terrorists-is-almost-impossible-but-the-door-must-always-remain-open-rBKyklv9838HuN7Zdx011N/pagina.html

62 "Pope talks airstrikes in Iraq, his health, possible U.S. visit" by Francis X. Rocca (Catholic News Service, 8/18/2014) http://www.catholicnews.com/services/englishnews/2014/pope-talks-airstrikes-in-iraq-his-health-possible-u-s-visit-cns-1403469.cfm

63 Left unclear is whether Pope Francis envisions more limited and carefully targeted uses of violence as a last resort; or whether he has in mind such measures as nonviolent peacekeeping, civil society acts of nonviolent resistance and protest, or initiatives by Islamic religious leaders and faith communities to deter membership in ISIS.

interreligious spirituality and commitment, and its accompaniment by a Vatican video illustrating the beauty and endangerment of "our common home". It is crucial to mobilise nations, peoples, communities and members of faith traditions, by awakening imagination, inspiring new identities and creating wider worldviews.

In this vein, it is important to note that public symbolic actions by recent popes go beyond "teaching" in the sense of pronouncements and documents. Symbolic actions and events creatively reach out to those of many faiths, and span divisions that spawn violence. One example is the well-publicised prayer vigil for peace in Syria that Francis held in St. Peter's Square in September 2013. He was joined by 100,000 peace advocates, even as international leaders debated the possibility of military action. Another example is the prayer of three successive popes – John Paul, Benedict, and Francis – at the Western Wall or "Wailing Wall" in Jerusalem, the remnants of a platform on which the Second Temple was built. Their widely circulated and iconic images represent Christian repentance of suffering caused to the Jews, as well as hope for peace between Israelis and Palestinians. The latter message was brought home powerfully (and controversially) by Francis's additional visit to the "wall of separation" in Bethlehem.

2017 World Day of Peace Message

Each document of the Catholic Church relating to peace and war since Pope John XXIII's *Pacem in Terris*, through the Council document on *The Church in the Modern World* to the US bishops' letters *The Challenge of Peace* and *The Harvest of Justice* has given progressively more space to the issue of nonviolence, all the way to the 2017 peace message.

Pope Francis's World Day of Peace message issued on 1 January 2017 has gone beyond previous papal statements in laying out a robust substantive theological and pastoral articulation of nonviolence. The following reflects on what makes this message historic and how it can serve as a key resource for a foundational Church document on active nonviolence.[64]

That Pope Francis consciously chose "nonviolence" as the theme of his message to the world on New Year's Day 2017, is powerful. The pope unabashedly pointed out that "nonviolence" is what Jesus taught and modelled and said, "To be true followers of Jesus today also includes embracing his teaching about nonviolence."[i] The pope is signalling a true return to the sources for the Catholic Church: Sacred scripture and the traditions of the early Church. Just as the return to the sources (*ressourcement*) by theologians and philosophers such as Henri de Lubac, Jeanne Ancelet-Hustache, Yves Congar, Marie-Thérèse d'Alverny, Marie-Madeleine Davy and Karl Rahner fuelled the renaissance of Catholic theology and the magnificent documents of the Second Vatican Council, so today the pope is returning in a fresh way to the sources.

First, he is reading the Gospels attentively and finds his inspiration there. He says for example: "Jesus himself lived in violent times ... But Christ's message in this regard offers a radically positive approach. He unfailingly preached God's unconditional love, which welcomes and forgives. He taught his disciples to love their enemies and to turn the other cheek. When he stopped her accusers from stoning the woman caught in adultery and when, on the night before he died, he told Peter to put away his sword, Jesus marked out the path of nonviolence. He walked that path to the very end, to the cross."[65] Pope Francis is not using natural law theory as the basis of the Church's teaching on war and violence; he is going straight to the Gospels , e.g. the Sermon on the Mount is described as the "manual" for this approach to peacemaking. Such a shift enables a clearer statement by Pope Francis that "peacebuilding" is expressed "through active nonviolence".

---

64 "Why Pope Francis' World Day of Peace Message is Such a Breakthrough," by Terrence Rynne (10 April 2017) https:// nonviolencejustpeace.net/2017/04/10/why-pope-francis-world-day-of-peace-message-is-such-a-breakthrough/

65 Ibid.

And we might extend this to say clearly that constructive "peacebuilding" is distinct but complementary to nonviolent resistance. He also reflects on the lived tradition of the early Church and how they confronted persecution with courageous nonviolence and how they stunned the world, prompting massive conversions to Christianity.

The third source of inspiration for Pope Francis is the living witness of believing, nonviolent Christians across the world. He says: "Nor can we forget the eventful decade that ended with the fall of Communist regimes in Europe. The Christian communities made their own contribution by their insistent prayer and courageous action. Particularly influential were the ministry and teaching of Saint John Paul II. Reflecting on the events of 1989 in his 1991 encyclical *Centesimus Annus*, my predecessor highlighted the fact that momentous change in the lives of people, nations and states had come about 'by means of peaceful protest, using only the weapons of truth and justice'."[66]

As the Pope reclaims Jesus's teaching on nonviolence, he is saying that in the face of violence and war: no more quiescence, no more anguished acceptance, no more standing on the side wringing hands. Instead get in the middle of the fray and fight violence with the "weapons of truth and love".[67] He underlines the teaching with the penetrating words of Benedict XVI: "Love of one's enemy constitutes the nucleus of the Christian revolution."[68]

Additionally, the pope's message is not a simply "religious" appeal. The title of the message is "Nonviolence: A Style of Politics for Peace". The Pope is making nonviolence not just the keynote of a Christian's faith in Jesus, he is saying that nonviolence is effective in the real world of politics — and is superior to and more effective than violence. The world never gets to peace through violence and war but only begets more violence and war. As Walter Lippmann wrote:

66 Ibid.

67 Ibid.

68 Benedict XVI, Angelus, 18 February 2007

"...the abolition of war depends primarily upon inventing and organizing other ways of deciding those issues which hitherto have been decided by war."

Since publishing the 2017 World Day of Peace message, Pope Francis has used the word "nonviolence" in various statements and interviews. Even more substantively, the pope has promulgated historic, nonviolent positions, including making the death penalty inadmissible[69] and condemning the possession, as well as the use, of nuclear weapons.[70]

Episcopal Pastoral Letters and Statements

Though the focus of this discussion has been on post-Vatican II popes, it is important to realise that the most effective "official" teachers of Gospel nonviolence in local contexts are the local episcopacy, accompanied by clergy, religious, pastoral ministers, catechists, community workers and members of base communities. Their existential perspective is frequently very different from that of high-level Vatican teachers, heads of state and international leaders who have the power and prerogative to deliberate about unleashing their considerable military arsenals (or even a UN peacekeeping force) against less powerful aggressors.

For example, in Medellín, Colombia (1968), the Conference of Latin American Bishops named the support by political authorities of an oppressive elite as a major source of violence, and recognised structural injustice as a form of

---

69 Linda Bordoni, Pope Francis: 'death penalty inadmissable', Vatican News, August 8, 2018: "Pope Francis has approved a new revision of paragraph number 2267 of the Catechism of the Catholic Church, according to which "a new understanding has emerged of the significance of penal sanctions imposed by the state," thus "the death penalty is inadmissible." The decision was announced by the Congregation for the Doctrine of the Faith in a 'Letter to the Bishops' dated 1 August and signed by the Prefect, Cardinal Luis Francisco Ladaria. https://www.vaticannews.va/en/pope/news/2018-08/pope-francis-cdf-ccc-death-penalty-revision-ladaria.html

70 Joshua J. McElwee, "Pope condemns possession of nuclear weapons in shift from church's acceptance of deterrence," National Catholic Reporter, November 10, 2017.
https://www.ncronline.org/news/vatican/pope-condemns-possession-nuclear-weapons-shift-churchs-acceptance-de-terrence

"institutionalised violence". They called for a Church that is not only nonviolent, but in solidarity with those who are poor. In 1983, the bishops of the United States reflected their own cultural situation within a superpower nation, when they embraced Gospel nonviolence in the first half of their pastoral letter "The Challenge of Peace". Yet they went on in the second half to endorse a policy of "strictly conditioned" nuclear deterrence which placed the lives of millions and the health of the entire planet in jeopardy. "The Harvest of Justice is Sown in Peace", the US bishops' pastoral letter issued on the 10th anniversary of "The Challenge of Peace", was more critical of just war theory, called for "peaceable virtues" and underlined the potential of nonviolence to be a principle of political debate and government decisions. And in November 2017 the Vatican sharply answered the 1983 position by officially condemning the possession of nuclear weapons and shifting from an acceptance of the policy of deterrence.

Over the past half-century, the Church has increasingly declared that humanity must look beyond violence to solve the enormous problems we face. Following is a sample of statements by bishops and episcopal conferences on nonviolence.

Africa

- *Do not be afraid; rise above adversity.* This "message of encouragement and hope" was released by the Catholic bishops of South Sudan on 16 June 2016. It can also be found on the *Solidarity with South Sudan website.*
- Bishop Kevin Dowling C.Ss.R., Rustenburg, South Africa: *A Catholic vision of nonviolence for Africa*, 5 December 2016.
- Bishop Kevin Dowling, C.Ss.R., Rustenburg, South Africa: *Nonviolence and peacemaking: Lessons from Oscar Romero, Denis Hurley and Pope Francis* 25 January 2017.

Asia

- *Japanese bishops conference endorsed* the Appeal to the Catholic Church to recommit to the centrality of Gospel nonviolence and sent a letter to Cardinal Peter Turkson.

- *Ten Days for Peace (2017)*, a message from the president of the Catholic Bishops' Conference of Japan.
- *Catholic Bishops Conference of the Philippines (CBCP): The many names of God and the blessing of peace*, 30 April 2015: "To kill in God's name – this is one of the most painful contradictions of our time! ... Jesus is the incarnation of the supreme welcome of the other."
- *CBCP: Striving for a Just Peace, the moral road*, 11 July 2015: "All-out war is not the answer to the Mindanao situation. ... We want a Bangsamoro Basic Law that is rooted in social justice..."
- *CBCP: Statement on torture*, 23 June 2015
- *CBCP: On the killing of voiceless and defenceless lumads*, 11 September 2015, Your Brother's Blood Cries Out to Me from the Ground! (Gen 4:10)
- *CBCP: Pastoral appeal to our law enforcers: Appeal to reason and humanity*, 20 June 2016: "To kill a suspect outright, no matter how much surveillance work may have antecedently been done on the suspect, is not morally justified. Suspicion is never the moral equivalent of certainty, and punishment may be inflicted only on the ground of certainty."
- *CBCP: Ethical guidelines on proposals to restore the death penalty*, 14 September 2016: "To every man and woman is open, by the Saviour, Jesus Christ, the invitation to the fullness of life. Every man and woman is a person redeemed by God's own Son, made an adopted son or daughter of God, and heir to the promise of the Resurrection. This is the dignity of the human person. It is this dignity that the death penalty transgresses."
- *CBCP: Pastoral on deaths and killings*, 30 January 2017: "We, your bishops, are deeply concerned due to many deaths and killings in the campaign against prohibited drugs. This traffic in illegal drugs needs to be stopped and overcome. But the solution does not lie in the killing of suspected drug users and pushers. ... Every person has a right to be presumed innocent until proven guilty. Society has ways and processes to catch, prove guilty and punish perpetrators of crimes. This process must be followed, especially by agents of the law."
- *CBCP: Statement on Marawi, terrorism and dialogue*, 10 July 2017: "We all cry from our hearts: War in Marawi, never again! War in Marawi, no more! We

therefore call for the return to normalcy and peace in Marawi and its environs as soon as possible. ... The basis for peace and understanding already exists. It is part of the very foundational principles of both faiths: love of the One God and love of neighbor."

- *CBCP bishops oppose arming priests in response to the killing of priests*, 12 June 2018: "We are men of God, men of the Church and it is part of our ministry to face dangers, to face deaths if one may say that way. But we would do it, just what Jesus did."

Asia-Pacific

- Rose Marie Berger, *"Fiji archbishop advocates nonviolence to help stabilize social unrest"*, National Catholic Reporter, October 8, 2019.
- David Nussman, *"Hong Kong bishop: Rosary is 'nonviolent resistance' to evil"*, PagadianDiocese.org.

Europe

- Belgian bishops endorsed the "Appeal to the Catholic Church to Recommit to the Centrality of Gospel Nonviolence".
- *German Bishops Conference: "Gerechter Friede" ("A Just Peace")*, 27 September 2000
- *East German (GDR) Catholic Bishops' pastoral letter on peace (1983)*

North America

- "The Church is in the midst of a fundamental reappraisal of how to balance the Christian obligation to nonviolence with the need to resist evil in the world. ... The power of nonviolence, once relegated to the category of romantic idealism, has emerged as a potent force for social transformation and the building of lasting peace." -- Bishop Robert McElroy of San Diego, speaking after Pope Francis's remarks at a Vatican conference on nuclear disarmament held in November 2017.
- *The challenge of peace, USCCB 1983*, God's promise and our response, a pastoral letter on war and peace by the USCCB, 3 May 1983.

- *The harvest of justice is sown in peace, USCCB 1993*, a reflection of the USCCB on the 10th anniversary of the Challenge of Peace.
- *A statement to the Muslim community, Catholic bishops of Saskatchewan 2017*: "condemning violence, particularly violence in the name of God, whose name is peace", 30 January 2017.
- Baltimore's Archbishop William Lori's *pastoral letter on nonviolence* begins a dialogue in his archdiocese on nonviolence, racism and the struggle for justice based on the principles of Rev. Dr. Martin Luther King, Jr.

Latin America

- *Que en Cristo Nuestra Paz México tenga Vida Digna*, Mexico (2010)
- Conference of Latin American Bishops, Medellín, Colombia (1968); excerpts on *justice, peace and poverty* from final document, 6 September 1968 *(Excerpted by Gerald Schlabach)*
- Archbishop Oscar Romero, El Salvador: *The Church and Popular Political Organizations*: Third Pastoral Letter of Archbishop Romero, co-authored by Bishop Arturo Rivera y Damas, Bishop of Santiago de María, Feast of the Transfiguration (6 August 1978)
- Archbishop Oscar Romero, El Salvador: *The Church's Mission Amid the National Crisis*: Fourth Pastoral Letter (6 August 1979)
- Archbishop José Luis Escobar Alas, San Salvador: Pastoral Letter: *"I See Strife in the City"*: On the Occasion of the Feast of the Beloved Blessed Oscar Romero (24 March 2016)
- *Aparecida* (Bishops of Latin America and the Caribbean) #541-543: peace and violence issues are addressed; the power of love is contrasted with violence
- Writings of Dom Helder Camara of Brazil

2. Biblical Foundations of Nonviolence

Nonviolence and the Hebrew Bible

The Israelites were not simply more cheerful than the Babylonians who enslaved them; they saw the same world with the same violence, but they refused to resign themselves to it as "just the way it is". God, they thought, was a revolutionary who wanted to change the world. This is what salvation meant: not plucking a few survivors from the wreckage of the world and installing them in heaven, but creating a new heaven and a new earth. So God begins this grand revolutionary project by calling a goat-herder from Ur and gathering a small group of people around him.

The election of this ragged group does not seem a promising way to start a revolution. Scripture scholar Gerhard Lohfink explains it in terms of the nonviolence of God. Most revolutionaries use violence because they are short on time; there must be one grand upheaval in which the powers are overthrown. God, on the other hand, has all the time in the world. God is nonviolent, so God begins the transformation of the world by calling a small group to live differently so that people can see a beautiful life and join the movement voluntarily, not by coercion.

In the Hebrew Bible violence is closely associated with matters of God. Scripture does not camouflage the violence we do to each other. Instead, it exposes this violence. To achieve the goal of revealing in its pages a God of covenant and peace, the Bible does not hesitate to place this God in dangerous proximity to all types of violence. In so doing it demonstrates that covenant and peace have their price and cannot be regarded as something easily enjoyed or gently obtained. The Bible also reveals that the content of its pages is not simply a pious story, but an experience of salvation, which seeks to integrate all human reality, even in its most negative dimensions of violence, suffering and death.

The witness of scripture presents human history as full of violent experiences: wars, deportations, forced exile, interpersonal violence, the rape of women, abandonment of the most vulnerable. Throughout, God chooses the side of the poor, oppressed and exploited. But the language expressing God's justice and partiality for those who suffer emphasises God's power by using violent imagery that represents how the human family visualises power historically.

The God of the Bible is near us throughout history, debating and defying the violence that we do to each other. These stories include the human urge to have divine legitimation for the violence we inflict on others. Alongside this is also the profound and vital experience of a God who liberates, who makes a covenant and has a plan of life and peace, but at the same time punishes, avenges, rages and does not hesitate to dialogue with the people about violence, even giving the impression that we have found the legitimation we so misguidedly seek.

This perception does not fail to mark deeply the experience and spirituality of the people of the Bible, forcing it to raise questions that very much resemble ours today:

- If God appears linked to violence and if, on the other hand, biblical faith tells us God can only want and do good, must we conclude that violence is good and positive?
- How do we reconcile the revelation of a God of all mercy, witnessed to throughout scripture, with the image of a God who uses violence to show power? Which God do we believe in? Which God claims us as God's own, making of us all one family and inheritors to fellowship in the Spirit?
- At a time when violence threatens humanity and Earth, our common home, and where various sectors of society and the Church seek nonviolent solutions to the drama of conflict and violence, Christians face a dilemma: If our reading of God in history is that God is violent, then how can we be nonviolent? Must we choose between the God of the Hebrew Bible, who is sometimes depicted as wrathful and vengeful, and the God of Jesus, who reveals himself as redeeming love in the powerlessness of the cross?

God does not appear to humanity except through what humanity is. Through lenses marked by sin and hurt, the human being can often see only a violent God. The violence our eyes see in the God of the Bible is often the revelation of our own violence. Immersed in the sin of our own violence, human beings can only see a God who also interacts with us through violence.

This way of seeing God bears a distorted understanding of who God is and who we are as created in God's image. God reveals Godself to us in truth, even when this revelation shows our interpretation of God acting violently. God creates the creature with love and freedom. Therefore, God respects the paths and options that this freedom takes. God does not interfere or force human beings to do what we simply cannot, or to understand what we do not yet have the capacity to assimilate. Yet God accompanies and reveals Godself to the extent that the human being can bear, at the same time preparing us to take other steps and move forward in truth, life and light.

The God of the Bible is not like God's creatures. God does not feel obligated or indebted to a logic in which evil is paid with evil and good with good. Even when this seems to be the case — as in the *lex talionis*, where Moses attributes to the Lord "only one eye for an eye" — its hope is to limit, not increase, violence. Whenever a human being expects or demands from God predictable or symmetrical behaviour, we will often be systematically disappointed. God does not play the human game of the dynamics of retributive justice.

Neither does God imitate or mimic human justice, making it clear that God is divine and not human. Hence, God's revelation can often be felt as wrath. But this is not the final word. In so doing, God breaks our temptation to isolate God in a reductive mimicry and takes advantage of this to teach us that God is God, the totally Other, the different, not similar to human beings.

When the biblical story witnesses to the eruption of human violence with its tragic consequences — war, conquest and looting of a city — God often pushes back to challenge this violence. According to Moses, God will no longer consent to or even advise the extermination of the entire population of a city, or all the individuals who are in it. But God is portrayed as willing to order, for example, not to exterminate every person in a town but only the males (Deut 20:13); or according to Joshua, God is portrayed as supporting the subjugation and destruction of a city that is cursed, but without appropriating its treasures (Joshua 6:18). God reduces the violent desire of the people, forcing them to limit their own unbridled and predatory drives, in order to be able to see life beyond instinct, acquisition and domination.

One strand of the rabbinic tradition interpreted these attacks depicted in the Bible in such a way as to declare that military power should no longer be used by the Jewish people.[71] God's activity in history is always directed towards love and forgiveness without measure as the ultimate good for all creation (Isaiah 11). Even though we come to know God through the violence that marks human history, the God of the Bible actively leads us towards love and nonviolence. This is God's ultimate and final intention, and in the midst of the violence he "baffles" and "deconstructs" the concepts and images that Israel has about God.

God does not magically eliminate violence to move closer to love, but takes violence upon Godself in order to break this diabolical process. The hard questions that arise when we consider God's closeness to violence lead to the affirmation that the central message of scripture is "God is love". In the Christian story God consistently follows the path of meekness and peace in the incarnation, life, death and resurrection of Jesus. This is where God is fully revealed, not in revenge and violence, but in the place of the victim.

The nonviolent practice of God makes a way, even amid violence, that inspires and illuminates any human desire for nonviolence. Since violence imposes itself with the

71 "Reasoning with Violent Scripture: With a Little Help From Job" by Edward Kessler (Journal of Scriptural Reasoning, 2004, University of Cambridge) http://jsr.shanti.virginia.edu/back-issues/vol-4-no-1-july-2004-the-wisdom-of-job/reasoning-with-violent-scripture-with-a-little-help-from-job/

force of the sin of non-meekness, we recognize that meekness[72] will bear the scars of violence. To claim that the practice of meekness can stand outside historical experiences of conflict and violence is illusory and falsely romantic and idyllic. To wish for a peacebuilding that eludes and diverts from the paths of conflict is to lie to oneself and to the human condition. It is in the midst of conflict that love can open its way. This is the path that God has taken. And this will be the only possible way to teach the human being the difficult art of peace with patience and love.

To illuminate this trajectory in the Judeo-Christian tradition, we examine three key texts in the Hebrew Bible: Cain and Abel (Gen 4:1-24), the sacrifice of Isaac (Gen 22:1-19) and the Suffering Servant of Second Isaiah (Is 52-53).

Cain and Abel (Gen 4:1-24): "Two brothers before God"

Cain is the first human born of a human. Cain and Abel's conflict leads to the first violence, a murder.

The biblical text then presents the two siblings, Cain and Abel, with different occupations. Cain is linked to agricultural practice and Abel to pastoral. This difference of activities will characterise a difference of attitudes, because in the development of individual vocations, human beings develop their own perspective from their experience with the environment. In the case of the biblical account, Cain and Abel demonstrate different religious practices, which may indicate different perspectives in the religious-moral sphere as a result of the activities developed. The division into two distinct functions also leads to different sacrifices for different religious practices. Each cult belongs to a culture. There are, therefore, two altars and two cults.

---

72 Glen Stassen points out that wherever the word praeis ("meekness") appears in the Bible, "it always points to peacefulness or peacemaking," while Clarence Jordan preferred to render it as "completely surrendered to the will of God" (Stassen, 49, citing Jordan, 1974, 24-25). Reflecting on Paul's use of this term, Raniero Cantalamessa notes, "Meekness ("prautes") is placed by Paul among the fruits of the Spirit (Galatians 5:23).

Verses 4b and 5 tell us that the Lord reacts differently to the offerings of the brothers. However, it is not clear why there is divine rejection of Cain's offer. This raises a lot of questions for us to consider. One interpretation is that the divine reaction could be a challenge to the sedentary-agricultural practice, demanding that it leave behind its attitude of domination and certainty about human ability in controlling our surroundings. Instead, God seems to privilege the attitude of Abel, a nomadic shepherd who, in his fragility and unstable activity, offers the true cult that pleases God in its understanding of humility before God's ultimate sovereignty.

The prophet Amos denounces the religion used to mask inequalities and placate the conscience of the rich (Am 5:21-23). In this case we find the Lord rejecting the worship of Israel, demanding justice instead of the opulent offering. The Lord, in the voice of the prophets, rejects not the offerings in themselves, but the spirit with which they are placed before God. God is not manipulated by the quality or quantity of the offerings, but demands true worship, the practice of love, justice and fidelity. The sin of Cain can be understood in these terms, rather than in the quality of his offering. As an eponym of the Cainites, Cain would be the one who gave rise to the worship that would later be severely condemned by the prophets of Israel, for their distance from the practice of justice and fidelity to the Lord.

Another hypothesis lies in the theme of the enemy brothers, inviting us to look at the expressions of this relationship. Cain, feeling inferior to the younger brother, allows himself to be invaded by hatred against his brother. In Cain we see the mimetic desire (René Girard's phrase meaning a desire for what somebody else has or wants)[73] in its most perverse form: converted into envy, resentment and, finally, hatred. Mimetic desire leads Cain to escape the otherness that seems to divide and tear him apart. Like Adam and Eve, Cain does not accept divine

---

73 See René Girard's Things Hidden since the Foundation of the World (Stanford University Press, 1987) and I See Satan Fall Like Lightning (Orbis, 2001) for Girard's work on mimetic theory, violence, and sacrifice.

sovereignty, refuses to obey it and makes of himself a god. Otherness is denied in Cain, both in the person of Abel and in obedience to the divine mandate.

The God of Israel is sovereign and has motives that escape God's subjects. The God of Israel reveals himself as the great Other, "an Other over which the human being has no power, is immutable, does not surrender to the impatient pursuits of [humanity]"[74] and yet the Lord does not fear the otherness arising from this relationship with humans; on the contrary, God accepts participation in the dialogical experience, in a process that helps humans to deepen their "problems and to solve them through an experience more and more correct and complex".[75]

God dialogues with Cain to try to conquer sin and his "downcast countenance". This witnesses to the intimate drama between Cain, God and consciousness, the drama of every human being. Divine guidance urges Cain to acknowledge the way he has favoured the spread of sin. He is asked to develop his conscience by trusting God and kinship. Becoming aware that sin is at the door is the imperative that imposes total responsibility for the dynamics of its choice. God proposes to Cain "to do right", but Cain does not let himself be convinced. The divine proposal is the protection of the sinner's life. Abel's murder will be an extension of Cain's sin. In the dialogue given in verses 9 and 10 Cain responds casually and provocatively about his brother. His reply — "Am I my brother's keeper?" — is already revealing his distance from familial love. The indifference present in his response brings us a clue that Cain is not sorry for his act.

In the account of the Fall, God asks, "Where are you?" In this text the question changes focus: "Where is your brother?" Before God the responsibility demanded at this moment is with regard to the sibling. The question is novel. It is a social, relational question. The experience of God passes through the experience with the sibling, the social.

---

74 Maria Clara Bingemer, Alteridade e Vulnerabilidade, São Paulo: Loyola, 1993, p.82.

75 Juan Luis Segundo, O dogma que liberta. São Paulo: Paulinas, 1991. p.83.

God does not follow Cain's evasions and reacts to murder with punishment. The cry of vengeance comes from the earth on which Abel's blood was spilled. Here we enter another fundamental reflection in our text. Blood and life belong to God alone. When a person kills another, they attack their own divine power. The blood spilled on the ground cries out directly to the Lord of Life. The divine judgment concerning Cain is more terrible than that concerning Adam and Eve. Here we have an action that cannot be reversed: sibling murder. The earth, the motherly base of life, drank the blood of a brother. The earth itself denies Cain the power to bless it. The earth cannot be Cain's home. The consequence is the life of the fugitive, deportation from that land.

Cain ploughed the soil, offered his fruit, but also brought the blood of his brother to the ground. This blood cries against him from the very soil, which denies Cain its fruit. He is banished from the ground. The divine curse casts him away from the earth: *hä 'adämä*. Cain will become a wanderer, wandering through the land uncultivated and deserted. The desert will be the absence of divine protection; it is a material and spiritual desert.

But Cain does not have the last word. Surprisingly, God places Cain under his protection. God places a sign on Cain. This sign is not a stigma; on the contrary, by it Cain is re-assumed into divine protection. It is a mark that not only protects him, but also removes him from the cycle of punitive human justice. Because of the murder he has committed Cain is separated from God but also, incomprehensibly, kept under God's protection. So God models the protection of the sinner, the guilty one, the aggressor, not merely the pure, the innocent or the victim.

The sacrifice of Isaac (Genesis 22:1-19)

The texts are found in Genesis, chapters 12 to 25, and show the beginning of the process of formation of the Hebrew people. Because they keep a great chronological distance from the "time of origins", these texts cannot be treated as forming a "biography" of Abraham and Sarah, but rather as a record of the origin of the Hebrew people as beginning in God or, more precisely, the relation of a small family nucleus with the God it discovered.

The biblical account describes a migrant trajectory for Abraham and Sarah. They would have left Ur, in the region designated as Chaldea or the land of the Chaldeans (where Iraq is now, near the Persian Gulf), moved south to Assyria, reaching the city of Haran. Then, according to the account, Abraham and Sarah would have descended to Palestine, passed through Egypt and returned to Palestine, a country in which they would have died (in the city of Hebron).

All this wandering was explained as a design of God (cf. Gen 12:1). Abraham and Sarah respond to a call. Their tribe or clan was one of the many groups that migrated along that route, looking for better lands. Having many gods, these groups immediately began to see God as Other, as otherness, as Unique, as One who knows the best destiny for the people, who intervenes, proposes and "dialogues", without being confused by the ideas that individuals can invent.

This seems to be the meaning of Genesis 17:7, when the author of the text attributes to God the phrase "I will be God to you". To be God means to be alone, to be the sovereign, to be that absolute on which Abraham and Sarah are called to place all their trust. To be the centre of life, to take the place of the deities conceived and projected by human beings, this is what the God of Abraham and Sarah wants.

Accepting the conditions of God implies faith in this same God. It is a wager on this promise and we place in it the hope of a better future. On the other hand, Abraham and Sarah should not remain passive, waiting. They are called, even without understanding or knowing clearly where everything will go. God simply requires us to trust, and everything will follow. The land that Abraham and Sarah sought so much, the son that biologically (in natural conditions) they could not have, and the respect and admiration of long and lasting offspring: all this is promised by God to Abraham and Sarah (Gen 12:2-3).

The certainty of faith would still have to be developed and confirmed in the challenges that life imposed. Abraham and Sarah were already older when they departed (Gen 12:4 and 16:2). Since hearing the promise of God, Abraham and Sarah lived in the confrontation between faith and reality. God's promise was rationally incomprehensible: from an elderly husband and wife a great people would be born!

Finally, chapter 21 of Genesis tells of the birth of Isaac, the rightful heir of the promise. The conflict with his nephew Lot was ended by Abraham and Sarah's decision to divide the land, leaving Lot to choose his share (Gen 13:9). This and other episodes are indicative of how Abraham and Sarah were assuming God's logic, changing their criteria and positioning in accordance with what was established by the divine will. Nevertheless, the most forceful demand made on Abraham and Sarah is presented in the sacrifice of Isaac (Gen 22:1-19), a trial set by God. God wants to examine the intensity of their faith and therefore submits them to a test that constitutes a requirement that God does not intend to lead to full compliance. Yet for Abraham and Sarah the divine command is most earnest. It is about being or not being faithful to the God of the Promise, manifesting it in the cultic sacrifice. From these first two verses of the text we can draw some conclusions. First, the narrator's concern to warn that it was a trial, revealing an intention not to hurt the ears of the readers and to show that Adonai is not a bloodthirsty god. Second, in this way the narrator shows that Abraham and God see the same event from different viewpoints. For the former it is a question of the right sacrifice due to God; for the latter, it is about faith in God's promise. The fidelity of Abraham and Sarah to what they believed to be the design of God made them a model of faith.

Abraham and Sarah not only become heirs of God's blessing through Isaac, but become a source of blessing for future generations. The narrator of the epic sacrifice of Isaac does not have in mind doctrinal formulation but the demarcation of a boundary between worshipful and reverent action towards the omnipotent and the murder of human beings. Henceforth it is clearly established that what the Lord wants is distinct from what the gods/idols made by the neighbouring tribes and clans of Israel ask for.

If the sheer number of explicit prohibitions on the shedding of blood and the sacrifice of human beings indicates that Israel has had to combat this violence for a long time, it also shows unequivocally that the God of Abraham and Sarah does not legitimate violence, nor does it fit into the frame of human interests. God alone is Lord and only God can decide sovereignly about the beginning and the end of life. God alone is the first and last word about everything that exists.

Second Isaiah: The suffering servant (Isaiah 52-53)

The theme of human suffering is treated in a new way, when compared with other texts of the Hebrew Bible, in the four Songs of the Servant of YHWH. In the poems of Deutero-Isaiah the themes of suffering, pain and sacrifice — strong and constant interpellations in the journey of the people of Israel — are given a meaning that is unique throughout the history of the Hebrew people. It is a moment of maturity in intertestamental literature, of depth of thought and faith before the mystery of human pain. In the poems of the Suffering Servant we find a new element in the dimension of pain and destruction: the prophet discovers the divine power to transform the element that generates death into a renewing factor of life. He discovers in pain a means of repairing injustice, transformed into oppression and annihilation of the people, and turns it into a prophetic advertisement.[76]

The first poem introduces the person of the Servant. He is Elect, chosen by Adonai, who assigns him a task in the salvation of the people. For this mission the

---

76 "The figure of the Suffering Servant emerges after 587 BC, when the Jewish people were exiled in Mesopotamia. The king of the Babylonian empire, Nebuchadnezzar, after conquering and destroying Jerusalem, deported a large number of skilled Israelites to his capital, Babylon. With the disappearance of the sacrifices in the Temple of Jerusalem, the exiled community felt totally destroyed; they began to believe that the Babylonian gods were more powerful than YHWH, or that YHWH himself had rejected his people because of their sins. The author of chapters 40 to 55 of the book of Isaiah was addressing a dispirited people and giving them a message of consolation." Joan Morera Perich, Dismantling the Hells. Practicing the Nonviolence of Jesus Today (Christianity and Justice Study Center , booklet 169, October 2018).

Lord prepares him by giving him his Spirit. The prophetic spirit surrounds him and assists him to manifest what is right. The Servant is a man whom God sustains to act with discretion and steadfastness in the execution of deliverance. The vocation of the Servant has its source in God. The gift of the divine spirit (*rûah*) becomes the basis of the Servant's activity and also his motivation.

The text indicates that it is God who takes the initiative and chooses the Servant, supports him and guides him towards the mission of establishing on earth the mispat — the right, the moral law founded on the relationship between the people and the Lord.

Next, the song presents seven denials describing how the Servant will perform the mission. The attitude of the Servant reveals a law that contradicts the harsh law of the world, which decrees the death of the marginalised, the broken and the weak. The servant goes ahead with his mission and, although bruised, does not hurt others; though overwhelmed, he does not oppress. The song emphasises the character of nonviolence present in the servant's attitudes. His mission will be guaranteed without the use of violence.

Finally, we hear a promise from the Lord: The Servant will not be broken until he has built the toro. The purpose towards which his mission is directed will be victorious over any and all obstacles and occasions of suffering, oppression or death. The mission will be filled with struggle and may cause him serious pain and discouragement, but he will not be annihilated while it is being fulfilled. The Servant takes the first step towards his mission through resistance to oppression. In resisting, the Servant breaks the chain of violence; the oppression is not reproduced. It affects him, is received by him, and, at the same time, is annihilated through his attitude of resistance and nonviolence.

In the second song, it is the Servant himself who foresees his suffering. In view of his prophetic vocation, the Servant speaks of his calling and destiny, linked to the pronouncement of the Word (v. 2). His mission is linked to the national restoration of the chosen people — "to bring Israel back and to be the light of the nations!" His vocation is to be "the Servant" in order to carry out his mission of gathering the dispersed people and announcing to the peoples the existence and will of the one God. His training comes from the Spirit of the Lord. His equipment is not weapons of war, but the weapons of a prophet: his tongue is like the arrow, and a sword to proclaim the word of God. Though the Servant feels he has toiled in vain, he acknowledges the futility of suffering (v. 5) and reaffirms his trust in the Lord and his understanding that the mission entrusted to him is great (v. 6).

In the third song, the servant's voice sounds like that of a wise and faithful disciple. His specific message is that with his courage (v. 6) and his confidence in divine assistance (vv. 7-9) he will bear misfortunes (vv. 5-6) and will certainly count on the triumph of the Lord (v. 9). The poem begins by presenting the mission of the Servant and the nature of his vocation, it continues by highlighting the obedience and pertinacity of the Servant and concludes by presenting his absolute trust in Adonai.

In verse 4 the Servant defines himself as a disciple of God, someone who every morning receives his lesson, which has a renewed connection with God every day. It is this relationship of intimacy and constancy that gives him the fibre to resist the oppressors who persecute him. His discipleship is a vocation to serve the weak, so it is important to keep an eye on the Word of the Lord.

The Servant hears the Word of the Lord and proclaims it to the community. He is in a difficult situation, because his word is the Word that requires awareness and transformation of reality according to the plan of God. Enmity, aggression, violence, insults and contempt arise, but despite this, the Servant maintains his attitude of fidelity to the Lord. Something totally new arises: instead of lamentation we get the acceptance of suffering. The Servant acknowledges himself victimised, beaten, reviled and annihilated, but in the name of the mispat himself, his mission to bring righteousness to the nations. The Servant consciously assumes suffering. He perseveres because he has found new firmness.

The Servant believes the Lord will come to his rescue, so he accepts the suffering, giving his yes to the will of the Lord. The certainty of final victory and of his election and vocation offers him firmness and strength in the face of suffering and enmity. His certainty does not come from the contradictions and reactions of reality but from his trust in the Lord. The Servant does not believe that any of his enemies can truly defeat him. Condemnation itself does not mean defeat because his support comes from the Lord, who will help him by performing true justice. Here we see the Servant of YHWH taking up his mission and carrying it out. Union with God, the attitude of listening to what God has to say, leads him to another vision of justice: the righteousness of God. This certainty leads him not to retreat from oppression, but to stand firm, to denounce the iniquity of the system that governs the world. The Servant knows that his vocation and consequent mission require him to be prepared for the worst, for misunderstanding, injury and annihilation, for condemnation by historical judgment.

The fourth song presents the Servant as "a man of sorrows," "acquainted with suffering" (v. 3ab); who not only suffered physical pain (vv. 5a, 4cd) but also moral pain (v. 3ef); a victim of slander, being righteous (v. 11c); counted among the transgressors (v. 12d). He was unjustly condemned (vv. 4, 8) and violated (v. 7), to the point of losing human appearance (v. 14). His end is brutal, to be finally buried among the wicked (v. 9).

It seems that the prophet, in describing so much suffering and contempt, does not want, as Job did, to simply remember the suffering of the righteous. The context leads one to believe that he intended to announce something else, totally new in antiquity, revealed for the first time to the world by the Lord, through his prophet (v. 13). He is a righteous man who willingly gives his life to obtain forgiveness for his people.

At the same time that the Servant is a mediator of reparation, he makes the sufferer's suffering the material of his restorative offering, thus transforming his pains into a remedy for his own wounds (v. 11ab); and by offering himself for many (v. 12) also becomes a remedy for their wounds (v. 5d). Deutero-Isaiah makes this figure, unique in the Hebrew Bible, the mediator who carries upon himself "the punishment that will bring peace to the people" (v. 5c).

The question that arises is how to explain the value and effectiveness of the Sacrifice for reparation before God? The prophet himself seems to have sought to answer this problem in his speech. It is the love of Adonai that reaches everywhere and also supports the mission of the Servant as mediator. The mediating sacrifice of the Servant brings salvation and healing in an unsurpassable way (vv. 5d, 12e), for all sinners, because this is the desire of Adonai. God leads and surpasses all limits in the attainment of his designs (v. 10f).

The efficacy of the Servant's sacrifice, guaranteed by the Lord's verdict of magnificence and reward, seems to reveal the mediating sense of salvation from suffering, while at the same time explaining the grace of return. The biblical word has a double nature. It is, at the same time, divine and human. Also it is communitarian. To the people of the Hebrew Bible, both the sin of society and the sin of the individual are against God, against each component of the group and against the social group itself. Therefore, the responsibility of this sin and its consequences is both that of the individual and the community. The human being, created by God, is capable of violence. God cannot be accused as responsible for the evils that we generate by the misuse of our freedom. In this sense, we observe that injustices are rooted in the violation of God's will. We know that the prophet calls upon every individual to leave the way of sin, to ward off misfortune and to encourage the nation to forsake injustice and keep the law in order to enjoy better days.

We identify the Servant of YHWH as a corporate personality: as an individual who represents a community, which has an identity that turns to its own attitudes; and an individual character, or the collective attitudes of all people. Thus, there is a journey from the individual to the community in these songs. The idea of the Servant, according to Carlos Mesters,[77] is inspired by the prophet Jeremiah, the great Sufferer, who never bowed his head before his oppressors and who did everything to uphold hope in the people. Mesters argues that the figure of the Servant of YHWH helps in discovering in his mission the mission of God's own people, who put themselves at the service of the Lord, and, as a consequence, suffer insults, slander and all kinds of oppression. At that historic moment, the people of Israel also reposition themselves, stand before all these reflections and renew the Covenant with the Lord. The people of the captivity were God's servants; they did not allow Nebuchadnezzar to steal their ideals, but instead maintained their ideals and their hope for a society based on law and justice.

The search for the identity of the Servant leads us to resolve the question as to the mission assigned to him: not so much *who* is the Servant but what is his mission. He accomplishes his mission not with bow and sword, but renewed with the spirit of gentleness, meekness and steadfastness in suffering.

As a prophecy, the servant's songs contain the new seed with the full force to propel it into the future: These songs have an eschatological dimension in the sense that at the moment the seed is issued it inaugurates a new birth. The songs give birth to a new mode to be consolidated or embodied in the new kind of human being announced to the Israelites in the person of the Servant.

As we stand before the conception of the intrinsic relationship between the individual and community of the people of Israel, we also begin to understand better the question of the identity of the Servant. This double character — personal and collective, individual and communal — is also present in the figure of the Suffering Servant. This helps us to understand that he is not just one of the mediators of salvation who figure in the history of Israel, but is in all of them in different ways, centred on the personification of the Suffering Servant, which reflects a dialectical interaction between individual and community.

---

77 Carlos Mesters, La misión del pueblo que sufre: Los cánticos del siervo de Dios en el libro del profeta Isaías (Trans. T. Pérez, Madrid:Ediciones Paulinas, 3rd edition, 1983)

Another fundamental aspect of our analysis concerns the Sacrifice of Reparation presented in the poems. The Sacrifice of Reparation — the 'asam — is a precondition for reparation for faults and the consequent lifting of punishment presented in the Priestly Code (Lev 5:14-16). The immolation of the "lamb of reparation" for the forgiveness of sins is refigured here as the voluntary offering of the Servant. Its historical mission becomes the offering of its own life for the salvation of its people from slavery, for the restoration of rights and justice for its people.

The offering of life and its immolation make sacrifice the greatest religious act — life, the highest good of humanity, being voluntarily surrendered to the deity makes it the religious *act par excellence* — recognition of and submission to divinity. For Israel it is gift, fellowship and atonement. The suffering of the Servant was recognised as an effective vicarious sacrifice for reparation of the sins of many. It points to a new meaning for suffering in the economy of salvation of Israel at the same time that it discovers a new economy. All the guilt acquired implies, at the same time, a responsibility to God. Every perverse action directed against the human being is also directed against God.

The people "strayed from the path", turned away from the Lord, led their lives far from God's commandments, set their own criteria for decision-making and allowed themselves to be guided by idols. If the sin of an individual is capable of bringing about the misery of the community in the Hebrew Bible, the reciprocal can also be true: the community can have its sins forgiven, it can find salvation through the repairing act of an individual who offers his or herself in reparation for the whole.

Such salvation is possible because of the understanding of individuality and solidarity of the human person that regulates the individual-community relationship in Israel. Deutero-Isaiah prophesied about the Suffering Servant. More than a "scapegoat" burdened with the sins of the group, the author saw in him the "lamb of reparation" sacrificed (Is 53:7) to obtain forgiveness of sins (Lev 5:16). The novelty lies in having discovered in suffering an effective character for mediation. He is "the righteous one" whom God meets by the rivers of Babylon, among the deportees, to deliver the people from exile.

It was not the altruism or the philanthropy of the Servant that dictated his sacrificial attitude of his own life as mediation — it was Adonai's desire to restore righteousness as part of the plan for salvation. This prevents the death of the Servant from being judged as failure. His mission, the surrender of his life for sinners, mirrors the order of the Lord and the revelation of divine power. The Servant of YHWH, as mediator, thus takes on a new character for the understanding of the people of Israel. The community's renewal comes in a plan of salvation that does not require the elimination of the enemy, but occurs through the depth of connection with God and the desire to accomplish God's salvific plan.

In the Servant of YHWH, we see the highest expression of justice and fraternity. Through the Servant's apparent defeat, the most complete and definitive victory is realised: victory over the powers of death, oppression, violence and the denial of life that comes from the "other". The Servant of YHWH tells of a faith in the human person that is effective in concrete ways, which recognises that final victory is not given to the forces of death; so there is always the possibility of recovery from sin. Restoration of law and justice passes through the person-community of the Servant of YHWH — with the surrender of his own life for the cause of all, which is the cause of God, in the assurance of the definitive power of God.

What God? What violence?

Having reached the end of this brief journey through some paradigmatic texts on the revelation of God in the Hebrew Bible and its relationship with violence, we must point out some conclusions that, although they do not end the task of reflection, reposition its direction.

We can say categorically that the God of the Bible does not use violence. The experience of the God of the Bible is that God does not want death, but life. However, this God allows human beings to engage the divine from what is our existential reality, and this reality includes the practice of violence.

Indeed, the reality of bloody wars and human sacrifices, for example, is an integral part of the lives of the people of Israel, as with so many other societies and nations throughout history. What is striking, therefore, is not so much the content of the narrated text, for example that of Isaac's sacrifice, asked of Abraham, but its insertion in the trajectory of experience and reflection of a people gradually realising that their God is the God of life; and, perhaps most important, that in the maintenance and glorification of life God partners intimately with human beings. To this end, this God, who seems to demand of the frightened and submissive human being a sacrifice that surpasses all normal ethical demands, ends up replacing the human victim with a lamb. That is, God seeks people where they are in terms of religious and ritual violence and makes them go one step further towards respect for life as a whole, with the realisation that God does not want the sacrifice of humans. In the same way, sacrificial rituals with bloodshed of animals are not aimed at stimulating violence, but at regulating and limiting it, within a historical context that makes use of it to signify the relationship of humanity with the divine. The slaughter of beasts as an offering to the Lord was not a demand of God, but a concession to the violent nature of humans. Cain's fratricide is the expression of what we are capable of in relation to our fellow humans, and God meets us at the point where we are, in order to allow access to the communion that will give us the fullness of life.

All this, in essence, points to what is original in the experience of Israel: the experience of the absolute otherness and transcendence of God. The great mark of the experience of the God of Israel is to find the way beyond henotheism and monolatry to the affirmation of faith that God is One and Holy, that is, different, separate. God does not number among human beings, nor are God's thoughts identical with those of the human being (cf. Is 55:8). God is God and not human, although God comes to meet us where we are to make us have access to communion with God's life; to open to us the experience of the central commandment of the Law of Holiness: Be holy as I am holy! This is how God, in acknowledging the murder of Abel, does not kill Cain and, despite holding him accountable to his justice, does not recognise the right for anyone to eliminate his life. Cain is marked with the sign of belonging to the Lord, who is the One to assert Godself as the owner of life and death. In the same way, Abraham, faced with the terrible demand of having to sacrifice his own son, does not end his experience before a godlike Moloch or Chemosh, who would feed on sacrifices of human lives, the silent idols that are satisfied with the violence perpetrated in their name. Cain receives the revelation that this God is another and different, disliking violence against human life. This does not mean that the Hebrew Bible fails to show us God ensuring accountability and correcting God's creatures. However, what we receive from the Hebrew Bible is the deeper accountability that God imposes, making it pedagogical, establishing parameters and ensuring a horizon for when restrictions will end.

God ensures accountability not by killing or eliminating but by engendering again, that is, making mercy an encompassing trait and saving us from destructive escalation. God comes to bear on Godself the accountability that another would merit so that the excess of mercy puts an end to violence, even justified violence. Then, yes, the image of the God of the Hebrew Bible, whose mercy no longer wants sacrifice, shines brightly. Then, yes, the vocation of the human being created by God for peace, not for violence, glows with new light. The human task is revealed as this: to be the bearer of God's merciful accountability and the pardon of grace; to bear a deficit in revenge, even when considered just; accepting loss with the patience and compassion that bear conflict without giving in to the temptation to eliminate it violently, and without demanding full reimbursement for what was lost.

In the Hebrew Bible the figure of the Servant of YHWH is paradigmatic in terms of this maturity of the experience of a God who is both just and merciful, whose love "exceeds" the violence and even the equity of "armed" justice. Even more, Isaiah critiques Israel for trusting in military strength for security rather than in God's ways (31:1-5, 32:15). This critique is a repeated pattern, as Jewish scholar Reuven Kimelman has pointed out (Ps 44:7, 20:8, 1 Sam 17:45, Zech. 4:6).[78] Hence, Isaiah ties the Suffering Servant to shifting the community to trust in God's type of justice and security, as well as ushering in the time when "nation shall not lift sword against nation nor ever again be trained for war" (2:4-5). This mysterious Servant figure, whose exact origin and significance leads exegetes to different interpretations, nevertheless opened the way for the desire and practice of the first Christian communities to identify him with Jesus of Nazareth, he whom they recognised and proclaimed as the Son of God. The path of Jesus Christ is the path of nonviolence, and yet one on which violence is inscribed. The God of the Bible is manifested as merciful and nonviolent, but always encountered within the manifestations of violence in human history, never outside them.

It is to the nonviolence of Jesus that we now turn.

---

78 Kimelman, Reuven, "Nonviolence in the Talmud," In Roots of Jewish Nonviolence, edited by Allan Solomonow, 24-49. Nyack, NJ: Jewish Peace Fellowship, 1985.

Nonviolence and the Christian Bible

The growing consensus of contemporary scriptural and theological research is that Jesus proclaimed and lived nonviolence. This judgment is based on a clear understanding, first, of the realities of his time and his calling to respond to them.[79]

---

79 Numerous seminal works by theologians and scripture scholars illuminating the nonviolence of Jesus have been published since the mid-20th century, from Lisa Sowle Cahill to James Douglass, from Leonardo Boff to John Dominic Crossan, from Albert Nolan to Eileen Egan, from John Dear to Ched Myers, and from Rev. Emmanuel McCarthy to Eli Sasaran McCarthy. Here are a few highlights of this contemporary research.

Robert Daly, SJ, in his work on nonviolence in the New Testament and the early church concludes that there is little scholarly doubt that the message of nonviolence is central to Jesus's life and teaching as well as part and parcel of the faith in early Christianity. Citing the work of Rene Coste, he summarizes a broad consensus of gospel criticism when he affirms: 'It is an incontestable fact that Christ did preach nonviolence, both as a condition and as a consequence of the universal love that he taught us.'" (Robert Daly, SJ, "The New Testament and the Early Church," in Nonviolence: Central to Christian Spirituality, ed. Joseph Culliton (New York: Edwin Mellen Press, 1982), 41. Many influential moral and systematic theologians have incorporated this New Testament scholarship into their work. Edward Schillebeeckx, for example, concluded that based on scripture scholarship Jesus died because of the way he lived -with nonviolent resistance. (Edward Schillebeeckx, Christ: The Experience of Jesus as Lord, New York: Crossroad, 1980.)

Bernard Haring's 1986 volume, The Healing Power of Peace and Nonviolence, is a clarion call to Christians to embrace nonviolent action. Fr. Haring, recognized as one of the finest moral theologian of the twentieth century, rooted his research in the work of a set of scripture scholars who helped him to see vividly the nonviolent Jesus, including Rudolph Schnackenburg, Rudolph Pesch, Norbert Lohfink and Heinrich Spaemann. They found that nonviolence is at the heart of the gospel. (Bernard Haring, The Healing Power of Peace and Nonviolence, New York/Mahwah, NJ: Paulist Press, 1986.).

Another important contribution to this area of study was the publication in 1972 of John Howard Yoder's book The Politics of Jesus, called by theologian Stanley Hauerwas " the most important work of theology of the twentieth century." Using the latest tools of historical/critical biblical scholarship, bridging the gap between scripture studies and moral and systematic theology, and drawing on the work of C.H. Dodd, Hans Conzelmann, Rudolph Schnackenburg, John L. McKenzie, SJ, Robert Margenthaler, Robert North, SJ, Krister Stendhal and Hans Dieter Betz, Yoder concluded that Jesus taught an ethic informed by the sociopolitical realities of first century Palestine whose content consisted most importantly of nonviolence and love of enemy and that this is normative for Christians. (John Howard Yoder, The Politics of Jesus. 2nd ed., Grand Rapids, MI: William B. Eerdmans, 1994.)

The moral theologian Richard Hays, exploring the moral vision of the New Testament, recognizes that the call to nonviolent peacemaking, while not easy, stretches people beyond what is typically considered "realistic" or "natural." He wrote: "God broke through the borders of our standard definition of what is human and gave a new formative definition in Jesus." (Richard Hays, The Moral Vision of the New Testament, San Francisco: Harper San Francisco, 1996, 105.)

The scripture scholar and theologian Walter Wink also made definitive contributions to a revitalized understanding of the nonviolence of Jesus. Through careful exegesis of New Testament texts — including the "hard sayings" of Jesus like "Turn the other cheek" (MT 5:38-41) — he illuminated Jesus's "third way" of nonviolence as an active and transformative alternative to either violence or passivity. Wink's pioneering exegesis and theological analysis has dramatically underscored the centrality of Jesus's programmatic nonviolence. (Walter Wink, Engaging the Powers: Discernment and Resistance in a World of Domination (Minneapolis: Fortress Press, 1992), 175ff.)

The birth, life and death of Jesus as portrayed in the New Testament took place within the context of official and ever-deepening Romanisation in Jesus's Jewish homeland. The Jews were an oppressed people, kept in line by the threat of violence. Tax revenue was regularly sent to Rome to help finance Rome's wars of expansion. Herod's additional taxes went to build elaborate buildings and cities. From every side the people in the countryside were being squeezed. Debt forced many off their precious parcels of land.

It was not surprising that after Herod died in 4 BCE, just after Jesus's birth, their anger sparked a violent revolt. The capital of Galilee, Sepphoris, the home of wealthy landowners, was attacked and its armoury raided. In response, the Roman general Varus sent part of his army into Galilee under Gaius and he "routed all who opposed him, captured and burnt the city of Sepphoris and reduced the inhabitants to slavery". Sepphoris was four miles from Jesus's hometown of Nazareth. Jesus no doubt grew up hearing the story of "The Day the Romans Came", when Rome struck terror into the hearts of the people.

Rome's imperial power was military, economic and political, but also religious, theological and even eschatological. The Romanisation of Israel involved a clash between empire and colony, but also more profoundly between the Kingdom of Rome with its human vision of civilisation, and the Kingdom of God as the divine vision of creation. But how could a God of distributive justice tolerate a world of imperial injustice? God declares in the Torah that "the land is mine; with me you are but aliens and tenants" (Leviticus 25:23). Israel's Romanisation involved not just a human and colonial struggle against imperial violence and oppression, but a divine and eschatological struggle for justice and peace on earth (Luke 2:13-14).

The economics of this time of Romanisation come through in Jesus's parabolic discourse. His parables, as a rhetoric of nonviolent challenge, invited his listeners to think about the results all around them: from the *tenants* in Matthew 21:33-39 and the *labourers* — who stand in the marketplace looking for work all day — in

Matthew 20:1-16 to the *debtors* in Luke 16:1-7 and the *bandits* in Luke 10:30-37. More succinctly, those who had something got much more, and those who had nothing lost even that, as articulated in the warning aphorism of Matthew 13:12 and 25:29.

The incarnation of Jesus enters the deepest level of this fundamental clash.

Both sides of this clash focused on an individual person who embodies the vision and incarnates the advent of this ultimate earthly transformation. In Rome's vision, its dawning Golden Age was incarnated in Augustus Caesar, the bringer of Roman peace, who is portrayed as both human and divine. Israel's eschatological understanding and hope focused on expectations of the Messiah, a human leader suffused with divine power to deliver his people from imperial oppression.

The context of Jesus's life and teaching was a clash therefore between not only a great empire and a small colony, but between two fundamentally different visions for the ultimate destiny of the human race, two diametrically opposed approaches for establishing peace on earth. It is helpful to keep this context in mind when we reflect on Jesus's nonviolence.

"Love your enemies" is theological

"You have heard it said, 'You will love your neighbour and hate your enemy.' But I say to you love your enemies and pray for those who persecute you; so that you may be children of God. For God causes the sun to rise on the bad as well as the good, and sends the rain on those who do good and those who do evil." (Matthew 5:43-45).

Love of enemies is not just human ethical teaching or conventional human wisdom. It is deeply theological. It is revealed in the sacred scriptures and confirmed in Jesus's lived experience with God. Jesus's nonviolence rests on his deep, passionate communion with God. Jesus teaches and practises nonviolence because he has come to know that God, his Everlasting Parent, Abba and Amma, is nonviolent.

Jesus's teaching on "love your enemies" is distinctive because it is so all-embracing, so far- reaching and so rooted in his theological vision. It rests on bedrock. When we drill down to bedrock we find the sure, solid base on which we can build. Jesus points out that the creator of the universe, the source and power of all, is nonviolent. If the creator of all is nonviolent – as Jesus says, "God sends the rain on the good and the bad and shines the sun on the just and unjust" – then we are on solid ground if we act as God acts. God has created all and cherishes all. From Genesis 1 we learned that all human beings are made in the image and likeness of God. That is the reason all human beings have innate dignity. Every human being is a *sacrosanct* creature.

Jesus was deeply versed in the Jewish scriptures. The evangelists portray Jesus as one who speaks in a way that continually calls to mind passages from the Jewish scriptures. Luke's account (Luke 24) of Jesus's encounter with two disciples on the road to Emmaus after the events of Holy Week tells us the lens he used to interpret the scriptures. The disciples were despondent and confused. As they walked along, Jesus came up to them and walked beside them, but they did not recognise him. He began to explain to them how to read the scriptures. He said, "How slow you are to all that the prophets have told you. Did not the Christ have to suffer and then enter his glory?" (Luke 24:25-26). Then starting with Moses and going through all the prophets, he explained to them the passages that were about himself. They said after he had left them, "Were not our hearts burning within us as he explained the scriptures to us?" (Luke 24:32). Jesus focused on a key to understanding the Jewish scriptures as a whole – on the violence willingly suffered by him, the messiah. There is no sense of retribution from God against those who committed the violence to his highly favoured one. Instead, the violence that was willingly suffered led to glory.

Jesus seemed to understand that in the long development of his peoples' scriptures, understandings of God's relationship to violence and retribution had varied and changed. On one hand, the seeds of the idea that divine restorative justice interrupts the predatory logic of blood vengeance were already planted in the primal narrative of Genesis, with God's "protection" of the murderer Cain (Gen 4:15). On the other hand, the deity portrayed sometimes in the Hebrew Bible appears to approve of, and even inspire, bloody war on enemies. The historical context and developing understandings of God in the face of suffering, are important to note — disasters such as exile were interpreted within a traditional worldview which assumed difficult circumstances should be attributed to divine anger. In particular, before monotheism (belief in one God) fully developed, there was an understanding that a community's fate depended upon the comparative strength of its deity. But Jesus never cites these texts, preferring the witness of the prophets. He had come to see that there is no violence in God, and that testimonies that sanction such were actually projections of vengeful and violent human beings.

It is worth reflecting on the scriptural passages that Jesus does emphasise, which follow the "golden thread" woven through the five adjectives describing God in Exodus 34:6: "The Lord is merciful, gracious, faithful, forgiving and forever steadfast." For example, Jesus:

- ignores some texts (e.g. most of Numbers, Judges or Joshua);
- is selective with others (for example, he does not mention the 28 "thou shalt nots" in Leviticus 18-20, but does cite 19:18: "You must love your neighbor as yourself");
- and occasionally redacts out themes of retribution in others (as in his citation of Isaiah 61 in Luke 4:18-19, in which he deliberately omits the last line of 61:2b: "... and the day of vengeance of our God").

Jesus affirms the indiscriminately compassionate God who begins to emerge in the prophetic books, who is ever faithful to the covenant, persisting in love despite human hardness (such as Hosea's metaphor of a husband's fidelity to an unfaithful wife). Jesus embraces Second Isaiah's idea that not only will God refuse to use violent force against humans, but will send a suffering servant, who will show humanity a new way and kind of power to deal with violence: "he submitted to be struck down and did not open his mouth though he had done no violence and spoke no word of treachery" (Isaiah 53:7-9). Jesus sought to embody this conviction that God's salvation intends nothing less than to rescue us from our violence and ideologies of vengeance.

A call to "love our enemies" takes us into the upper reaches of human nature and its capabilities — the upper reaches transformed by grace and the power of God. It is integral to the fulfilment of our salvation story.

"Love your enemies" includes political enemies

Some hear Jesus's teaching and take it to mean personal enemies and that it does not apply to enemies in other countries or ethnic groups. They understand therefore that it has nothing to do with politics. It is only about interpersonal dealings. However, the Gospel of Luke, in particular, makes clear that the teaching applies to any and all who are perceived as enemy and therefore is eminently political. The Gospel of Luke deepens our understanding of just what Jesus means by this radical demand.

Luke highlights one group in particular that was perceived by contemporary Jews as their enemy — the Samaritans. The beginning of antipathy towards the Samaritans goes back centuries. It originates with the conquering of the Northern kingdom by Assyria in 722 BCE. Many inhabitants of the Northern kingdom were transported to Assyria but quite a few in the middle kingdom of Samaria were left behind and were thought to have intermingled with gentiles over the years. While Samaritans were generally understood more broadly as Israelites (albeit of mixed heritage), there were long-standing religious tensions regarding scripture, temple location (the Samaritans built a temple on Mount Gerizim) and priesthood. The antipathy grew even more intense during the period of Hasmonean kings. In his expansive wars of conquest John Hyrcanus (134-104 BCE) burned the temple on Mount Gerizim and totally destroyed the Samaritan city of Shechem.

Luke tells us that Jesus travels through Samaria on his way to Jerusalem; this is in itself notable as such a route would typically have been avoided by Jews, and aligns with Jesus's deliberate nonviolent inclusiveness. Jesus experiences the antipathy of the Samaritans towards the Jews just as he has begun his trek to Jerusalem.

"As the time drew near when Jesus would be taken up to heaven, he made up his mind and set out on his way to Jerusalem. He sent messengers ahead of him, who went into a village in Samaria to get everything ready for him. But the people there would not receive him, because it was clear that he was on his way to Jerusalem." (Luke 9:51-53).

Just to be on the way to Jerusalem was enough to be shut out by the Samaritans. Even more clearly does the latent violent antipathy between the peoples emerge from the reaction of his disciples, James and John.

"When the disciples James and John saw this, they said: 'Lord, do you want us to call fire down from heaven to destroy them? Jesus turned and rebuked them. Then Jesus and his disciples went on to another village." (Luke 9: 54-56).

Jesus rebuked them. Violence is to have no place in their practice or in their hearts. All this time they had been with him, seen his example and heard his teachings and they still instinctively turned to violence as the ready response to an offence.

In the next chapter, Chapter 10, Jesus, still on his journey to Jerusalem, in response to a teacher of the law who is trying to trap him, tells the parable of the Good Samaritan. The teacher of the law has asked Jesus "Who is my neighbour?"

Jesus describes a man severely beaten by robbers and left half dead whom a priest and a Levite had noticed and walked on by. He then describes "a Samaritan who was travelling that way came upon the man, and when he saw him his heart was filled with pity. He went over to him, poured oil and wine on his wounds, bandaged them; and then he put the man on his own animal and took him to an inn, where he took care of him. The next day he took out two silver coins and gave them to the innkeeper. 'Take care of him,' he told the innkeeper, 'and when I come back this way I will pay you whatever else you spend on him." And Jesus concluded, "In your opinion, which one of these acted like a neighbour towards the man attacked by robbers?" The teacher of the law answered: "The one who showed him mercy" (Luke 10: 33-37).

The conjunction of the words "Samaritan" and "neighbour" shattered all conventions. Jesus challenged viewing the Samaritans — and indeed any group — as enemy and the deeper issue of dividing people into outsiders and insiders.

In Chapter 17:11 Luke writes: "As Jesus made his way to Jerusalem, he went along the border between Samaria and Galilee" emphasising again his location in Samaria. He came upon ten men suffering from a dreaded skin disease. He healed them and then the text describes that only one returned to him, thanking him and "glorifying God in a loud voice". (Luke 17:15). That one was a Samaritan, an *allogenes*, an outsider, and popularly perceived as an enemy.

Luke makes clear that the category of enemy refers to everyone who is typically seen as *allogenes* — not our kind, outsiders, those who threaten us, those who are "other". He is communicating that Jesus does away with those categories. All are to be embraced as our brothers and sisters if we are to be children of God. Wars begin in the minds of human beings. Not seeing others as allogenes puts us on the path to peace.

A surprising gift awaits people who practise love of enemies; so-called enemies often have important lessons to teach us when we are open to them.

For example, when Jesus engages the Samaritan woman at the well (John 4) in honest dialogue, it leads to respect, reconciliation and communion. When he listened to the entreaties of the Syrophoenician woman (Mark 7:24-30) to heal her daughter, he was awed by her faith and did what he had not planned on doing. Both model nonviolence: the woman acts on behalf of her daughter — the most vulnerable in society — and Jesus, who engages with her, really listens and is changed.

Luke goes even further to illuminate Jesus's teaching on love of enemies. Even more resented, if not hated, by his people are members of the occupying army of imperial Rome. Luke, however, describes three instances in which persons who were also leaders in the army of Rome, centurions, did some acts worthy of admiration. The first example is in Capernaum, when a centurion sent some Jewish elders to ask Jesus to come and heal a beloved servant who was very ill. The elders recommended him highly to Jesus explaining that he showed love for the Jewish people and had even built a synagogue for them. Jesus healed the servant and commended the centurion for his faith (Luke 7:2-10). The second example Luke describes is a centurion at the foot of the cross who, just after Jesus gave up his spirit, acknowledged the hand of God and proclaimed that Jesus was indeed an upright man (according to Luke's version). (Luke 23:47). The third example is from the Acts of the Apostles, written by Luke (Acts 27:1-28:16). A centurion, Julius, was given the responsibility of delivering Paul to the authorities in Rome. Luke describes Julius's great kindness to Paul. At one point in the tortuous journey Julius proposed an alternative plan to prevent the shipwrecked sailors from killing Paul and the other prisoners.

No one is beyond the pale of the nonviolent love of Jesus and later of his disciples. All — gentiles, Samaritans, Romans, even those who mocked and scourged Jesus — are their siblings. All are the children of God who is their Everlasting Mother and Father. None should be killed or harmed by Jesus's followers. They are to be loved, overwhelmed by love. Jesus's teaching on nonviolent resistance is much more than most forms of pacifism, which require only that we refuse to harm or kill our enemies. It invites us to love them — and show that love through active resistance and outreach. As Martin Luther King said, "Love of our enemies is the key to the solution of the problems of the world."[80]

But surely this is an impossible ideal. How can weak human beings live this way in a world full of conflict? The answer is that Jesus's teaching does not end there. He insists that "love of enemy" is the right stance. It is the right posture in which we reflect the will of God. But he does more than get us in the right posture. He gives us a set of proactive practices that make love of enemy practical. But another section of the Sermon on the Mount, the verses just before the teaching on "love of enemies", shows us how we can make the revolution a reality. Jesus's reading of the scriptures brought him to the realisation of just how powerful and steadfast and nonviolent his God is. Further reading and study and reflection on his people's experiences brought him to understand the power of nonviolent direct action.

Jesus taught creative, nonviolent direct action

Matthew 5: 38-42: "You have heard it said 'an eye for an eye, a tooth for a tooth'. I say to you, do not return violence for violence. Instead, if someone strikes you on the right cheek, turn to him your left. If someone presses you to go one mile, go a second mile. If someone takes your tunic, give him your cloak as well."

Too often in the history of Christianity, this passage has been wrongly seen as a teaching of passivity in the face of evil. When correctly understood it is just the opposite, as Pope Benedict XVI has pointed out.[81] It is a teaching on how

---

80 "Loving Your Enemies," Martin Luther King Jr., 31 August 1952 (The Papers of Martin Luther King, Jr. Volume VI: Advocate of the Social Gospel, September 1948 - March 1963, Clayborne Carson, Susan Carson, Susan Englander, Troy Jackson, and Gerald L. Smith, eds.)

81 Pope Benedict, Midday Angelus, Feb. 18, 2007. He says this "love your enemies" is the "magna carta of Christian nonviolence; it does not consist of surrendering to evil--as claims a false interpretation of 'turn the other cheek' (Luke 6:29)--but in responding to evil with good (Rom. 12:17-21), and thus breaking the chain of injustice."

to assertively, creatively resist evil and oppression without becoming like the oppressor. It makes "love of enemies" practical and doable.

Consider each of the verses in turn. "You have heard it said, 'an eye for an eye and a tooth for a tooth'." Jesus is citing the Scriptural tradition on how to respond to hurt and violence. Even the score but only equally, tit for tat, as part of a law intended to prevent the escalation of violence. It had been a big advance over an earlier mindset of "if someone takes your eye, take their body" — i.e. respond with increasing or overwhelming violence and teach their whole community a lesson they would not forget. Yet even this good intention still often led to the community getting stuck in cycles of violence.

Hence, the second verse: "I say to you, do not respond with violence for violence." The verb *antistenai* has frequently and unfortunately been translated as "do not resist" — accentuating the interpretation that Jesus is teaching us to be doormats in the face of evil — contrary to the way he himself acts. The verb *antistenai* means, literally, "stand against". Throughout the Bible standing against means standing militarily against an opponent. The verse is better translated as "do not respond to evil with evil" or "do not respond violently to evil done to you".

Consider the next three verses first as a whole. They each describe a harm done to someone, fairly common harms that could have happened to anyone listening to Jesus. As tightly drawn examples in a series, they prompt the listener to think of more examples.

The first example, of someone striking another across the right cheek describes someone backhanding another with a demeaning slap. (It is taboo in the culture to use the left hand in such a situation.) The right cheek can only be reached by someone's right hand with a backhanded blow. Jesus is most likely describing someone in a superior position, a slave owner to a slave, an abusive husband to his wife, dealing a demeaning blow to a perceived inferior. How to respond? The expected reaction might be to cower or to swallow the insult to avoid more blows. Jesus says instead, to turn the other cheek — be willing to risk a fist to the face. Imagine someone on the receiving end of an insulting backhanded blow, looking at the abuser in the face, communicating not only that he is not cowed, he asserts his equal dignity, and thus, discovers his power. This interrupts the logic of humiliation and calmly calls on the abuser to rethink his behaviour as inconsistent with their own dignity.

Such an action is not only not passivity, it is creative nonviolent direct action designed to surprise the opponent, illuminate shared equal dignity, and invite a change in behaviour.

The second example describes a situation in which one person is taking another's tunic, the garment under the cloak, as a pledge in a lawsuit. (Jewish law, as a protection for the destitute and to avoid the risk of death from exposure, forbade taking the heavy outer garment or cloak of another, unless to use as a pledge for a loan, in which case it had to be returned every evening because it is what an impoverished person uses to sleep in overnight). Jesus describes the poor person, reduced to destitution by law proceedings, taking off the cloak as well, in effect stripping naked as a protest to the entire proceeding. The poor person may be destitute but maintains the ability to take the initiative and graphically communicate the injustice of the situation.

The third example describes the custom of *angareia*, whereby occupying soldiers may at any time press subject peoples and/or their pack animals into service to carry their heavy packs. The soldier may perceive the Jewish civilian as nothing better than a pack animal. Imagine his surprise when that person surprises him with an independent spirit, takes the initiative and marches on for another mile. Occupied, perhaps, but still, in a real way, free.

Jesus is teaching a new way: not fight, flight or accommodate, but wield nonviolent power designed to remove fear from within the ones wielding it, remove perceptions of inferiority and break through the enmity.

Note how the passage of Matthew 5:38-42 is structured. It is similar in all 14 triads that make up the Sermon on the Mount.[82] First Jesus states the accepted, customary standard of action in simple declarative sentences. In this case, "an eye for an eye and a tooth for a tooth" etc. Then he states what not to do, what gets people into an increasingly negative cycle and bind. In this case, "don't respond to violence (evil) with violence (evil)." Then finally imperative verbs, actions that can be taken to get out of the cycle of violence: Turn, give, go a second mile; go well beyond what the conventional wisdom would have you do. This is what St. Paul will call surpassing righteousness — daring, life-affirming actions in the face of evil.

In the Sermon on the Mount Jesus is speaking directly to his disciples. The rest of the crowd is gathered round and overhearing Jesus's words. Jesus is calling his disciples to his way of life, the way of nonviolence. They in turn will demonstrate that way of life to the people and encourage them to follow as well. It is not, as some will later term it, an impossible ideal. It is the hallmark of discipleship. Following that way of life, a life of nonviolent, creative love, is possible because of the gift of grace and love from God. As we read in Luke: "For He himself is kind to the ungrateful and the wicked" (Luke 6:35). It is to live in the free, bracing air of the kingdom of God.

Jesus formulates these practical approaches that move humanity well beyond the eye-for-an-eye tradition, which had been accepted wisdom for centuries, not just by his creative reading of oral and written tradition. Recent events in the political world would have informed his embrace of nonviolent direct action. Jesus did not invent nonviolent direct action. His own people were practising it. Josephus informs us that the Jewish people had, in addition to violent resistance, tried nonviolent resistance as well.

A well-known example of nonviolent resistance was prompted by two famous

---

82 Glen Stassen, "The Fourteen Triads of the Sermon on the Mount (Matthew 5:21-7:12)," Journal of Biblical Literature 122, no. 2 (Summer 2003): 267-308.

teachers in Herod's time, 4 BCE, Judas and Matthias and their students. Herod had erected a large golden eagle, the key symbol of the Roman army, over the great gate of the Temple. Forty young students went up and chopped it down. The event was deliberately planned. The event was aggressive and bold in defiance of Herod and his practices of collaboration with Rome. Yet they did not offer any armed resistance to the military force sent to apprehend them but courageously waited for the attack. Herod had them and their teachers burned alive.

Another celebrated example was against Pilate in Jesus's time, 26 CE. Pilate had introduced into Jerusalem at night images of Caesar attached to the army's standards. A multitude of people went to Caesarea to implore him to remove the standards. Josephus writes: "When Pilate refused them, they fell down prostrate on the ground and continued immovable in that posture for five days and as many nights. On the next day Pilate sat on his tribunal, in the open marketplace, and called to him the multitude, as desirous of giving them an answer and then gave a signal to the soldiers, that they should all by agreement at once encompass the Jews with their weapons, so the band of soldiers stood around about the Jews in three ranks. The Jews were under the utmost consternation at that sight. Pilate also said to them that they should be cut to pieces, unless they would admit of Caesar's images, and gave intimation to the soldiers to draw their naked swords. Whereupon the Jews, as it were on one signal, fell down in vast numbers together, and exposed their necks bare, and cried out that they were sooner ready to be slain, than their law should be transgressed. Hereupon Pilate was greatly surprised at their prodigious superstition and gave the order that the ensigns should be presently carried out of Jerusalem."

In the face of imminent violence and bloodshed the Jewish people courageously stood their ground. They refused to co-operate in the evil. They also remained completely nonviolent and non-threatening to Pilate. Pilate was amazed at and admired their courage. They appealed to the better angels of his nature and succeeded in reaching him with their common humanity. This was classic nonviolent direct action.

Nonviolent direct action was alive and well in Jesus's time. He recognised it as a powerful alternative to violence. He not only taught it to his disciples, he practised it. The best way to understand the *teachings* of Jesus is to observe Jesus's *life*, the way he *practises* nonviolent direct action.

Jesus resisted structural and cultural violence

Jesus not only taught nonviolent direct action, he used it himself. He utilised the methods of nonviolent direct action to resist and overcome the structural and cultural violence[83] that was baked into his society. Structural evil extends beyond the evil that people do; it extends to institutions, systems, laws and policies that harden injustices in place. The main pillars of daily life for most Jews were Torah, Sabbath and Temple. But the role of, and traditions associated with, these institutions were already subject to debate and conflict in first-century Palestinian Judaism. Many shared Jesus's view that these institutions were being controlled by the elites for their own social and economic interests, to the detriment of the majority, particularly the poor and marginalised.

The seventh day of the week, the Sabbath, was the day when the creator himself looked at his creation and pronounced it good and then rested. It was intended by God to be such a day for his people, a day of rest and rejuvenation. Instead, through complicated interpretations it risked becoming a day for the authorities to pronounce judgments on people and place unnecessary restrictions on them.

Mark's Gospel, Chapter 3: 1-6, describes Jesus entering a synagogue and encountering a man with a withered arm. Some people present were intent on seeing Jesus do something to violate the Sabbath. Jesus did not ignore or shy away from the potential conflict. He called the man up to the front and asked the people: "What does our law allow us to do on the Sabbath? To help or harm?

---

83 Cultural violence includes the language, narratives, attitudes, habits, norms, ethical frameworks, symbols, customs and traditions which legitimate structural and direct violence.

To save a man's life or to destroy it?" No one replied. Mark describes Jesus as angry as he looked around but at the same time sad for those who opposed him because they were so stubborn and wrong. Then he said to the man: "Stretch out your hand." He stretched it out and it was healed. Mark says the Pharisees left the synagogue and met some members of Herod's party and they made plans to kill Jesus (Mark 3:6).

The Sabbath was a day for celebrating release from slavery and bondage as well as from work. It was an appropriate day for healing. Jesus stood up to the Pharisees and members of the Herodian party who opposed him. He performed a "work" of mercy and compassion consistent with the purpose of the Sabbath. As a result he risked censure and even death at their hands. His public life had barely started and already he had become a marked man.

Another striking example of Jesus's resistance to the powers is described in Luke, Chapter 13. Jesus interrupts the Sabbath service, notices a woman who is bent and has been bent for 18 years. He feels compassion for her, calls her forward, puts his hands on her and at once she straightens up, praising God. He then defends his action in a very strong challenge to the synagogue leaders: "You hypocrites! Which of you would not let out your ox or your ass on the Sabbath to water it? And should this daughter of Abraham who has been in bondage for 18 years, should she not be released, freed from her shackles on the Sabbath?" Luke goes on to write that all the people rejoiced at what he had done.

In the same way there was debate and a number of rules within first-century Judaism regarding ritual purity laws and notions of inclusion and exclusion — in particular in relation to the Temple (understood as God's house). These included elements of one's type of work, family, behaviour, contact with animals and physical health. What is clear from Jesus's ministry, activity, teaching and social interaction including table fellowship, is that he aims to challenge such conceptual boundaries and to disregard them in his behaviour. He explained his stance. "It is not what goes into a man that condemns him but what comes out of him." (Mark 7:15).

Jesus vigorously contested the way the scribes were interpreting the Torah. Jesus took a stance based on the teaching of Isaiah that the Jewish religion was to be the light for the nations (Isaiah 2:2-4). He based his stance on Abraham and Sarah, the progenitors of all the nations, who were to mediate the divine blessings to all the nations of the earth. Jesus had come to fulfil the law and the prophets, not do away with them. It pained him that so many were being excluded from the kingdom of God over notions of purity and impurity. Jesus believed that holiness was not staying pure but developing the virtue of compassion. He gave sight to the blind man and thus allowed him to worship in the Temple. So also with the lame man and the woman who suffered from the flow of blood, making her impure. Jesus touched the leper instead of abiding by a fear of impurity. After healing the leper, Jesus sent the person with leprosy to the priest for a judgment of cleanliness to make sure the healed one could rejoin the community of faith. Jesus acted in a straightforward, nonviolent way to undercut misguided authority. Jesus counselled the people to not be afraid. "Do not let your hearts be troubled or afraid." (John 14:27).

After working to renew their communities across the length and breadth of Galilee, healing and gathering people into renewed communities, he decided to deal not just with the presenting problems but to turn his attention to the underlying causes. He set his face to Jerusalem.

Jesus chose to oppose and challenge the way the Temple was being run. He had a gift for choosing actions that struck people forcefully and memorably. He chose actions that spoke his message even more clearly than his words — symbolic and prophetic actions. On his way to Jerusalem, near Bethphage and Bethany, he sent two of his disciples to the village opposite to untie a young donkey which he then rode into the city. He rode the donkey over the Mount of Olives, across the Kidron valley, and up to the Temple mount — the action spoke louder than words that his was a royal claim, a new kingdom, a new kind of king, who exerted power without violence. The movement intentionally fulfilled the passage of Zechariah: "Rejoice greatly, O daughter Zion! Shout loud Jerusalem! Lo, your king comes to you; triumphant and victorious is he, humble and riding a donkey, on a colt, the foal of a donkey. He will cut off the chariot from Ephraim and the horse from Jerusalem; and the battle bow shall be cut off, and he shall command peace to the nations; his dominion shall be from sea to sea, and from the River to the ends of the earth" (Zech. 9:9-10).

This was a counter-symbol to Pilate, who at the same time was entering Jerusalem on his war horse. As Benedict XVI wrote: "But even in Zechariah's day, and still more by the time of Jesus, it was the horse that had come to signify the might of the mighty, while the donkey has become the animal of the poor." The oracle of Zechariah describes a new kind of king, one of nonviolence who bans war horses and chariots and battle bows, brings peace to humanity, and ends war.

According to the Synoptic Gospels, Jesus then entered the Temple and performed another action charged with meaning. Mark wrote:

"Jesus entered the Temple and began to drive out those who sold and those who bought in the Temple. He overturned the tables of the money-changers and the seats of those who sold pigeons; and he would not allow anyone to carry anything through the Temple. And he taught and said to them: 'Is it not written, 'My house shall be called a house of prayer for all the nations?' But you have made it a den of thieves'" (Mark 11 15-17).

Jesus defends his bold action in the Jerusalem Temple by citing two prophetic traditions that articulated his own double critique of this institution under Roman occupation. He appeals to Isaiah 56:3-8 to remind the leaders that the Temple was meant to be the city on the hill whose light would reach all nations. And he adds an allusion to Jeremiah 7:1-14 (itself delivered from the gate of the Temple), which censured the nation's stewards who used the cult to exploit and profit from the people, warning against relying on ritual purity if accompanied by social injustice. Jesus was passionately dedicated to the wellbeing of the poor, and stood against the political economy of the Temple when it siphoned off the resources of vulnerable people into the purses of some of the priests and elites (as illustrated by his lament over the "widow's mite", Mark 12:40-44). He calls for "mercy not sacrifice" in Matthew 9:9 and thus challenges the cultural myth of redemptive violence. His action in the Temple is the culmination of Jesus's life-long obedience to God and civil resistance to imperial and religious injustice. It triggered the violence of the powers and the Empire to come down on him.

To this point we have seen a few different sides of Jesus's nonviolence.

We have seen him use nonviolence to confront the human tendency to regard those who are different from us as allogenes, outcasts and enemies, removing one of the main triggers of violence from people's minds. This is preventive peacemaking: before the violence starts cascading down.

We have seen him teach his disciples how to cut the ground from under the tendency to respond to violence with violence; to respond to violence and aggression by meeting it with creative nonviolence. This is *intervention* peacemaking: interrupt the cycle of revenge and violence before it can really get going.

We have seen how he uses nonviolent direct action to address and change the underlying causes of violence. He knows that a peacemaker sometimes has to be first a peace disturber. The problems afflicting people have to be brought out into the open and those in power have to be shaken out of their complacency before the problems can be resolved. Not just Jesus but also Gandhi, Dorothy Day, Hildegard and Jean Goss-Mayr, and Nobel laureates Martin Luther King, Wangari Muta Maathai and Leymah Gbowee were first seen as peace-disturbers before they were recognised as peacemakers.

When people are feeling unjustly treated, when they feel like outcasts in their own homes, when they have been deprived of the means of caring for themselves and their families, anger is bound to fester and fester until it erupts in violence. Jesus tried to heal festering wounds such as these. This is *civil resistance* peacemaking: addressing the structures of violence embedded in a society, exposing them, disturbing those responsible and rallying a tidal wave of positive alternatives. He could see the future, that if his people let the anger continue to build and they exploded with wrath, the power of Rome would descend on them like a sledgehammer. We have seen him try to reach those who were causing the injustices. He galvanised the power of the people and used powerful symbolic, prophetic action to try and break through to the powers.

Finally, the Gospels instruct us in a nonviolent approach to bringing about reconciliation and healing *after the harm has been done*, after the injustice has been committed. This is reconciling peacemaking.

Jesus practised nonviolence to reconcile and heal

Jesus, faithful to the Biblical tradition that increasingly focuses on the needs of all stakeholders, gives his followers an alternative process to the rabbinic or Roman law courts for pursuing justice: nonviolent restorative justice instead of retributive justice. His approach centres first on the victim and then on the offender. It assumes that a crime is not just a violation of law but more importantly a violation of a person. It sees that justice is secured only when the offender holds her- or himself accountable *and* victim and offender are reconciled.

The teaching is found in Matthew 18: "If your brother or sister has sinned against you, arise and point out the fault when the two of you are in private, and if they listen to you, you have won your brother or sister. If you are not listened to, take with you one or two others so that the case may be decided through the evidence of two or three witnesses. If they still refuse to listen to them, tell it to the congregation. But if they do not listen to the congregation, then regard such a one as a Gentile or a tax collector" (Matthew 18: 15-17).

Note first the emphasis on the victim. In a typical retributive justice system the emphasis is all on the offender — proving their guilt and assigning an appropriate punishment. It is assumed that punishing the offender makes the victim whole. Not much attention is paid to the wounds endured or needs accrued to the victim from the assault or the offence. The victim's pain deserves attention. Furthermore, in this approach agency is given to the victim. It assumes that the victim has power and authority — as long as they are ready to take the initiative and will not be revictimised by the offender.

The key line of the passage is: "Arise, and confront the one who has sinned against you." In the typical retributive justice system the offender may never really hear or understand what their offence has done to the victim. In the restorative justice system the offender is fully confronted with the totality of what they have done. This first step, if successful, helps the offender save face through a private approach. Without the shaming dynamic that comes from the presence of peers, the offender may be able to respond more sincerely. Through negotiation the parties work things out themselves. The goal is to regain the offender if they listen and take full responsibility. If they do so, the victim will know that he or she has been fully heard and understood.

If the offender is not, however, won over, the violated party can pursue a series of steps that steadily increase community pressure on the offender. The first recourse is to bring along one or two witnesses. If the offender still refuses to listen then bring to bear the entire community in loving, but firm nonviolent coercion.

More recent experiments with "peace circles", "healing circles" and "community justice conferencing" confirm the effectiveness of these restorative justice practices. Often the peer pressure of family, neighbours, colleagues and other stakeholders provides the needed push to a stubborn offender and opens the way to a productive discussion identifying the needs of all stakeholders and a path forward for the victim and offender, as well as appropriate recompense from the offender.

In the worst case scenario, the offender dismisses the pain of the victim and the testimony of the community. In that case, the "lost sheep" does not want to be found and has made himself or herself an outsider and not responsible to the community. Treating the offender then as a "Gentile or tax collector" is not necessarily punitive. It is recognising that a different approach to engaging with the offender is required. Jesus was called a "friend" of tax collectors and sinners; the community re-engages with the offender in the same way Jesus engaged with the socially excluded — reaching out to them and proclaiming the good news to them anew.

The saying in Matthew 18:20, "For where two or three are gathered in my name, I am there in the midst of them" is significant. In the difficult and challenging redemptive process of supporting victims to take moral initiative, and holding offenders accountable, for the health of the whole discipleship community — Jesus will be "in our midst".

In this way Jesus teaches us still another facet and kind of peacemaking. This is *"after the harm has been done"* peacemaking, which also functions to prevent or minimise future harm. The aim is to nonviolently renew, rebuild and strengthen the community through reconciliation.

An even surer way to rebuild, renew and strengthen the community is through the daily practice of forgiveness.

Forgiveness and restorative justice

Just after Jesus's teaching on victim-offender reconciliation, Peter asks an important follow-up question: "Then Peter went up to him and said: 'Lord how often must I forgive my brother or sister if they wrong me? As often as seven times?' Jesus answered: 'Not seven, I tell you, but 70 times seven'" (Matthew 18: 21).

Jesus, in teaching us the Lord's Prayer, points out that forgiveness is two-sided. It is a gift before it is a task and failure to forgive nullifies the benefits of God's forgiveness: "Forgive us our debts as we have forgiven our debtors."

It does not ignore or overlook evil. It begins by explicitly naming and confronting evil — and then meeting it with unconditional love. Successful Truth and Reconciliation commissions begin with the recitation of the crimes done to real, individual persons, followed by admittance of the crimes by the perpetrators, bringing into light of day not only the acts but the public recognition of psychic wounds that continue to afflict those who suffered. The people harmed have the opportunity to emerge from their grief, and if they can find it in their hearts to forgive, to start again, perhaps even with those who have perpetrated the violence.

Hannah Arendt, the famous Jewish political philosopher, has suggested that forgiveness is a political initiative that she attributes to Jesus and the only response to violence that ends the chain of reciprocal recriminations from revenge. It refuses to play that game and instead cancels it.

Jesus's teaching that disciples should forgive 70 times seven is the mirror reverse of Lamech's claim in Genesis that he would exercise revenge 70 times seven (Gen. 4: 23-24). Forgiveness breaks the cycle, looks at the perpetrator in a new way and restores the offender to good standing. It is a supremely free and creative act.

Jesus's words on the cross — "Abba, forgive them, for they know not what they do" — sum up this packed teaching on forgiveness. Jesus at one and the same time shed any trace of blame and hatred from his spirit, kept his followers away from retribution and maintained the perpetrators were true children of God.

In all these instances and types of peacemaking: preventive peacemaking, intervention peacemaking, *civil resistance* peacemaking and *"after the harm has been done"* peacemaking, Jesus is acting in the political/public sphere. The following example shows how he used nonviolence to directly defend others.

Jesus demonstrated how to defend nonviolently

A common way people dismiss the legitimacy of nonviolence is by asking a person who believes in nonviolence the following question: "But what would you do if a loved one was being threatened with violence? To stand by and do nothing makes the passive observer worse than the one threatening the violence, does it not?"

The assumption behind the question, of course, is that the only way to protect someone threatened with violence is with intervening violence.

On at least one occasion Jesus walked right into a situation of horrific threatened violence and modelled the practice of direct unarmed civilian protection. A mob of men stood armed with stones ready to stone to death a woman whom they had caught in an act of adultery. They felt completely righteous — they felt their own law commanded them to act. They said to Jesus:

"Teacher, this woman was caught in the very act of committing adultery. In our law, Moses commanded that such a woman must be stoned to death. Now, what do you say?" (John 8:4-5).

First note the courage of Jesus. He did not shrink away from the scene; he walked right into the middle of it. Then, note his coolness under fire. Then notice his creativity. One does not respond in such a situation with nonviolent creativity unless one has practised so acting — if violence has not been disavowed consistently, i.e. without cultivating the virtue of nonviolent peacemaking. He did not use superior force to overcome their violence. He did not threaten. He bent down in front of them and began silently writing something in the dust — a classic diversion-of-attention move. We don't know what he wrote, and it does not seem to matter. He let the situation cool, put them back on themselves. John's Gospel says that he then stood up. He must have looked at them but probably not in a condemnatory or angry way — that would have further inflamed the situation. Probably a composed, benign face. He then put them back on their heels with a simple statement of truth:

"The one among you without sin, cast the first stone" (John 8:7).

Then he bent over again and resumed writing. He did not intensify the standoff by staring at them or challenging them. Instead he let his words sink in. John wrote:

"They all left one by one, the older ones first" (John 8: 9).

The younger ones' hyped-up energy evidently took a little longer to cool.

John's Gospel gives us a classic picture of nonviolent action at work in the teeth of a threat of violence, transforming the violence. With a restorative justice lens, he challenges them to acknowledge their shared role in sin and harm. It is our own Divine saviour — fully human, in action. Since then faithful Christians and countless others have shown how we can confront violence and overcome it without violence. People have shown it in the personal sphere. They have shown it time and time again in the political sphere. It is a myth that the only way you can stop a gun is with a person who has a bigger gun. That approach usually leads to escalation. The cycle of violence is real and a deadly no-exit. As Pope Francis pointed out in an Angelus address in 2013: "War brings on war! Violence brings on violence."

Jesus and violence against women[84]

The issue of gender violence endemic in Biblical texts is one that must be critically examined and understood. To ignore these problematic passages that seem to sanctify gender violence is to ignore the voice and experience of the Bible's women victims. In so doing — in seeing how gender violence that targets women in particular ways is exercised and sanctified through biblical narratives — we can gain better insight into contemporary phenomena that do likewise. In this way, the Bible can serve its sacred purpose as a guide to help us identify death-dealing practices in our world that require transformation so as to defend life and dignity.

Critically, an important aspect of Jesus's ministry was to acknowledge the women around him, including those who were survivors of violence, and to affirm their inherent dignity, worth and wisdom. As acknowledged by John Paul II in *Mulieris Dignitatum*:

"In the eyes of his contemporaries Christ became a promoter of women's true dignity and of the vocation corresponding to this dignity. At times this caused wonder, surprise, often to the point of scandal: 'They marveled that he was talking with a woman' (John 4:27), because this behaviour differed from that of his contemporaries."[85]

Throughout the gospel accounts, Jesus's ministry to, with and led by women is noted in several ways. First, he notices women in a distinct way and brings them healing throughout his ministry (Matthew 8, Luke 18). He refuses to comply with ancient laws that cast some women as impure, crossing social bounds of acceptability to be with, and bring a healing touch to, women who faced social ostracism (Mark 5, Luke 13, John 4). Despite the important activities of Jesus to witness and bring healing to women survivors of violence, the Christian

---

84 "Following Her Lead" by Susan Hayward, excerpt www.nonviolencejustpeace.net.

85 http://w2.vatican.va/content/john-paul-ii/en/apost_letters/1988/documents/

ethical tradition has not historically offered adequate attention to the problem of pervasive forms of violence against women and girls, and sexual violence experienced by those of all genders.[86]

Jesus often pointed to women around him who were models of faith (Luke 18, Luke 21). It is perhaps not surprising, then, that his female disciples were often among the few who recognized Jesus for who he was during his ministry, stood vigil with him during his crucifixion, were the first to whom he appeared after his resurrection (Mark 16), and were subsequently the first to preach the good news — the central call of Christian faith. Women were not only central in Jesus's ministry during his life on earth, with women accompanying Jesus and his male disciples in public on their travels and providing hospitality to them throughout (such as Mary and Martha), but were critical ministers of his teachings following his death, resurrection and ascension. In the Acts of Apostles and epistles, several women are named as key leaders of early Christian communities, such as Phoebe in Rome and Junia, whom Paul describes as "distinguished among the apostles" (Romans 16:9), as prophetesses (Acts 21:9), missionaries and founders of churches, such as Priscilla (1 Cor 16:19).[87] Other historical sources further illuminate the critical role women played as leaders in the early Christian movement.

Moreover, we have several examples from the texts of women serving as leaders of nonviolent resistance. The first comes from Exodus. When Pharaoh orders midwives Shiphrah and Puah to kill Hebrew sons when they are born, they refuse to obey, even lying to the Pharaoh when asked in a courageous act of deception for the cause of life (Exodus 1).

---

86 Marie M. Fortune, *Sexual Violence*, 47-48. As Fortune notes, this may be due to the fact that authoritative Christian ethicists have been predominantly male and this issue has not been a priority for them, as it is one that primarily affects women and girls.

87 For more, see Hans Küng, *Women in Christianity*.

Jesus and a culture of nonviolent service

When Matthew, Luke and John wrote their Gospels the revolt against Rome had already happened (66 to 70 CE) and Rome had already unleashed its whirlwind of violence. The Jewish revolt had been totally crushed, 500 a day crucified, the Temple demolished, the scaffolding up the mountain towards the fortress Masada had been constructed and the last holdout rebels had perished. Mark was probably written before the other three Gospels, perhaps just as the revolt was beginning or perhaps just after the destruction of the Temple. The readers of the Gospels therefore knew Roman domination well. After the destruction of Jerusalem, Rome, under Vespasian, instituted a tax that would go towards the maintenance of a pagan shrine placed on the site of the ruined Temple. Rome issued a coin called "Judea Capta" meaning "Judea captured and supine", which pictured a Roman soldier brandishing a spear over a kneeling female. The early readers of the Gospels knew well how Rome lorded it over subject peoples and kept them craven.

The Gospels therefore, looking back, portray Jesus as quite prescient about what Rome represented and the threat that was looming if the cycle of violence escalated on both sides. In his mind's eye he could see the destruction that was coming, was deeply moved by the anguish that was coming to his people and lamented their failure to follow his way of peace. Luke wrote: "When Jesus came within sight of the city, he wept over it and said: 'If only you had known the ways of peace! But now your eyes are held from seeing. Yet the days will come when your enemies will come upon you with barricades and shut you in and press on you from every side. And they will dash you to the ground and your children with you, and leave not a stone within you, for you did not recognize the time and the visitation of your God" (Luke 19: 41-44).

But the Gospels, especially Mark, are equally clear that Jesus presented to his followers a way that would be a complete antithesis to Rome's way of threat and domination. He called them to form a counter-community of nonviolence and service. Mark wrote:

"As you know, the so-called rulers of the nations act as tyrants and lord it over them. But it shall not be so among you; whoever would be great among you must be your servant, and whoever would be first among you shall make himself a slave to all. For the Son of Man has not come to be served but to serve and to give his life to redeem many" (Mark 10: 42-45).

He put a child into their midst, the least powerful figure in their culture, with no rights, and he said that they were to live as children — recognising their littleness but also their great power for good and for others. He treated women, another group with few rights and little power, in ways distinctly different from the way his society treated them. After his resurrection he even sent Mary Magdalen as his witness to the male disciples (John 20:11-18). All, even those with little standing in his society, were included in his circle and in his ministry.

On the night he was betrayed he called them together to give them additional lessons on how to build a nonviolent community that would serve as an antithesis to Rome and successive imperial powers. He highlighted the absolute necessity of building a community of compassion and nonviolent service. He understood that no one can be nonviolent in splendid isolation. We need others to model for us nonviolent behaviour. Thus he identified the beatitudes, which offer core dispositions, virtues and practices for us to cultivate in daily life. We need colleagues in the nonviolent fight to pick us up when we get discouraged. We need a community to remind us of the way that Jesus showed us.

In John's Gospel, he then modelled for them one more time how he wanted them to live. He, their Master, got down on the floor with a container of water and some towels and began to wash their feet, removing the dust from their feet and sandals. He said:

"Do you understand what I have done to you? You call me Master and Lord, and you are right, for so I am. If I, then, your Lord and Master have washed your feet, you also must wash one another's feet. I have just given you an example that as I have done, you also may do" (John 13: 12-15). Thus he gives them a "new commandment, that you love one another as I have loved you" (John 13:34).

For all those reasons he called them together to give them and us a memorial of his nonviolent way. He took bread, broke it, blessed it and gave it to them saying, "Take and eat; this is my body given up for you" (Luke 22: 19). He did the same with the cup of wine and then said, "Do this in memory of me." Whenever you come together and share my body and blood, you are to remember my life, how I acted. Act as you have seen me act — resist structures of violence, show people how to return love for hate, spurn arms, show compassion for the poor and the outcasts, be willing to endure pain and suffering for my sake. Lean on one another. His model of inclusive, nonviolent community building meant breaking bread and sharing the cup with even his betrayer: "The hand of my betrayer is with me at this table" (Luke 22:21).

He then got up from the table and led them out to do the other key action for building a nonviolent culture. They went out to pray. At all the key moments of Jesus's public life he felt the need to take his community off by themselves to pray — to stay in constant communion with the God who loves all, to keep fresh and alive the spirit that enlivens all. It was to prayer that he turned on this night of threat and coming violence.

Jesus lived a life of nonviolent love

Jesus spent much of the evening before his arrest in prayer in the Garden of Gethsemane. He knew what was building against him and he was in great distress. In Mark's description we have here the only time in Mark that Jesus calls his Abba:

"My soul is sorrowful even unto death…Abba God, all things are possible for you. Take this cup from me, but not what I will but what you will" (Mark 14:33, 36).

He was terrified at what might be coming. Luke wrote: "As he was in agony, he prayed even more earnestly and great drops of blood formed like sweat and fell to the ground" (Luke 22: 44).

He is afraid — with good reason. Rome loomed on his horizon.

The depth of his prayer in the garden prepared him to face what was coming. (Luke wrote in 24:43 that an angel came to strengthen in him in his agony.) He got up and went forward to meet his fate. Judas, his friend and betrayer, went directly up to him and gave him a kiss so that those sent to arrest him would know which one was Jesus. In each of the Gospel versions Jesus responded with nonviolence and sorrowful resignation. Matthew wrote that Jesus responded: "Friend, do what you came for" (Matthew 26: 50). Jesus called the one who betrayed him "friend", still not excising him from the book of life.

The disciples accompanying him were afraid. One of them, identified in John's Gospel as Peter, drew a sword and hacked at the ear of the high priest's servant. Jesus's response was immediate. According to Matthew's Gospel he said: "Put your sword back in its sheath. All who take the sword will die by the sword. Do you not know that I could call on my God, who would at once send 12 legions of angels?" (Matthew 26: 52-53).

If ever there was a time when using violence in defence would seem to be justified, it would be at this moment — but Jesus sees it differently. He knows what violence does. It produces more violence and moves us off the path of salvation. He has consistently opted for a better way and he does so here. He confronted violence with the unarmed power of truth and love. According to Luke's Gospel Jesus said, "Enough of this" (Luke 22:51) and then Jesus touched the man's ear and healed him. These are his last words to the disciples before his death. "Enough of this" and "Put away the sword." At this pivotal moment he rejected the violence option and chose nonviolence. He expected his followers, once they saw how he behaved in these climactic moments, to do the same.

He was then handed over, first to the high priest and the Sanhedrin. As the trial scenes unfold, Jesus continues to respond forthrightly and with dignity. When a soldier feels free to slap him for the way Jesus answered the high priest, Jesus responded calmly but assertively, "If there is some offence in what I said, point it out; but if not, why do you strike me?" (John 18:23).

He was then handed over to Pilate, who alone, as the official representative of the empire, had the power over life and death. In his response to Pilate he made it clear that he was a king but a different kind of king, one who rejected the tired power of the sword to intimidate and dominate. John wrote that Jesus said to Pilate: "My kingship does not come from this world. If I were a king like those of this world, my followers would have fought to save me from being handed over to the Jews" (John 18: 36).

Pilate then handed him over to the soldiers. The full, ugly power of the empire was unleashed on him. That power was meant to intimidate and control. Matthew says the whole cohort of soldiers, hundreds of soldiers, surrounded him. They scourged him, beat him, spat on him, mocked him. He refused to be intimidated. He refused to hate. He refused revenge. He showed them and us how to be human in the face of the greatest inhumanity.

They then led him to the cross — their ultimate tool of humiliation and control.

Jesus's going to the cross is the final action of one who throughout his life acted nonviolently to remove the causes of suffering for his people and stand in resistance to the powers. Jesus constantly risked the hatred, fear and violence of the powers in charge but kept right on going. The cross is the direct result of his ethic of nonviolent resistance and action. The cross cannot be understood apart from his life.

Jesus died because of the way he lived. He died because he confronted the powers of evil and showed us a new way to fight. In so doing he upset the powers-that-be. The cross is a sacred symbol because it stands for a historical life given fully, and to the end, for the liberation of humankind through nonviolent power.

As Pope Francis has written: "My Christian faith urges me to look to the cross... Violence is not answered with the language of death. In the silence of the cross, the uproar of weapons ceases and the language of reconciliation, forgiveness, dialogue and peace is spoken."

There is no word of Jesus more often repeated in the Gospels than his words urging his disciples to follow him along the road to the cross. e.g. Matthew 10:38, 16:24, Mark 8:34, 10:31 Luke 9:23, 14:27. He is really saying to them and to us to follow his way of life even at the risk of such barbaric suffering and with the risk of our entire life's work coming to, apparently, nothing. To imitate the cross is to accept suffering rather than deny the truth. To imitate the cross is to be loyal to the life practice of nonviolent, redemptive love.

The Risen Jesus shares nonviolent love

The disciples, in fear, had run away when Jesus was arrested in the garden of Gethsemane. Most of the resurrection accounts begin with fear. When the risen Jesus first appears to his friends, they are hiding behind locked doors, fearing for their lives, utterly shaken by their loss. He appears to them and there is no note of recrimination, no reproof, no anger at their abandonment of him. Jesus shows them what he has always shown them — unfathomable love, the same love that he shares with his Abba. He says to them, "Peace be with you." What begins with fear, is transformed into a moment of great joy. John wrote: "On the evening of the first day of the week, when the doors were locked where the disciples were, for fear of the Jews, Jesus came and stood in their midst and said to them,

'Peace be with you.' When he said this, he showed them his hands and his side. The disciples rejoiced when they saw the Lord. Jesus said to them again, 'Peace be with you.' As Abba God sent me, so I send you" (John 20: 19-23).

Jesus commissioned his disciples, and through them, us, to continue his work of building the kingdom. At the Last Supper Jesus told his disciples that they would do greater things than he had done. He dared to leave the work of building the kingdom of heaven to a small group of fallible human beings. John's Jesus deliberately connected resurrection with peace, a peace that does not deny Jesus's agony and death. The risen one gives us peace as we take up our cross — as we follow in his footsteps. He stood against structures of oppression. He bound up people's wounds. He gathered people in banquet and celebration. He used the power of nonviolent action to build the kingdom of God. As we follow his way, we too will glimpse the joy of the resurrection.

In summary, the Gospels show Jesus as a full-spectrum nonviolent peacemaker. He teaches us how to *prevent* violence before it starts, by refusing to treat anyone as an outsider or enemy. He teaches us how to intervene with creative, disarming nonviolent action when things get hot, breaking the cycle of violence. He demonstrates *civil resistance* peacemaking, attacking structural violence, bringing it into the open, using nonviolent power to change the equation. He demonstrates *after-the-harm-has-been-done* peacemaking — how to nonviolently reconcile parties who have been estranged. He shows how to neutralize personal violence and *protect others* with the power of creative nonviolent action. He calls us to form a *culture and community of nonviolent service* that builds sustainable peace and will be an antithesis to regimes of domination through violence. Finally, he shows us how to live a *life of nonviolence to the full* and to the end.[88]

---

88 Although focused on the Gospels in this section, there are considerable resources in other parts of the Christian Bible. See Willard Swartley, *Covenant of Peace: The Missing Peace in New Testament Theology and Ethics*. Grand Rapids, MI: Eerdmans Publishing, 2006. Some of the Christian scriptural sayings that get misused to legitimate violence can be found briefly addressed here: http://www.catholicpeacefellowship.org/downloads/summer04.pdf, p. 12-16.

3. Towards a Theology of Nonviolence

Just as scripture scholarship has increasingly illuminated the centrality of nonviolence to the life and mission of Jesus, theologians are increasingly elucidating the theology of nonviolence, including in light of the classic categories of systematic theology, including creation, anthropology, Christology, pneumatology, and ecclesiology.

Creation and Anthropology

In the beginning, Genesis tells us, one God created everything with words.

The first creation story in Genesis is often compared to the Babylonians' *Enuma Elish*, but the contrasts are more important. For the Babylonians, creation came about through a war among the gods; the earth was created from the dead body of the slain goddess Tiamat, and humans from the blood of her murdered servant Kingu. Violence is the way things are. In Genesis there is no rivalry among gods, no primordial violence on which to impose order. Creation is good, and human beings are made in the image of God who declares this goodness.

Peace, in other words, is ontologically primary; nonviolence is the nature of creation. Human beings will sin, but sin is a distortion of what really is. As Augustine would later argue, evil has no being; it is a privation of good, not a mere lack but a privation, meaning good existed first and then was taken away. Humans are fallen, but that means that there is something good to fall away from, unlike in the *Enuma Elish*, in which rivalry and violence are present from the start. The Fall means that the way things are is not the way things are meant to be, or really are, in God's eyes.

This is not all. Embedded in the primacy of nonviolence is the ultimacy of nonviolence; the ontology of nonviolence is inseparable from the eschatology of nonviolence. The Fall means that the way things are is not the way things are meant to be, and therefore there is hope that things might yet be transformed to reflect their true nature. Any theology of nonviolence therefore looks simultaneously to the beginning of creation and to the final end of creation in the eschaton.

Creation is good and without violence

Creation, as narrated in Genesis 1, is good. While it is not necessary to take the first chapter of the Bible as a historical narrative, it expresses a theological intention — it is a poetic affirmation that God created everything in good order and considered it "good" (Gen 1:4, 10, 12, 18, 21, 25, 31).

In the first chapter of Genesis, there is no violence. In contrast to the *Enuma Elish* where rivalry and violence are present from the start, in this first biblical creation narrative there is peace and nonviolence between the different creatures on earth.

All creatures in the first chapters of Genesis are vegetarians — not even lions or eagles use violence to kill and eat. Nor do humans eat the meat of animals. It is only after the Flood that God enables humankind to hunt, kill and eat animal flesh: "Every moving thing that lives shall be food for you" (Gen 9:3 ESV).

It seems that as long as creation was as good as intended by God "in the beginning", it was characterised by a complete absence of violence, which is one key aspect of nonviolence. Thus, nonviolence is what God intended — and is a memory and a representation of the goodness of the beginning.

The human being made in God's image

Human beings are not only part of God's good creation but are even made in God's image (Gen 1:27) and therefore have a special responsibility regarding the goodness and nonviolence of creation.

Humans are created "in the image of God". This means not only that the Bible's first chapter attributes a very high value to humankind, in comparison with other creatures, but also the highest responsibility. Some argue that the "image" referred to in this text is comparable to the "image" an absent sovereign might place in representation of himself. So the text would suggest that humans are "representatives" of God on earth and have to act according to God's interest in creation.

Moreover, the human being is made for kinship: to be brothers, sisters and family to all. Humankind is created in the plural, but without any mention of estrangement, enmity or violence between them. As children of the one God we are all called to be a family bound by kinship and affection. We are to recognise each person as a sacred gift, and thus to act as and treat others as gifts. This is especially true in situations of conflict to avoid obstructing the movement of gift and becoming possessive, which would engender estrangement, enmity or violence.

Biblical scholar Phyllis Trible notes in her close reading of Genesis 1:27 "that God created humankind in God's image; in the image of God created-he him; male and female created-he them."[89] The passage is poetic but for Trible the switch from singular to plural pronouns in the passage reveals that humanity consists of two creatures, male and female; not as one creature with double sex. For many feminists such as Trible, Genesis 1:27 is the foundation of an egalitarian anthropology in which male and female are created to reflect the image of God equally. The creation story found in Chapter 2 and 3 of Genesis referred to as the "Fall" offers a radically different account of humanity. Unlike the earlier

---

89 In Michelle A. Gonzalez, *Created in God's Image: An Introduction to Feminist Theological Anthropology* (Orbis Books, 2007) p. 5.

narrative, in which humanity appears on the sixth day, this account places humanity at the front and centre of creation, formed from the dust of the earth and the breath of God, and it is placed in the Garden of Eden to care for it.[90]

The powers, though created for good, have fallen

The ontology of peace is even true concerning sin, which is a distortion of what really is.

The fall of human beings did not only result in individual sins but also in sinful social structures. The powers and principalities that originally were part of the good creation turned — through human sin — into destructive forces threatening not only the life of human beings but also the creation as a whole (Rom 8:38; Gal 4:3; Eph 2:2; Col 2:20). Among these fallen powers, we can discover patterns of human scapegoating persecuting single individuals as well as friend-enemy patterns channelling internal violence to the outside of a particular group. Anthropologists have called such patterns "closed societies" or ethnocentric worldviews.

Today scientists recognise a "parochial altruism" as one of the oldest and most stable forms of social life. Human beings are more likely to live in solidarity with each other if they are committed to a group that understands itself over against other groups. Parochial patterns characterised early tribal wars as well as the rising nationalisms in our own day. They also provide the foundations for understanding these somewhat artificial divisions as the way things ought to be, and worthy to be violently upheld and defended.

The "sin of the world" challenges us personally and corporately. While creation is good and initially reflects its grounding on the God who desires nonviolence

---

90 Ibid, p. 10.

for all life therein, the impacts of the Fall are experienced interpersonally and structurally. Social structures that govern interactions in the political, economic, cultural and even religious dimensions of social life, these too are impacted by the impulse to rule and impose order through violent coercion and domination. The Psalms and the prophets witness to the terrible injustices and harm that rulers and their armies, merchants and their taskmasters, inflict on their subjects and employees. Structural violence is sustained by the people who go along with the practices of unjust structures without questioning their consequences on entire populations, especially the vulnerable. Through structural violence our parochial patterns of determining who belongs in our spheres of beneficence and solidarity turn into violence towards the other.

Amid the "fallen" situation of the present, we must not forget the suffering of creation as described exhaustively by Pope Francis in his encyclical *Laudato Si'*. Violence and nonviolence are topics deeply related to the "integral ecology" (LS 137) proposed by him, because any violence against nature affects or will affect the most vulnerable of our sisters and brothers. At the same time, any use of violence against humans destroys this deep ecological relationship with our common home. Nonviolence denotes a paradigm of the fullness of life at the heart of reality. It is the power of love in action that celebrates the sacredness of life and actively works for the well-being of all. It challenges sin — including the structural sin of injustice — with faith and hope.

Together, we are called to grow in the way of our nonviolent God as revealed in the Judeo-Christian scriptures.

Christology

The early Christians employed different interpretive approaches for reading the Hebrew Bible. They often allegorised passages, such that war against the Amalekites was an allegory for war on sins. They tended not to read violent passages morally, either to reprove God and the Israelites or to justify their own acts of violence, but rather to read them as affirmations that God acts in history to rescue his people. Above all, Christians have read such passages through the lens of what Jesus Christ definitively revealed about God: that God redeems the world by absorbing, not legitimating, its violence.

The culmination of the revelation of the way things are, and the way God is, occurs in the life, death and resurrection of Jesus Christ. Christ is not just one more witness to the power of nonviolence. Christians believe that Jesus Christ is the very incarnation of God. The central drama of cosmic history is the incarnation in human history of the all-powerful Creator of the universe as a helpless baby born to a poor couple in a barn, and the redemption that follows from his life, death and resurrection.

Jesus taught and lived nonviolence. His death on a cross indicates a willingness on the part of God to suffer violence rather than deal it out. His resurrection shows that violence does not have the final word, and that revenge is not on God's agenda. The entire drama of the incarnation and the redemption operates with a nonviolent logic of kenosis; rather than use power to overcome resistance coercively, God empties Godself and turns the logic of power on its head, absorbing the violence of the world rather than perpetuating the cycle of retribution.

The work of René Girard is helpful in unpacking the logic of redemption. Violence, Girard famously posits, is contained by human societies through scapegoating; rivalries would threaten to blow society apart if the rivals did not unite against a weaker victim. All societies maintain order by creating unanimity around the idea that the victims deserve what they get. God achieves a decisive breakthrough in human history by revealing through Jesus Christ that this scapegoating mechanism is a lie. Christ reveals the innocence of and our interconnectedness with the victim, because the resurrection reveals that the victim is God.

Incarnation

We encounter God in Jesus the Christ. God is incarnated in history amid the suffering of individuals and societies. Christ is thus truly our peace (Eph 2:14). In meeting Jesus, we have the capacity to discover a precious gift of peace that is not to be hoarded or monopolised. It can and must be shared with the entire world and should remain in dialogue with the wisdom of the world. In and through Christ Jesus, God's pedagogy of peace takes on flesh, reveals a face directed towards those most in need, and points to a path that we can follow in our daily lives and within our communities — conflicted not just on occasion, but endemically with violence and strife. We discover at once the message, example and wisdom of God's peace in Jesus.

These reflections on the incarnational nonviolence of God in Christ unfold in four steps. First, we examine the good news of peace that Jesus walked and talked, focusing on key passages such as "Blessed are the peacemakers." Second, we reflect upon Jesus as a wounded healer of peace. The "cross" to which he was nailed is a key to understanding the nature of violence in our world, for it is also our cross and a sign of our vulnerability amid the violence of systems and structures, on which we crucify and are crucified.

Third, we discuss how Jesus's way of reconciliation can break cycles of violence through solidarity and humanisation. Fourth, we consider in a Christological key the nonviolent discipleship of Saint Óscar Romero and the reverberations in El Salvador today of that witness and the witness of all the women and men martyred there. These final words are just examples of the self-manifestation of God's call for nonviolence that, like unpremeditated but brightly lit beacons of hope, are discoverable *within* the ongoing historical struggles of the people of God.

Peace in the New Testament

In the Christian Gospel we encounter a gift of peace that is neither wholly otherworldly nor merely worldly; it is rather a real human offer of divinely incarnated peace. "Have no anxiety about anything, but in everything, by prayer and supplication with thanksgiving, let your requests be made known to God. And the peace of God, which surpasses all understanding, will guard your hearts" (Phil 4:6-7). This peace challenges us in our personal relations, in the widespread incidence of social violence and even with respect to defamation and bullying spread over the internet.[91]

Virgilio Elizondo related the story of the Galilean Jesus in the light of three principles: the Galilean, the Jerusalem and the Resurrection. Here we reflect on those principles in the light of God's offer of peace in Christ Jesus.[92]

Jesus and many of his disciples were Galilean. It was a unique form of religious and cultural identity in Palestine of the first century. The Galileans were generally not wealthy and cosmopolitan but came from an ethnically diverse, downtrodden community that had for centuries struggled to maintain this unique identity in the face of fierce opposition from more than one side. Elizondo is not without a historical warrant in comparing them to the Mexican Americans in the United States today. The New Testament speaks specifically about a "Galilee of the

---

91 In *Gaudete et Exsultate*, Pope Francis compares calumny to terrorism. Cf. N. 73: "Detraction and calumny are acts of terrorism: a bomb is thrown, it explodes and the attacker walks away calm and contented. This is completely different from the nobility of those who speak to others face to face, serenely and frankly, out of genuine concern for their good."

92 Virgil Elizondo, *Galilean Journey: The Mexican-American Promise* (Maryknoll, N.Y.: Orbis, 1983, 2000, 2002). See also his essay "Jesus the Galilean in Mestizo Theology," Theological Studies 70 (2009): 262-280 as well as the other fine essays in that issue, especially that of Michael Lee.

Nations/Galilee of the Gentiles" (Matthew 4:15; see also Acts 13:13-52). Elizondo shows that this usage is rooted in a vision of peace from the prophet Isaiah that is then incorporated into the Gospel of Matthew:

"The prophet Isaiah (9:1-2) refers to "Galilee of the Gentiles". Isaiah also speaks of universal salvation for all the nations, of a new era of peace and harmony, and even of a new heaven and a new earth. The influence of Isaiah's perspective in the New Testament seemed to suggest a unique and unsuspected role for Galilee in God's salvific plan for the restoration of unity within the human family, a unity and harmony that had been destroyed by sin since the very beginning of creation (Gen 3-11). The relative unimportance of Galilee seemed to fit with the idea that the Gospel is absurd to many, that the ways of God appear as foolishness to the wise of this world, and that the redemptive grace of God is an unexpected gift."[93]

The Gospel of Matthew thus links discipleship to Jesus with a Galilean exemplarism. These *mestizos* from the first century are not heralded as being objectively better than Samaritans or others. But their highly particular struggle to maintain a Galilean identity speaks with equal eloquence to an existential problem of humanity that will be illuminated by God's revelation in Jesus Christ.[94]

We arrive therefore at Jesus's Sermon on the Mount, which in Matthew reads: "Blessed are the peacemakers, for they will be called children of God."[95] In both accounts, Matthew and Luke, Jesus blesses the peacemakers and also embodies

---

93 Virgil Elizondo, "Jesus the Galilean Jew in Mestizo Theology," 271.

94 In his Easter Vigil homily of 2014, Pope Francis said in a similar vein: "In the life of every Christian, after baptism there is also a more existential 'Galilee': the experience of a personal encounter with Jesus Christ who called me to follow him and to share in his mission. In this sense, returning to Galilee means treasuring in my heart the living memory of that call, when Jesus passed my way, gazed at me with mercy and asked me to follow him. It means reviving the memory of that moment when his eyes met mine, the moment when he made me realise that he loved me. Today, tonight, each of us can ask: What is my Galilee? Where is my Galilee? Do I remember it? Have I forgotten it? Have I gone off on roads and paths which made me forget it? Lord, help me: tell me what my Galilee is; for you know that I want to return there to encounter you and to let myself be embraced by your mercy."

95 Matthew 5:9. Cf. Pope Benedict XVI, Jesus of Nazareth, I, 84-85.

peacemaking. His very birth in Luke heralds "glory to God in the highest and on earth peace to those on whom his favour rests" (Luke 2:14). When his public ministry begins and he preaches a message of discipleship in expectation of the coming of God's reign, those who follow him are called not only to an individual path to salvation. In belonging to Christ, one is also invited to belong to the new reign that also blesses and embodies peace (*shalom*) in the *ekklesia* and in the world (Cf. I Chronicles 22:9f). This community must not only profess peace but offer testimony internally and externally to its palpable and transformative presence in their unity.

How do the disciples turn this peace into a reality? One cannot sit by idly and expect it to happen on its own. But it is also not a matter of blind activism. It is a spiritual path that requires expertise, prudence and the discernment to avoid premature discouragement. On this very point, Pope Francis writes in *Gaudete et Exsultate*:

"Peacemakers truly 'make' peace; they build peace and friendship in society. To those who sow peace Jesus makes this magnificent promise: "They will be called children of God" (Matthew 5:9). He told his disciples that, wherever they went, they were to say: "Peace to this house!" (Luke 10:5). The word of God exhorts every believer to work for peace, 'along with all who call upon the Lord with a pure heart' (cf. 2 Tim 2:22), for "the harvest of righteousness is sown in peace by those who make peace" (Jas 3:18). And if there are times in our community when we question what ought to be done, "let us pursue what makes for peace" (Rom 14:19), for unity prevails over conflict.[96]

Peace is both a process that encompasses the very activity of discipleship and one of its most cherished and fragile fruits. If the community of disciples does not struggle for peace with one another they will not be able to "make" peace in and for the world. Peacemaking is not a vague wish. It is an arduous commitment to

---

96 *Gaudete et Exsultate* 85.

maintain a childlike devotion to God's peace even when surrounded by wolves.[97] Pope Francis emphasises the need to be frank and speak up about the violence around us when it seems easier to ignore that reality and move on.[98] Jesus and his Galilean disciples were aware from the outset of the perils involved in the sowing of peace: "From the days of John the Baptist until now, the kingdom of heaven suffers violence, and the violent are taking it by force" (Matthew 11:12).

The peacemaker offers words and an example of religious reform. The man mocked as King of the Jews enters into this hub of cosmopolitan religion on an ass. The symbolism of the entry into Jerusalem expresses the subtle but revolutionary power of the Resurrection principle.

Less subtle, perhaps, is the incident about the moneychangers in the Temple of Jerusalem reported in John 2:13-3:22. There Jesus shouts: "Take these out of here and stop turning God's house into a marketplace." (John 2:16). Jesus is agitating for peace in the midst of corruption and violence. In this scene he is visibly angry. Where does prophetic and fraternal correction fit into the matrix of peacemaking? Jesus's reform of the idolatrous cult is not at its core antinomian rebelliousness but rather a condition for the possibility of real peace. Otherwise, the sanctimonious will always have the upper hand in arguing for a status quo that is riddled with structural violence. Accordingly, Pope Francis makes a distinction between the "tranquil, artificial and anaesthetised peace" in which anyone can put up his or her own "do not disturb" sign and Jesus's witness to peace.[99]

---

97 *Gaudete et Exsultate* 89: "It is not easy to 'make' this evangelical peace, which excludes no one but embraces even those who are a bit odd, troublesome or difficult, demanding, different, beaten down by life or simply uninterested. It is hard work; it calls for great openness of mind and heart, since it is not about creating 'a consensus on paper or a transient peace for a contented minority', or a project 'by a few for the few'...We need to be artisans of peace, for building peace is a craft that demands serenity, creativity, sensitivity and skill."

98 The Joy of the Gospel 227: "When conflict arises, some people simply look at it and go their way as if nothing happened; they wash their hands of it and get on with their lives. Others embrace it in such a way that they become its prisoners; they lose their bearings, project onto institutions their own confusion and dissatisfaction and thus make unity impossible. But there is also a third way, and it is the best way to deal with conflict. It is the willingness to face conflict head on, to resolve it and to make it a link in the chain of a new process."

99 Morning meditation from Tuesday, May 16, 2017 in the chapel of Santa Marta, "Tranquility is not Peace," published in: L'Osservatore Romano, Weekly ed. in English, n. 22, 2 June 2017.

He states: "The peace that Jesus offers is 'a real peace' because it is rooted in the Cross, and therefore enables one to overcome all of life's many daily tribulations, including suffering and illness, without falling into mere stoicism or playing the martyr."[100]

Or, as Saint Óscar Romero put it, "It is very easy to be servants of the word without disturbing the world: a very spiritualised word, a word without any commitment to history, a word that can sound in any part of the world because it belongs to no part of the world. A word like that creates no problems, starts no conflicts."[101]

In the Gospel of John, the disciples are called to receive the peace that Jesus embodies: "Peace I leave with you; my peace I give to you. Not as the world gives do I give it to you. Do not let your hearts be troubled or afraid" (John 14:27). Jesus communicates that inner peace is both the presupposition and the result of outer peace. You cannot fully have one without the other.

We turn below to the wounded condition of Jesus as a peacemaker. Let us first recall how this dynamic also reflects the third principle in Elizondo's Galilean dialectic of peace. God's messenger of peace does not die peacefully in a cancer ward surrounded by admiring pupils. He is killed by jealous ruling authorities in Jerusalem. The incarnate God suffers physically unto death and, some would argue, even a spiritual condition of being abandoned. By any human measure, he would be a candidate for revenge after tasting the agony of innocent suffering and the inhumanity of torture. His words from the cross nonetheless do not evince any such bitterness: "Abba, forgive them. They don't know what they are doing" (Luke 23:34). What is most striking about this familiar Lucan message regarding the cruciform origins of divine mercy is that it extends even to an offer of forgiveness to a fellow sufferer who may not even be innocent: "*Today* you will be with me in paradise" (Luke 23:43). The dynamic Gospel of mercy

---

100 Ibid.

101 Romero, "The Fourth Work of Justice and Peace," Lent Sermon 4

and forgiveness is proclaimed from the cross and links heaven and earth in its immediacy and radicality.

The post-Resurrection story of Emmaus is a key to incarnational nonviolence and serves as a lens to make sense of the attractive life, the violent death and the foretold but still surprising resurrection of the Lord. In encountering the Risen One, the gift of peace is made manifest to the disciples:

"The joy that is born in their hearts derives from '[having seen] the Lord' (John 20:20). He repeats to them: "Peace be with you" (v. 21). By then it was obvious that it was not only a greeting. It was a gift, the gift that the Risen One wants to offer his friends, but at the same time it is a consignment. This peace, which Christ purchased with his blood, is for them but also for all, the disciples must pass on to the whole world. Indeed, he adds: 'as Abba God sent me, so I send you'. The Risen Jesus returned to his disciples to send them out. He had completed his work in the world, it was then up to them to sow faith in hearts so that God, known and loved, might gather all God's children from the dispersion."[102]

The work of nonviolence and building peace thus begins on the road to Emmaus and ends only with the return to God. The encounter and the breaking of bread on the way to Emmaus prepare Jesus's followers for the manifold challenges that await them.

Christ's peace is through Christ's wounds

Remember too that this same scene includes the disclosure of the resurrected Jesus's wounds.

"On the evening of that first day of the week, when the disciples were together,

---

102 Pope Benedict XVI, General Audience, 11 August 2012 http://w2.vatican.va/content/benedict-xvi/en/audiences/2012/documents/hf_ben-xvi_aud_20120411.html

with the doors locked for fear of the Jewish leaders, Jesus came and stood among them and said, 'Peace be with you!' After he said this, he showed them his hands and side. The disciples were overjoyed when they saw the Lord. Again, Jesus said, 'Peace be with you! As Abba God has sent me, I am sending you.' And with that he breathed on them and said, 'Receive the Holy Spirit' (John 20:19-22)."

Here Christ's offer of peace is literally connected to his wounds.

A fundamental aspect of the kerygma of the nascent Church was the proclamation that Christ, the Risen One, was Jesus himself, who had been crucified:[103] "Jesus of Nazareth was a man accredited by God to you by miracles, wonders and signs, which God did among you through him, as you yourselves know. This man was handed over to you by God's deliberate plan and foreknowledge; and you, with the help of wicked men, put him to death by nailing him to the cross. But God raised him from the dead, freeing him from the agony of death, because it was impossible for death to keep its hold on him" (Acts 2:22-24; see also Acts 3, 13-15; 1 Cor 15, 3ss and John 20, 25-28).

This proclamation is central to affirming the historical nature of the resurrection of Jesus which, in turn, allows us to affirm the transcendent and eschatological dimension of his Church; a presence that is not "visible and empirical, but [...] a transcendent presence lived in history".[104] It is the presence and not the absence of Jesus that gives birth to the Church. The conception of a Church that takes the place of an absent Jesus in the expectation of the Parousia is a conception that denies that the resurrection took place within history. This historical continuity also legitimises the nonviolence of the Gospels and gives it a transcendent and eschatological dimension as a core value of the early Christian communities. It is the nonviolent Jesus murdered on the cross who rises from the dead.

---

103 Cf. J. Sobrino (1982), "El Resucitado es el Crucificado. Lectura de la resurrección de Jesús desde los crucificados del mundo" en J. Sobrino, ed. Jesús en América Latina: su significado para la fe y la cristología, UCA editores, San Salvador, pp. 235.

104 P. Richard (1998), *El movimiento de Jesús antes de la Iglesia. Una interpretación liberadora de los Hechos de los Apóstoles*, Santander: Ed. Sal Terrae, p. 31.

The passion and resurrection

The passion and death of Jesus were initially disconcerting for some disciples, who in the book of the Acts of the Apostles still ask after the resurrection: "Lord, are you at this time going to restore the kingdom to Israel?" (Acts 1:6) — a questioning that inquires about the political project that equated the Kingdom of God with the Kingdom of Israel.[105] St. Paul speaks even of the madness of the cross, something that the first communities gradually came to understand as wisdom that leads to the resurrection: "For the message of the cross is foolishness to those who are perishing, but to us who are being saved it is the power of God" (1 Cor 1:18) and "For the foolishness of God is wiser than human wisdom, and the weakness of God is stronger than human strength" (1 Co 1:25).

It is possible to read the passion from a nonviolent perspective, taking the Suffering Servant Songs in Isaiah again as one's point of departure.[106] In the first song (Is 42:1-9) it is said that the Servant is sent to be light: "I, the Lord, have called you in righteousness; I will take hold of your hand. I will keep you and will make you to be a covenant for the people and a light for the Gentiles" (Is 42:6; 49:6) and it is already mentioned that his nonviolent attitude will finally bring justice to the peoples of the earth: "In faithfulness he will bring forth justice; he will not falter or be discouraged till he establishes justice on earth" (Is 42:3-4). However, the third and fourth songs (Is 50:4-9 and Is 52:13-53:12) present the Servant subjected to a punishment that seems cruel and unjust but is delivered by God. The fourth song, finally, speaks of the exaltation of the Servant who has experienced the torment (Is 52:13) and becomes the justification for many (Is 53:11).

---

105 P. Richard (1998), *El movimiento de Jesús antes de la Iglesia. Una interpretación liberadora de los Hechos de los Apóstoles*, Santander: Ed. Sal Terrae, p. 28.

106 Cf. J. Morera Perich (2018), *Desarmar los infiernos. Practicar la noviolencia de Jesús hoy*, Cuadernos CJ, no. 207, Barcelona: Cristianisme i Justicia, pp. 6-13.

The figure of the Servant of YHWH is paradigmatic in terms of this maturity of the experience of a God who is both just and merciful, whose love "exceeds" the violence and even the equity of "armed" justice. This mysterious figure, whose exact origin and significance leads exegetes to different interpretations, nevertheless opened the way for the desire and practice of the first Christian communities to identify him with Jesus of Nazareth, he whom they recognised and proclaimed as the Son of God. The path of Jesus Christ is the path of nonviolence, and yet one on which violence is inscribed and marked. The God of the Bible is manifested as merciful and nonviolent, but always encountered within the manifestations of violence in human history, never outside them.

The nonviolent confrontation, in opening spaces for integration, delegitimises the myth of redemptive violence, which believes in the destruction of those who are considered "enemies" because it is not able to imagine the possibility of a change.[107] The experience of being "disarmed" by the testimony of nonviolent resistance is reflected in the confession of the Gospel's centurion: "And when the centurion, who stood there in front of Jesus, saw how he died, he said, 'Surely this man was the Son of God!'" (Mark 15:39).

Resurrection in a wounded world

When asked about the meaning of the crucifixion and resurrection of Jesus in our time, it is fundamental to talk about the suffering of the peoples as the body of Christ suffering today and as an understanding of the historical continuity of the salvific action of the passion and resurrection. We can speak of the cross as a reality of individual people, but also as a reality of entire peoples: "What does it mean for the history of salvation and in the history of salvation the historical reality constituted by the majority of oppressed humanity? Can it be considered historically saved, when it continues to carry on itself the sins of the

---

107 Ibid., p.16.

world?"[108] Because of that, "it is right to speak about the 'crucified God' but just as necessary or even more so to speak about the 'crucified people'. This also gave the situation of Majority World ("Third-World") peoples a theological status."[109]

The crucifixion and resurrection reveal at once the tragedy of the victims and the hope in the justice of God. The violence exerted on the crucified peoples is a cry that rises to heaven and the resurrection is the confirmation that the cry has been heard and the suffering redeemed by the action of God (Cf. Acts 7:34).

But how are we to respond to the violence exerted on the crucified peoples in a world "engaged in a horrifying world war fought piecemeal"?[110] The resurrection affirms that violence unjustly exercised is not the destiny of humanity and announces that God is capable of transforming the injustice that creates victims by inflicting violence and suffering.[111] And that announcement becomes a hope that is historically realised when Jesus's "path of nonviolence [...] [is] walked [...] to the very end, to the cross, whereby he became our peace and put an end to hostility (cf. Eph 2: 14-16)."[112] That path is a path of liberation (Luke 4:18) fully illuminated in the resurrection. If God has resurrected Jesus, faith in the resurrection implies setting up conditions for the victims to come down from the cross and to have life in abundance, even if that process involves giving one's life through nonviolent love (John 10:10-11).

---

108 I. Ellacuría (1994), "El pueblo crucificado" in I. Ellacuría and J. Sobrino, eds. (1994), *Mysterium liberationis. Conceptos fundamentales de la teología de la liberación*, Vol. 2, Madrid: Ed. Trotta, p. 189.

109 J. Sobrino citing I. Ellacuría in J. Sobrino (1993), *Jesus the Liberator. A Historical-Theological Reading of Jesus of Nazareth*, New York: Orbis Books, p. 254.

110 Pope Francis (2017), "Nonviolence: A Style of Politics for Peace," Message of His Holiness Pope Francis for the celebration of the fiftieth World Day of Peace, no. 2, https://w2.vatican.va/content/francesco/en/messages/peace/documents/papa-francesco_20161208_messaggio-l-giornata-mondiale-pace-2017.html

111 Cf. J. Sobrino (1999), *La fe en Jesucristo. Ensayo sobre las víctimas*, Madrid: Ed. Trotta, p. 52.

112 Pope Francis, op. cit., no. 3.

Reconciliation

The resurrection is a call to reconciliation:

"For Christ's love compels us, because we are convinced that one died for all, and therefore all died. And he died for all, that those who live should no longer live for themselves but for him who died for them and was raised again. [...] Therefore, if anyone is in Christ, the new creation has come: The old has gone, the new is here! All this is from God, who reconciled us to himself through Christ and gave us the ministry of reconciliation: that God was reconciling the world to himself in Christ, not counting people's sins against them. And he has committed to us the message of reconciliation" (2 Cor 5, 14-15, 17-18).

Reconciliation in history is not, however, an easy process. In most societies struggling to rebuild after armed conflicts or prolonged periods of repressive regimes the word "reconciliation" itself can have multiple meanings and therefore find enormous resistance. Violence always involves wounds and deep divisions whose healing is usually slow and painful. The division between victimisers and victims can continue even after the formal end of a conflict. Nevertheless, despite everything, the historical and transcendent reality of the resurrection announces that it is possible to transform violence. "Whoever accepts the Good News of Jesus is able to acknowledge the violence within and be healed by God's mercy, becoming an instrument of reconciliation."[113]

Breaking cycles of violence through solidarity and humanisation

Reconciliation necessarily involves forgiveness, in the same way that the Suffering Servant, the Crucified One, is capable of forgiving his executioners (Luke 23:34). It is an act of love that goes beyond all logic and all interests and whose deeper

---

113 Pope Francis, op. cit., no. 3.

meaning has been revealed in the resurrection. It is the hope that nonviolent love can transform violence and open the way to full life.[114]

Forgiveness is freely given and, as such, opens both the possibility of acceptance and rejection by the other party, as shown in the contrasting attitudes of the centurion and those who derided Jesus. Indeed, given that conflict — in many ways — is part of every human community's life, the search for justice and reconciliation is always demanding creative nonviolent approaches. But from the logic of the resurrection, only forgiveness which is accepted after honest recognition of the commission of sin, injustice, or violence can lead to the transformation of structures. True reconciliation implies that transformation.[115]

A fundamental aspect of this process, and nonviolence in general, is the recognition of the humanity of the other. When the other stops being an enemy and spaces are opened for the consideration of his or her humanity, the path of forgiveness and reconciliation can begin. And it is always a two-way process. The victimiser recognises the humanity of the victim and decides to stop the violence and the victim opens the heart to the recognition of the victimiser's humanity and to the possibility of a common future shared in justice. It is a process that begins in the sphere of interpersonal relationships but transcends them to engage in social structural change, including the state level and also the sphere of international relations. From this perspective, reconciliation has always a political dimension, understood from the historical realisation of the Kingdom of God[116] and from Jesus's preferential option for the poor.[117]

---

114 Cf. J. Sobrino (1992), *El principio misericordia. Bajar de la cruz a los pueblos crucificados*, Santander: Ed. Sal Terrae, p. 105.

115 Ibid., p. 107.

116 Cf. J. Sobrino, *Jesus the Liberator*, op. cit., pp. 67-104.

117 Cf. G. Gutiérrez (1990), "Pobres y opción fundamental" in *Mysterium liberationis. Conceptos fundamentales de la teología de la liberación, Vol. 1*, Madrid: Ed. Trotta, 303-322.

Witnessing

Peace and reconciliation are thus not to be considered separately from Christ's wounds. The invitation to touch his wounds is an invitation from the wounded prophet of peace to *be* an *ecclesia crucis* in the world today.[118] Today among the poor of Latin America, for example, we find cycles of violence such as the gang warfare that cripples the youth in El Salvador, the United States and beyond; the decades of internal violence and the ensuing conflict between the FARC and the government in Colombia; and the Andean Indigenous peoples whose land and water rights are being sold by politicians and oligarchs to multinational corporations. Those who profess to belong to the wounded peacemaker are also invited to lead the people of God out of these cycles of violence into a lasting "peace on earth" willed by and in communion with God.

Let us recall just a few aspects of Saint Óscar Romero's bountiful legacy in witnessing to Christ the peacemaker. As Jon Sobrino explained, Romero "did not insulate himself from the reality of his society". He did not succumb to the temptation of unreality and did not "confuse the world of spirituality with the world of the invisible". Rather he immersed himself in the Spirit of God amid "the special place from which he prayed and meditated": the reality of El Salvador and its poor women and men.[119] Romero's peace-making and nonviolence were immersed in these realities of the search for justice and dignity for those who had been excluded.

Romero is the Salvadoran Church's architect of peace, a peace that was needed so desperately during his lifetime and no less so in our day. Moreover, he took to heart what the CELAM General Conference in Medellín had said about the necessary link between peace and development and applied that lesson directly

---

118 John 20:27. Cf. Roberto Goizueta, *Christ Our Companion*.

119 Jon Sobrino, S.J., "Monseñor Romero, A Salvadoran and a Christian," Spiritus: A Journal of Christian Spirituality, vol. 2:2 (Fall 2001), 143.

to his ministry.[120] How did San Romero invoke the peacemaker? Interestingly, he dedicated his Third Pastoral Letter to the Feast of the Transfiguration, a date that also marks a patronal feast day for the nation of El Salvador. As Margaret Pfeil has convincingly demonstrated, San Romero invokes the event of the transfiguration before the unjust rulers of his land as a prefiguring of incarnational peace.[121] He reminds them that the task of peace follows from the very name that has been given to their land:

"We want to end our reflections by contemplating the splendid vision of peace offered by the transfigured Lord. It is striking that the five persons chosen to accompany the divine saviour in that theophany on Mount Tabor were five men of aggressive temperaments and deeds. Moses, Elias, Peter, James and John can be described in the terms used of Christians at Medellin, *they are not simply pacifists, because they are capable of fighting, but they prefer peace to war.* Jesus channelled the aggression of their temperaments towards a rich work of construction, of building up justice and peace in the world. Let us ask the divine Patron of El Salvador to transfigure in the same way the rich potential of this people with whom he has chosen to share his name. To be his instrument for bringing about this transformation in his people is the reason for the Church's existence. That is why we have tried to reaffirm its identity and mission in the light of Christ. Only by being what he wants it to be will the Church be able to give more intelligent and effective service and support to the just aspirations of the people. 'This is my Beloved One: Listen to him' (Mark 9:7 and parallels). The voice of God on Mount Tabor is the best guarantee there is for the Church's mission among women and men, which is to point out Christ as the Beloved One of God and only Saviour, and to remind them of the supreme duty of listening to him if they want to be truly free and happy."[122]

---

120 Medellín documents, 20-27.

121 Margaret Pfeil, "Oscar Romero's Theology of the Transfiguration," Theological Studies 72 (2011): 87-115.

122 Archbishop Óscar Romero, "The Church and Popular Political Organisations," Third Pastoral Letter of Archbishop Romero, co-authored by Bishop Arturo Rivera y Damas, Bishop of Santiago de María, Feast of the Transfiguration, August 6, 1978, 24.

Romero's message to foster peace in El Salvador thus applies equally to his advocacy of nonviolence and his witness literally unto death on behalf of an agrarian reform that would give life to the campesinos who were being murdered in more ways than one. But all those working towards peace, says Romero, need to let their efforts be channelled and chastised by Jesus's refracted light of peace. This applies to the rulers and those under their rule, to the military and to the pastoral workers, to the bishops and to the lay people. In his lifetime there was great conflict in all of these areas. He invoked the transfiguration not as a quick fix but only to get all the parties to think about the witness of Christ in their lives.

Archbishop José Luis Escobar Alas of San Salvador is a successor to San Romero and wrote in 2016 a pastoral letter on his Feast Day entitled I *See Violence and Strife in the City*.[123] The letter does not analyse all the causes of violence in El Salvador today but acknowledges both Romero's on-going witness to the end of violence in El Salvador and the need to address the new challenge of gang violence in that light. Alas too invokes Christ the peacemaker. He cites for example the parable in which Jesus stops a group of men who wanted to stone a woman caught in adultery.[124] He notes how Jesus's example is also a call to take into account the leadership of women in Church and society.

Following Romero as a follower of Christ, Alas says, one can transfigure the Salvadoran cycle of violence that persists today. Social analysis was and is still needed. But the light of the peacemaker is equally necessary. In the end, Alas states: "I would venture to guess that the causes of social exclusion are primarily — in the words of St. Ignatius of Loyola — the three steps that the ruler of Babylon invites his followers to climb: wealth, honour and pride. These are the three steps, which in the view of St. Ignatius, lead to all the vices. They are the steps that blessed Archbishop Romero described in several of his letters and homilies as the worship of Mammon."[125]

---

123 Archbishop José Luis Escobar Alas, I See Violence and Strife in the City, Pastoral Letter of March 24, 2016.

124 Escobar Alas, I See Violence and Strife in the City #94, citing John 8:3.

125 Escobar Alas, I See Violence and Strife in the City #143, citing The Spiritual Exercises.

A witness to nonviolence like Romero can show us the path illuminated by the peacemaker, Jesus the Christ. Following that path and allowing that light to continue to shine in our own lives, families, neighbourhoods, cities and countries is up to us.

As Romero shows us, through Jesus we realise that we are brothers and sisters to all and that it is our responsibility to engage in God's "universal fraternity" (*Laudato Si'* 228). The ontological primacy of peace that is true for the whole of creation is also true for social structures. According to Saint Paul, the principalities and powers were originally good and part of their creation through Christ (Col 1:15-17).

While God has created every human being in God's image, and "the Son of God has united Himself in some fashion with every man" (*Gaudium et Spes*, no. 22), the Church has emphasised that a profound option for the poor is essential to the promotion of justice and the overcoming of violence.

The preferential option for the poor, said Pope Benedict in his opening address to the Conference of Aparecida, "is implicit in the Christological faith in the God who became poor for us, so as to enrich us with his poverty." It is therefore necessary to take the perspective of those persons who are poor as a starting point to any theology of nonviolence, because impoverished people suffer most from the different forms of violence present in our world. It is also decisive, in different circumstances and contexts, to assume the perspective of women, communities of colour, Indigenous people, children and all vulnerable people everywhere.

Pneumatology

Our God of unconditional, self-giving love calls all humanity to the nonviolent life. We who are the Church — the People of God — experience this call through the life and presence of Jesus and the creative power and guidance of the Holy Spirit. The Church seeks, and collaborates in building, the nonviolent Reign of God through the gifts, direction and promptings of the Holy Spirit.

The generative power of the Holy Spirit activates faithful nonviolence in our lives, our Church and our world. We experience the Holy Spirit's call to nonviolence and the gift of nonviolence through scripture, prayer, worship and service.

The Spirit in the Hebrew Bible

In sacred scripture, many symbolic images are used to convey the presence of the Holy Spirit, particularly those of wind, fire, water and Sophia Wisdom. The Holy Spirit is present in acts of creation and salvation, fundamentally shaping the eschatological meaning of word and sacrament in the Christian community.

"The Hebrew word for "spirit" (*rûah*) initially designated the wind, storm, or gentle breeze.[126] "*Rûah* also meant the breath in the human person, or life that was thought to be lodged in, or manifested by, breath (Gen 2:7)."[127]

At the beginning of the Book of Genesis, the Spirit or wind of God "swept over the face of the waters" (Gen 1:2; cf. Ps 33:6). This begins the creative act of God, establishing the context for a rich and enveloping sacramentality of all God's

---

126 M. John Farrelly, OSB, "Holy Spirit," in Michael Downey, ed., *The New Dictionary of Catholic Spirituality*, The Liturgical Press, 1993, 493.

127 M. John Farrelly. "Rûah brought rain to the fields from the Mediterranean or a sirocco from the desert and thus life or death to field and flock (Ezek 13:13; 1 Kgs 18:45; 19:12).

creation. The Spirit's wind issues forth in the breath of God animating the life of all members of God's creation, including humans. As scripture scholar Ellen Davis has noted, the poetic Genesis creation narratives highlight God's invitation to co-operation with God's ongoing creative dynamism.[128] This finds a later echo in 1 Cor 3:9, where human beings are invited to become *synergoi*, co-operators, with God in creative endeavours.

The thread running throughout scripture from Genesis forward is the building up of God's creation in love, which bears fruit in peace. Wherever life is fragile, God's Spirit strengthens and breathes dynamic, saving life into beings, relationships and communities, drawing them to God (cf. Judges 13:25, 15:14-15). Ezekiel, for example, calls on the breath of God to bring dry bones in the valley to new life: "Then he said to me: 'Prophesy to the breath, prophesy, mortal, and say to the breath: Thus says the Lord God: Come from the four winds, O breath, and breathe upon these slain, that they may live. I prophesied as he commanded me, and the breath came into them, and they lived, and stood on their feet, a vast multitude" (Ezekiel 37: 9-10).

Isaiah counts wisdom among the gifts of the spirit of the Lord that will be manifest in the awaited messianic kingdom, along with understanding, counsel, fortitude, knowledge, piety and fear of the Lord (Is 11: 2-3). With the Spirit of the Lord upon him, "he will bring forth justice to the nations" (Is 42:1). Like water on parched land, the Lord promises Israel that "I will pour my spirit upon your descendants, and my blessing upon your offspring". And on the day of judgment, Joel prophesies, the Lord will pour forth the Spirit on all: "Then afterwards I will pour out my spirit upon all humankind. Your sons and daughters shall prophesy, your old men shall dream dreams, your young men shall see visions; even upon the servants and the handmaids, in those days, I will pour out my spirit" (Joel 2:28-29).

---

128 Ellen Davis, *Scripture, Culture, and Agriculture*, Cambridge University Press, 2009.

The Hebrew Bible announces that the Spirit of Sophia Wisdom is at work in the world: "Although she is but one, she can do all things, and while remaining in herself, she renews all things; in every generation she passes into holy souls and makes them friends of God, and prophets; for God loves nothing so much as the person who lives with wisdom" (Wis 7:27). Of this passage, Elizabeth Johnson observes, "From the beginning of the human race's emergence into consciousness and responsibility, the breath of the power of Spirit-Sophia has been pervading the human heart and conscience, awakening the fire of affection for divine mystery and the flame of compassion wherever injustice eviscerates what that love requires in the world."[129]

Not every spirit, though, is of God. Because some are destructive, discernment of spirits is an important formative element in nonviolence.[130] Discernment, as Pope Francis writes, "is not a matter of applying rules or repeating what was done in the past, since the same solutions are not valid in all circumstances and what was useful in one context may not prove so in another. The discernment of spirits liberates us from rigidity. ...Without the wisdom of discernment, we can easily become prey to every passing trend (GE, 173). This is all the more important when some novelty presents itself in our lives. Then we have to decide whether it is new wine brought by God or an illusion created by the spirit of this world... At other times, the opposite can happen, when the forces of evil induce us not to change, to leave things as they are, to opt for a rigid resistance to change. Yet that would be to block the working of the Spirit".[131]

In the Hebrew Bible the Spirit is the breath of life that calls humanity to the nonviolent journey for peace rooted in justice.

---

129 Elizabeth Johnson, *Friends of God and Prophets*, Continuum, 1998, 40-41.

130 See also Pope Francis, *Gaudete et exsultate*, paragraphs 166-175. This whole section (para. 166-175) explicitly on discernment speaks to the prayerful disposition required for this, which is also an important aspect of the connection between pneumatology and nonviolence.

131 Pope Francis, *Gaudete et exsultate*, paragraphs 173, 168.

The Spirit in the Christian Bible

"The Spirit of the Lord is upon me, because he has anointed me to bring glad tidings to the poor. He has sent me to proclaim liberty to captives and recovery of sight to the blind, to let the oppressed go free and to proclaim a year acceptable to the Lord" (Luke 4:18-20).

From the beginning to the end of his earthly ministry, Jesus is inspired by the Spirit. "Luke particularly notes the outpouring of the Spirit in the conception and infancy of Jesus (Luke 1:35, 41, 67; 2:25-27), as he will later note the outpouring of the Spirit in the early Church" (Farrelly, 494). Mary's assent to the power of the Holy Spirit in the Incarnation and Joseph's assent to accept this family of Mary with Jesus in the womb portend the effect of the Holy Spirit's movement in and through those who walk with Jesus: it is dynamically relational and draws the lives of all who follow Jesus ever deeper into that "infinite charity which is the Holy Spirit" (Pope Francis, *Amoris Laetitia* 134, citing Thomas Aquinas, *Summa Theologica*, II-II 24.7).

Animated by this infinite love, Jesus models for his disciples what it means to be completely surrendered to God's will: ultimately it signifies openness to the movement and fruits of the Holy Spirit. The presence of the Holy Spirit accompanies the divine word given at Jesus's baptism and reaffirmed later at the Transfiguration: "You are my own dear One. I am pleased with you" (Luke 3:22; cf. Luke 9:35).

Following his baptism "full of the Holy Spirit", Jesus was "led by the Spirit into the desert, where he was tempted by the Devil for forty days" (Luke 4:1-2). Rejecting a worldly, violent power, Jesus witnesses to a different kind of reign. He faces these temptations with a disposition of complete surrender to God. The lures of power, possession and pride were no match for Jesus's humility, a key virtue in the spirituality and practice of nonviolence. Returning to Galilee, Jesus took up his public ministry, "and the power of the Holy Spirit was with him" (Luke

4:14). He reads from Isaiah and proclaims its fulfilment in him: "The Spirit of our God is upon me, because the Most High has anointed me to bring Good News to those who are poor" (Luke 4:18; Is 61:1).

At the point of his death, Jesus gives up his spirit, freely offering his life and love on the cross in the face of hate: "Into your hand, I commit my spirit" (Ps 31:5; cf. Luke 23:46). As René Girard notes, Jesus's dying and rising into new life interrupts the deadly cycle of mimetic violence. The same Spirit animating divine creation also empowers the crucified Jesus's resurrection. By the power of the Holy Spirit, death does not have the last word, and Jesus's nonviolent way of being permeates his community of disciples through his risen presence. "As the narratives of the Easter appearances make clear, henceforth [Jesus] is present through the power of the Spirit in word and sacrament, dwelling wherever two or three gather in his name, encountered as a stranger explaining the scriptures as he walks along the road, recognised in the breaking of bread, present where human wounds are touched and healed and, in a special way, served where the hungry receive bread, the thirsty drink, and the naked clothing" (Johnson, 209-210). Through his life, death and resurrection, Jesus draws his followers into a discipleship of nonviolence, sending them the Paraclete, the Advocate, the Holy Spirit, to strengthen them along the journey.

In John's Gospel in particular the eschatological nature of this gift of the Holy Spirit is clear, and it is explicitly linked to Christ's gift of peace:

"And I will ask the One who sent me to give you another Paraclete, another Advocate, to be with you forever. This is the Spirit of truth, whom the world cannot receive, because the world neither sees her nor knows her. You know her, because she abides with you, and will be within you …. Those who obey the commandments are the ones who love me, and those who love me will be loved by Abba God. I too will love them and will reveal myself to them. …. Those who love me will be true to my word, and Abba God will love them; and we will come to them and make our dwelling place with them. … This much have I said to you while still with you; but the Paraclete, the Holy Spirit, whom Abba God will send in my name, will instruct you in everything and she will remind you of all that I have told you. Peace I leave with you; my peace I give to you; but the kind of peace I give you is not like the world's peace. Do not let your hearts be troubled, and do not let them be afraid" (John 14:16-17, 23, 25-27).

"When the Spirit of truth comes, she will guide you into all truth. She won't speak on her own initiative; rather, she'll speak only what she hears, and she'll announce to you things that are yet to come" (John 16:13). The Holy Spirit is the first gift of the resurrected Jesus to his disciples, given to empower them on their mission of furthering Christ's peace and forgiveness, when he stands before them and says, "Peace be with you" (John 20:19-23).

One week after Jesus's first post-resurrection appearance to his disciples, he appears again to them, this time with Thomas present. Thomas makes a profession of faith, but only after touching Jesus's wounds. But why the wounds? Why not recognise Jesus by his face? His stature? His voice? These wounds are somehow at the heart of the Christian Gospel. They tell Thomas not only that this is Jesus whom he has touched, but that this is the God who came to be with and for them, even in suffering and death. ...Here is Jesus, with wounds eternally healed still among them. Here is Jesus, who had predicted he would take on the pain of all humankind, among them. Here is Jesus, whose wounds must represent, then, the wounds of all humankind, still among them. Here is Jesus, the face of God for them.

Here is Jesus, who has revealed that God's peace is intimately bound up with the paschal mystery of the nonviolent Way of the Cross and the Resurrection that has vanquished the absolute hold of death, evil and violence on humankind.

With the descent of the Holy Spirit upon the apostles, they take up Jesus's mission, which is characterised by nonviolence, as seen in the long lineage of

Christian martyrs in the first centuries of the Church. Filled with the Holy Spirit at Pentecost, Peter and John heal a person disabled from birth at the Beautiful Gate of the temple in the name of Jesus Christ (Acts 3:1-10). When asked to name the source of their healing power, Peter proclaims healing and salvation through Jesus Christ (Acts 4:5-12).

Nonviolence and the gifts of the Spirit

The language of charism, or the gifts of the Spirit, draws upon Paul's message to Corinth and figures prominently in the account of the Church's ministry and mission found in *Lumen gentium.*

As paragraph 12 puts it: "It is not only through the sacraments that the Holy Spirit makes holy the People, leads them and enriches them with his virtues. Allotting his gifts according as he wills ... he also distributes special graces among the faithful of every rank. By these gifts he makes them fit and ready to undertake various tasks and offices for the renewal and building up of the Church, as it is written, 'the manifestation of the Spirit is given to everyone for profit' (1 Cor 12:7)."

Lumen gentium relies on Paul's description of the diverse gifts freely given by the Holy Spirit for service to the Church. They may accent and coincide with natural abilities, but they are distinguished precisely as charisms by their essential direction towards the common good of the ecclesial community.[132] The Second Vatican Council's Decree on the Apostolate of Lay People (*Apostolicam*

---

132 Hans Küng, "The Charismatic Structure of the Church," in *The Church and Ecumenism, Concilium Vol. 4* (New York: Paulist Press, 1965), 51. See also the following contributions in *Retrieving Charisms for the Twenty-First Century,* ed. Doris Donnelly (Collegeville, Minnesota: The Liturgical Press, 1999): Margaret M. Mitchell, "'Be Zealous for the Greater Charismata': Pauline Advice for the Church of the Twenty-First Century," 22; John C. Haughey, "Charisms: An Ecclesiological Exploration," 2; and Avery Dulles, "The Charism of the New Evangelizer," 36. Finally, see René Laurentin, "Charisms: Terminological Precision," trans. Theo Weston, in *Charisms in the Church, Concilium Vol. 109,* ed. Christian Duquoc and Casiano Floristan (New York: The Seabury Press, 1978), 7-8.

Actuositatem) further specifies that believers have the right and duty to direct charisms towards the good not only in the Church but in the world as well.[133]

The humble, nonviolent surrender to God's love characterises the eschatological promise of God's reign. In Matthew 25:31-46, those who practise the works of mercy, feeding the hungry, visiting the sick and imprisoned, do so out of love for the person before them, not because they recognise Jesus. They manifest the fruits of the Holy Spirit at work in lives surrendered to God. With Mary, they have said "yes" to the Spirit's movement: " 'The Holy Spirit will come upon you, and God's power will rest upon you' " (Luke 1:35, 38).

The Spirit and the Trinitarian God

It is not possible to speak of the Holy Spirit without also speaking of the Holy Trinity. The Trinity is not an indecipherable dogma but a powerful articulation of the foundational relationality of God. The eternal communion of Creator, Redeemer and Sustainer is the ceaseless mutuality of ontological nonviolence in action. God is unconditional love that grounds, creates and maintains all life, rooted in the infinite goodness that the three Persons of the one God endlessly and inseparably share with one another and with all creation. St. Paul's frequent use of a tripartite greeting reflects this Trinitarian communion: "The grace of our Lord Jesus Christ and the love of God and the fellowship of the Holy Spirit be with all of you" (2 Cor 13:13).

As theologian Catherine LaCugna puts it: "Living trinitarian faith means living God's life: living from and for God, from and for others. Living trinitarian faith means living as Jesus Christ lived, *in persona Christi*: preaching the Gospel;

---

133 Decree on the Apostolate of Lay People (Apostolicam actuositatem), no. 3. See also John Haughey's account of the conciliar approach to the concept of charism in "Connecting Vatican II's Call to Holiness with Public Life," Catholic Theological Society of America Proceedings 55 (2000): 1-19.

relying totally on God; offering healing and reconciliation; rejecting laws, customs, conventions that place persons beneath rules; resisting temptation; praying constantly; eating with modern-day lepers and other outcasts; embracing the enemy and the sinner; dying for the sake of the Gospel if it is God's will. Living trinitarian faith means living according to the power and presence of the Holy Spirit."[134]

The nonviolent community of our Trinitarian God models how humanity is to be. The beloved community — God's own endless self-sharing — reveals how those of us made in the image and likeness of God are to live. We are called to be beloved community with one another, embraced and sustained by the beloved community of God.

The nonviolence of Jesus springs from this foundational understanding of God and the life God calls us to live. Jesus's nonviolence is rooted in his faithful response to the God of self-giving and infinitely relational love who has created a world that is good and who calls humanity to live in peace. "Jesus incarnates the liberating God, who takes sides with the poor and oppressed in a divine effort to bring life to all," writes John Dear.[135] Nonviolence is the way to God even as it is the way to one another. As LaCugna notes, the persons of the Trinity model the loving relationality into which Jesus invites his disciples. The Holy Spirit stokes the fire of God's love among all members of God's creation.[136]

Nurtured and guided by the Holy Spirit, nonviolence is a way of life that rejects the belief in violence, that transforms and resolves conflict, that fosters reconciliation and unity and that tirelessly seeks justice and peace for all. The way of nonviolence is a pilgrimage of discipleship that calls us to conversion,

---

134 Catherine LaCugna, *God for Us: The Trinity and Christian Life*, 2000, 400-01.

135 John Dear, *The God of Peace: Toward a Theology of Nonviolence*, Orbis Books, 1994, 43.

136 Catherine LaCugna, *God for Us: The Trinity and Christian Life*, 2000.

community, service and action. Nonviolence is a spiritual journey that invites transformation and healing at every level of our lives and our Church.

The Spirit and encounter

Spirit-led nonviolence is revealed through scripture. It is also disclosed through authentic encounter: the unexpected and sometimes life-changing exchange with another that transforms and heals, through which we can experience the "infinite charity which is the Holy Spirit" (*Amoris Laetitia* 134), as in this revealing contemporary example:

"One summer in Arizona, as temperatures reached 120 degrees, a group called the Samaritans sent volunteers to keep watch for any immigrants who might be in need or distress. When a group of 20 immigrants came walking along a dry river bed, a volunteer called out to them from a ledge on a hill and asked, 'Is anybody injured? Do you need any food? Do you have any water?' Suddenly the group of immigrants stopped. Unsure of who was speaking to them, they huddled together and deliberated awhile. Then slowly the leader began walking towards the Samaritan volunteers and said, 'We don't have any more food. And we only have a little bit of water. But if you are in need of it, we will share what we have with you.' "[137]

Even in situations of precarity and risk, encounter can create unexpected options for transformation, mutual solidarity and life itself.

In the Christian tradition, it is the encounters that Jesus has with others that serve as a paradigm for those who walk in his footsteps. Jesus calls his followers to repentance, to conversion and to lifelong discipleship. This experience of unexpected transformation, change of heart and a radical reorientation of one's

---

137 Daniel G. Groody, C.S.C., "Jesus and the Undocumented Immigrant: A Spiritual Geography of A Crucified People," Theological Studies, 70 (2009) pg. 298.

life is ignited by the encounter with Jesus who is the embodiment of love and mercy. Led by the Spirit more deeply into the life of Christ, we see the unveiled face of the living God (LaCugna, 378).

Something happens to those who encounter Jesus. John, Jesus's cousin, leaps with joy in his mother Elizabeth's womb encountering Jesus through his mother, Mary. The elders at the Temple are astonished by the 12-year-old Jesus's wisdom (Luke 2:41-52). There is the non-judgmental and egalitarian conversation Jesus had with the Samaritan at the well (John 4); the raising of a dead girl and the healing of a sick woman (Mark 5:21-43) — all of these exchanges bring new life and hope to those who suffered. Each demonstrates intimacy, acceptance, courage, gratitude and a shift to living life more fully in the service of the Beloved Community. These nonviolent encounters model for us a way of being with and for all others.

These stories also invite us to meet Jesus in a most personal manner. It is in our imagination, in the memories of sounds, scents, touch and emotions that Jesus stops for a moment with us on his journey. He takes us aside, spends time with us and pulls us into his life so that we can experience that beautiful gaze of love. It is that encounter with the enfleshed bearer of ultimate grace that we are invited to transformation and to a deeper spiritual reality.

We become that woman at the well. It is hot, it is dusty and we are filled with the scornful glances and whispered innuendoes of our neighbours, who look down on us and gossip about us. Our self-image, our self-worth, makes us despise ourselves. And this man, who could be like so many others who have abused us, speaks to us instead as an equal. He looks into our eyes as if he is our very brother who loves us, no matter what we may have done. We speak to him with contempt, expecting the worst. He responds with respect and directness, with humanness. He takes what no one else will take from us ... and fills us with an overflowing abundance of what we thought we would never have again: loving hope in our very existence.

We must become the disdained woman at the well who has lost hope. We must be the pregnant teen who runs to her cousin in absolute fright about her condition that will bring such shame and reproach. And we must be the arrogant teacher who is surprised by the innocent wisdom of a child, the despairing parent of a dead child or the sorrowing spouse who has lost her life partner. We are invited to feel our human pain and fragility, which we cannot escape alone. In the encounter with Jesus, we find the grace that transforms fear, despair, sorrow and unbearable pain into a new existence. To encounter Jesus is to invite him into our lives and to be assured that he lives within us. "Don't you know that you yourselves are God's temple and that God's Spirit dwells in your midst?" (1 Cor 3:16).

In the context of this experience of acceptance, intimacy and healing, Jesus's followers embrace his proclamation of the reign of God. This encounter transforms our deepest fears and insecurities into the possibility of hope, in the knowledge that God is doing something new in the world and that our role in this plan is essential. Fears and insecurities, which are often turned against others in acts of dominance, violence and exclusion, are overwhelmed by an encounter with absolute love and radical acceptance. In these encounters our personal fate and the fate of the communities we inhabit and shape are transformed. This is true in our lives. It is also true in the lives of the great cloud of witnesses who, for two thousand years, have encountered the God of nonviolence through Jesus Christ, guided by the Holy Spirit.

For 21 centuries, the Holy Spirit has called Christians in all parts of the world to a life of holiness. This has included responding to the challenges in their lives and their world with the humility and courage of nonviolence. Martyrs and saints — known and unknown — have dedicated their lives to actively following the Spirit's call to collaborate in building the already-but-not-yet nonviolent Reign of God. Despite its failings, the Church is called to be a community that "shares actively, freely, gratuitously and unrestrictedly its goods and charismatic gifts ... incompatible with physical, social and political acts of violence; with revenge, murder, rape, extortion, exploitation, war. Its political stance is pacifist and nonviolent."[138] The Church, as bearer of the Paschal mystery in the present day,[139] lives and teaches the mystery of reconciliation in the power of the Holy Spirit.

Ecclesiology

As followers of the Prince of Peace, the Church is called to be nonviolent. But the Church is not merely an aggregate collection of individual disciples; it is a community of people united as the Body of Christ. Is there something about the very logic of this union that witnesses to the nonviolence of God?

What is the Church for?

Scripture scholar Gerhard Lohfink explains the logic of gathering a People of God in terms of God's nonviolence. God sees the wreckage of the world post-Fall, the violence and chaos that have come about through human sin, and God wants to change the world. This is what salvation means: not plucking a few survivors from the wreckage of the world and installing them in heaven, but creating a new heaven and a new earth. God is a revolutionary. But God is not like human revolutionaries, as Lohfink underscores: "All violent revolutionaries have one basic problem: they are short of time. Individual lifetimes are limited, and the masses are often inert. If they want to see the new society of their dreams within their own lifetime, revolutionaries have to change the old society in a relatively short period of time, and that they can only do by violent means. The usual concept of revolution includes at least three elements: (1) that the masses are involved; (2) that the social overthrow happens relatively quickly; and (3) that it is brought about by open and direct violence".[140]

---

138 Don Gelpi, S.J., Experiencing God: A Theology of Human Emergence (Paulist Press, New York, 1978), 281.

139 Donal Harrington, "The Spirituality of Nonviolence," The Furrow, Vol. 42, N 11 (Nov. 1991), 617.

140 Lohfink, Gerhard. Does God Need the Church? Michael Glazier Publishing, 1999, p. 26.

God's principle of transformation is different. God, like all revolutionaries, desires the overturning, the radical alteration of the whole society — for in this the revolutionaries are right: what is at stake is the whole world, and the change must be radical, for the misery of the world cries to heaven and it begins deep within the human heart. But how can anyone change the world and society at its roots without taking away freedom?

God is nonviolent, so God begins the transformation of the world by calling a small group to live differently so that people can see a beautiful life and join the movement voluntarily, not by coercion. Salvation begins in the Jews, a chosen people meant to model a peaceful and reconciled life for the whole world, and the Church calls people into this unity. Salvation happens by attraction, not coercion, as William Cavanaugh explains: "This kind of attraction does not occur in a general and universal way, any more than one falls in love with men or women in general. Attraction to a saved life occurs when one can see a concrete community of people living out salvation, living reconciled and hopeful lives in the midst of a violent world. Rarely are people converted by well-argued theories. People are usually converted to a new way of living by getting to know people who live that way and thus being able to see themselves living that way too. This is the way God's revolution works. The Church is meant to be that community of people who make salvation visible for the rest of the world. Salvation is not a property of isolated individuals, but is only made visible in mutual love."[141]

Paul refers to the community of Christians as the "body of Christ". The Church is the continuation of the bodily presence of Christ on earth. The boundaries of that body are rarely clear, for the Holy Spirit is not confined to the visible Church. But the centre of that body is clear: the weakest members, Paul says, are the indispensable ones (1 Cor 12:22), and when one member suffers, all suffer together (1 Cor 12:26). Christ identifies himself with the victims of this

---

141 William T. Cavanaugh, "Pilgrim People" in *Gathered for the Journey*, ed. David McCarthy and Therese Lysaught (Grand Rapids, MI: Wm. B. Eerdmans, 2007), 88-105.

world (Matthew 25:31-46). In Girard's thought, the Church is that community that undoes the logic of violence by breaking the unanimity that proclaims the guilt of the victims. The Church identifies God with the victims of this world and thereby unmasks the scapegoating mechanism. Nonviolence is not for a few heroic individuals; it is lived in community by sensing the deep interconnection of all people, sharing the same nervous system in the cosmic Christ.

Siding with the victims of this world will provoke opposition. Nonviolence is not a tactic that always works in the short run, but we know with a broader, longer-term perspective it is in reality working. Christians must be prepared for suffering or even martyrdom, which is not merely a phenomenon deeply rooted in the past but a daily reality for Christians around the world today. Martyrdom is the ultimate witness to the truth of nonviolence. The martyr, in imitation of Christ, prefers to absorb the violence of the world rather than deal it out, in the secure knowledge that she or he is on the right side of history. The present and coming reign of God is nonviolent; the martyr decides to live that reality now. But the martyr is not alone; the witness of martyrs depends on a Church community ready to keep the memory of the martyrs alive as a proclamation of what God – and God's creation – is really like.

Church as sacrament of the future

As a reality that makes God's uniting of the world visible to the world, the Church is a sacrament. As *Lumen Gentium* says, "All those who in faith look towards Jesus, the author of salvation and the principle of unity and peace, God has gathered together and established as the Church, that it may be for each and everyone the visible sacrament of this saving unity."[142] The Church is, furthermore, "in Christ like a sacrament or as a sign and instrument both of a very closely knit union

---

142 *Lumen Gentium*, No. 9.

with God and of the unity of the whole human race."[143] It can be said that Christ is the sacrament of God, and the Church is the sacrament of Christ. The Church concretely manifests this claim when it is faithful to the nonviolent witness and teachings of Christ, who came to inaugurate the Kingdom of God.

The traditional "marks" of the Church indicate that the Church is characterised by its visible characteristics. The four marks are also signs of the nonviolence of God. The Church is, firstly, one because God is one. Violence divides, while God unites. The Church is, secondly, holy because God is holy. The Church is called to renewal and reform, to making manifest the nonviolent nature of God in its very life. The Church is, thirdly, catholic. It embraces all, and transcends the barriers that set people against each other. The Church is, fourthly, apostolic. It is called to be faithful to the nonviolent teaching of Jesus and the apostles, as found in the Sermon on the Mount. The four marks are "signs of originative gifts" and "emergent properties" of the not yet fully realised vocation of the Church.[144]

The promise of God's revolution is that history is moving towards the reconciliation of all things. But that reconciliation is not fully here yet, obviously. There is still plenty of violence and evil. After Jesus was gone, it was easy to look around and conclude "The Messiah has not come. The world is the same as it was." The only proof the early Christians could offer that the Messiah had indeed come was to live as if the world was already changed. The early Christians in Acts of the Apostles lived reconciled, nonviolent lives, praising God and sharing all their goods in common (Acts 2:42-47). They lived as if the future Kingdom was already here, because it is. Christ has already changed the world, and after ascending, the Holy Spirit has been poured out on all, making it possible that "your young people shall see visions, and your old people dream dreams" (Acts 2:17). The Holy Spirit has inaugurated the "last days", making it possible for people to live

---

143 *Lumen Gentium*, No. 1.

144 Stephen Pickard, *Seeking the Church: An Introduction to Ecclesiology* (London: SCM, 2012).

differently, to lead reconciled lives. True to his nonviolent nature, the event of Christ and the outpouring of the Spirit does not force anyone to change. Rather, people are invited to live a beautiful life now, not waiting to live reconciled, peaceful lives until everyone else does. We are invited to bring heaven to earth now — to show the future in the present — by living nonviolently. It is still the only proof Christians can offer that the Messiah has really come in Jesus of Nazareth.

It is an odd thing to be reminded that the Church — seemingly the most tradition-laden institution of the modern world, one rooted in the formative stories and experiences of its past - is fundamentally defined by the future. Rather than a barge being pushed from behind by a tugboat, the Church is a vessel guided into the future by a lodestar, a magnetic attraction to what lies ahead.

What lies ahead is the Kingdom of God. It was the beginning of the consummation of the Kingdom that Jesus proclaimed and inaugurated, and it is the reconciliation of the created order with God that Christians point to as the ultimate direction of history. It is the arrival of a "new heaven and new earth" (Is 65:17; Rev 21:1), in which sin and its effects have been effaced, and in which peace and love flow from unity with a loving and benevolent God.

All too often overlooked or marginalised, however, is the role of the Church in the unfolding of the Kingdom that began with Jesus and reaches completion when He comes again. While the Church does not build the Kingdom of God, nor is it itself the Kingdom of God, it nonetheless has an irreplaceable role in the unfolding of the Kingdom. By minimising the degree to which the mission and actions of the Church should be constituted by what God intends all humanity to become, the Church instead settles into dull conformity with the ends and means of the old age, that age whose end is proclaimed in the resurrection and completed in God's future time. When the role of the Church in the unfolding of the new era of God is properly reconfigured, many contemporary assumptions and habits stand ready for review and reconsideration.

Eschatology is not concerned primarily with the end of the world, nor about a post-historical utopia with no purchase on life today. As John Panteleimon Manoussakis writes, such dispositions serve as: "the perfect alibi for getting all too comfortable with the world in its current state. We have found the ideal justification for forgetting that this is not our home, our goal, our destination; that the categories of this world are not and should not be the paradigms and concepts of our thought. By exiling eschatology to a time beyond time, we have precluded ourselves from the wonderfully subversive effects of the future, of the reversals that the new might bring. Without an eschatological awareness in our interaction with the everyday, we cannot but be immune to surprise, and, therefore, to the kingdom of God, which has surprise as its very mode of manifestation (Matthew 24:27; Mark 13:36; Luke 12:40; 17:24)".[145]

Whether the Church is thought of as a "demonstration plot", a prototype, a beachhead or a "field hospital", the thrust of an ecclesiology mindful of its eschatological nature emphasises that within the Church people are supposed to start acting as if the Kingdom has already begun, and that the Church is called to show the world that a different way to live is possible *here and now*, even as the old order seeks to preserve itself against the onslaught of the coming Kingdom of God. The resurrection of Christ marks an irrevocable change in the created order, here and now, if only people had the courage to believe it and act as if it were so. If Christ has been raised, the fear of death — the ultimate limit on human hope and aspirations — should no longer hold sway. If all who follow Jesus will be taken up into God at some point in the future, the grave need not serve as a check on our life and work and most noble predispositions. If life is held only when it is freely given away (Mark 8:35; Matthew 16:24; Luke 9:24), then we need not kill any longer to protect it; by seeking to protect life with violence, we may be forgoing the experience of eternal life first exemplified by the resurrection.

---

145 John Panteleimon Manoussakis, "The Anarchic Principle of Christian Eschatology in the Eucharistic Tradition of the Eastern Church," Harvard Theological Review, 100:1 (2007), p. 33.

When the Church is properly aware of its eschatological character, it sees that following Jesus — his practices and priorities, dispositions and affections — is itself a crucial aspect of the Kingdom's unfurling in history. The Church does not cause the Kingdom to advance, but it is meant to show the world what human community starts to look like as the Kingdom becomes a lived reality. It does this in and through its sins, mistakes, wrong turns and reversals — it does this through showing what penance and reconciliation can make possible, by showing that the past need not have a death-grip on the present and future, and by imitating however it can the self-giving love of God towards one another and those outside its community.

The Church and countersign

While the Church has been called to be a countersign to the sin of the world, we must confess that the Church has sometimes been a countersign to the nonviolence of God instead.

The Church has often spent more of its moral and intellectual resources trying to justify participation in war and violence than to renounce it. In the Crusades, Christians blasphemously claimed that "Deus Vult" — God wills the carnage. The Church has sanctioned slavery, torture, the death penalty and forced conversions. Sexual violence against women and children has often been given cover in a patriarchal Church. In modern times, the Church has been riven by a narrow sectarianism that lauds killing on behalf of one's nation-state over the universal embrace of the Church catholic.

We cannot re-affirm the centrality of nonviolence to the life and mission of Jesus — and thus the life and mission of the Church — without confessing the ways the Church has betrayed its call to nonviolence throughout history. Indeed, our nonviolent journey requires ongoing metanoia — a profoundly transformative process as Church of turning away from the ways of violence — that includes acknowledging and making amends for this systemic betrayal.

The Church seeks to be faithful to the biblical witness of the God of nonviolence. But this same witness, the stories that reveal the God of nonviolence, clearly witness to humanity's sin of interpersonal and social violence. It is in the midst of these experiences of the harm we do to each other that God enters history in order to challenge violence, hold back a vengeful spirit, promote freedom from oppression and transform lives and communities. As an agent of this truth, the Church too must examine the ways its history is both touched by conflict and violence as a consequence of sin, while at the same time being gifted with the truth of a nonviolent God who wishes for us life abundant in love and hope.

Throughout human history our grandest plans for centralising power, promoting human progress and expanding the reach of our influence have met with the failure of our sinful propensity for violence, for the urge to impose our will on others through the subjugation and dehumanisation of those who do not think like us or adapt to our plans.

The Hebrew Bible reminds us that in the times of the Kingdom of Israel the people demanded a king. Having an earthly ruler represented the fulfilment of the promises of the Lord, of having arrived at a promised land and finally governing themselves according to the dictates of the Law. But this was judged by God to be a rejection of divine rule and the law, that which set them apart from the other kingdoms around them. On the contrary, the people asked for Samuel to request from Adonai a king: "We too must be like all the nations, with a king to rule us, lead us in warfare and fight our battles" (1 Samuel 8:20). Until then violence and conflict for the people of Israel had meant trusting God's plan and sovereignty, which in its infinite wisdom and mercy increasingly challenged humanity's violent will. But now the people were demanding that they too enjoy the benefits of an earthly ruler, one that would lead in battle, ignoring God's challenges and alternative vision. Samuel warns the people of the foolishness of their plan, for their benefit is not in becoming "like all the nations", but rather in being a people set apart to follow and trust a liberating God of life.

The prophets call out the distortions of our own totalising political projects. These projects tend to claim for themselves divine favour and blessing by establishing their justice and their contribution to the common good, while overlooking their failure or the harm they may do to others. Sin not only corrupts our historical projects, but also masks violence with the veil of necessity and progress. The prophets charged to call out this farce, while reminding us of God's mercy and purpose for peace and life, suffer the fate of being ridiculed, persecuted, jailed, exiled and sometimes even murdered.

The Church does not stand outside history. It is born of the historical experience of the community of believers accompanied by the Spirit, cleaving to the life, death and resurrection of Jesus Christ as the centre of history. Its practices and the tradition it moves forward have grounded history in many ways, shaped it for the common good, always hoping to bring the human family closer together as sisters and brothers and closer to life in Christ. But the Church's story also betrays the sin of the world, and the ways in which the Church has sometimes legitimated different forms of violence for the sake of increasing the faithful, resolving doctrinal conflict and protecting its material heritage.

A tradition of justified violence

The just war tradition has long been adopted as part of the Church's social ethics of war.[146] While the principles of just war sought to provide a framework for limiting wars, they have too often been used for justifying wars, leading to many deaths.[147] Augustine, who argued that killing could be a form of love, contributed to legitimating wars of the Roman Empire in the 400s. In 1095 at the Council of Clermont, Pope Urban II declared that there were wars that could be declared

---

146 Compendium of the Social Doctrine of the Church, 2004, #500,

147 Peter Partner 1998. *God of battles: Holy wars of Christianity and Islam*. Princeton, N.J.: Princeton University. See also R. Delahunty, "From Just War to False Peace," in 13 Chicago Journal of International Law, 1 (2012). This shows that consistent abuse can be traced from Cicero and the Roman Empire (7-10), the Medieval times with the Popes

not only as just wars but as holy wars.[148] In the medieval period the Church justified crusades against Muslims and blessed many young men with a promise of heaven as they went to fight in the crusades.

The 13th century saw the creation of inquisitions — included the Spanish, Portuguese, Mexican and Roman Inquisitions — which led to holy violence against persons deemed to be heretics or against Church doctrine (1560-1700). Close to 150,000 people went through the inquisition process and about 3,000 were executed.[149] The inquisitions targeted Christians who had converted from Judaism or Islam and were seen to be reverting to their old religion or practising a mixed religion. Others were convicted for going against official doctrines of the Church. The inquisitors operated under the legal basis of inquisitions established by Pope Urban IV in his bull *ad extirpanda* of 1252, which allowed for torture to extract confessions from heretics. By 1256 inquisitors were given absolution if they had used instruments of torture.[150] Inquisitions were banned in Europe in the early 19th century except in the Papal States.[151] The Church's department of inquisition was converted into the "Supreme Sacred Congregation of the Holy Office", and was renamed after the Second Vatican Council the "Congregation for the Doctrine of the Faith".

---

and Crusades (12-13), the years of conquest in the "New World" (14-15), and the modern period with the "sovereign state" logic of war (16-17). Even Hugo Grotius, key influencer of international law, acknowledged that "just war theory contributes to the likelihood and ferocity of war". 19. For a historical analysis of the misuse of just war thinking during the 20th century (such as WWI) see Johan Verstraeten, "The Just War Tradition and Peace Thinking 1914-1964" in *From Just War to Just Peace: Catholics between Militarism and Pacifism in Historical-Theological Perspective* (Kadok studies, 15), ed. Roger Burggraeve et al.(Leuven: Universitaire Pers, 1993). See also: Jonathan Glover, *Humanity. A Moral History of the Twentieth Century* (London: Pimlico, 2001).

148 Jonathan Phillips. 2014. *The Crusades, 1095-1205*. London: Routledge.

149 Edward Peters. 1998. "Inquisitions". *The First Crusade: The Chronicle of Fulcher of Chartres and Other Source Materials* (2 ed.). Philadelphia, PA: University of Pennsylvania Press.

150 Larissa Tracy. 2012. *Torture and Brutality in Medieval Literature: Negotiations of National Identity*. Boydell and Brewer Ltd, p. 22.

151 Jonathan Kirsch. 2008. *The Grand Inquisitor's Manual: A History of Terror in the Name of God*. San Francisco: HarperOne.

The Church tolerated slavery to a great extent and justified it based on scripture. Transatlantic slave traders sought ways of justifying the slave trade, following the expansion of colonies in the Americas and subsequent high demand for labour. Bishop Bartolomé de Las Casas initially endorsed slavery, though he later condemned it. Many popes issued bulls condemning unjust enslavement (although "just" enslavement was accepted), as well as mistreatment of Native peoples by Spanish and Portuguese missionaries. In their quest to capture more slaves in Africa, the slave traders held that enslaving Africans would bring them into contact with Christianity and save their souls.[152] What followed was more than 400 years of slavery in Africa and Latin America. According to the Trans-Atlantic Slave Trade Database, the number of captured Africans shipped to North America was 12.5 million; 10.7 million made it across the seas.[153] Many more millions of Africans were transported to Brazil and Caribbean countries.

The slave traders often used various scriptural justifications to perpetuate the lucrative slave trade industry. Reference was often made to Paul's Epistles which emphasised that Christian slaves had the obligation to serve their masters faithfully. For example, in his Letter to the Colossians (3:22), Paul states that: "Slaves, in all things obey those who are your masters on earth, not with external service, as those who merely please men, but with sincerity of heart, fearing the Lord." In Genesis 9:25-27 the story of the curse of Canaan has been used to justify slavery: "Cursed be Canaan! The lowest of slaves will he be to his brothers. He also said, 'Blessed be the Lord, the God of Shem! May Canaan be the slave of Shem." In Genesis 9:22 we read that it was Ham, the father of Canaan, who saw Noah naked, the latter having been drunk. Noah in turn curses Canaan. Extremist sectarian groups among Christian and Muslims identified black Africans as Ham's descendants. Anthony Pagden notes, "This reading of the Book of Genesis merged easily into a medieval iconographic tradition in which devils were always depicted as black. Later pseudo-scientific theories

---

152 Ross, William Stewart. 1880. *Christianity and the slave trade*. London: W. Stewart

153 Henry L. Gates, How Many Slaves Landed in US. New York: PBS

would be built around African skull shapes, dental structure and body postures, in an attempt to find an unassailable argument — rooted in whatever the most persuasive contemporary idiom happened to be: law, theology, genealogy or natural science — why one part of the human race should live in perpetual indebtedness to another."[154]

In South Africa the Dutch Reformed Church provided a Biblical justification for apartheid. They relied on Biblical verses such as Acts 2:5-11 and Revelation 5:9, 7:9, 14:6, among others, which according to them indicated that God divided people into different nations, languages and territories. The most frequently used text to justify separation of races is Acts 17:26: "From our one ancestor God made all nations to inhabit the whole earth, and he allotted the time of their existence and the boundaries of the places where they would live." According to South Africa's Truth and Reconciliation Commission (TRC): "Some of the major Christian Churches gave their blessing to the system of apartheid. And many of its early proponents prided themselves in being Christians. Indeed, the system of apartheid was regarded as stemming from the mission of the Church..."[155] The Dutch Reformed Church later publicly repented for this position.[156]

Colonialism became yet another tool of dominance against nations in the southern hemisphere. Many Africans, Latin Americans and Asians were subjected to the most dehumanising and violent experiences leading to the death and destruction of many people and their families.[157] Many colonialists came with Christian missionaries, in a sense giving blessing to the mission of colonialism. Religion was part and parcel of the state and evangelisation, especially in Spain, Portugal

---

154 Anthony Pagden. 1997. "The Slave Trade, Review of Hugh Thomas' Story of the Atlantic Slave Trade". The New Republic.

155 Truth and Reconciliation Commission, "Truth and Reconciliation Commission Final Report, Volume 4 Chapter 3." Pretoria: Government of South Africa.

156 BBC Despatches: Africa, November 19, 1997, http://news.bbc.co.uk/2/hi/despatches/africa/33032.stm

157 Robert Delavignette. 1964. *Christianity and colonialism*. Wheathampstead, Herts: Anthony Clarke Books.

and Great Britain.[158] In Africa, Latin America and Asia missionaries divided among themselves the conquered territories and spread their evangelisation with a blind eye to human rights violations carried out by colonialists.[159] The missionaries condoned racism and played within the supremacist ideologies advanced by the colonialists.[160]

In the light of these structural sins, Nigerian theologian Agbonkhianmeghe Orobator asks whether we can still honestly claim that the Church is a sacrament, and he argues that these various forms of violence at least obscure such an identity.[161] Perhaps it is better to claim this sacramental identity as more of an aspiration.

This critical theological reflection is an important consideration when reflecting on the nonviolent witness of the ecclesial body in the world today. In our ecclesial doctrines and practices, what kind of message do we send to the world?

Is the Church, in practice, a clear and vibrant sign of the unity of the human race? The Church concretely manifests this claim only when it is faithful to the nonviolent witness and teachings of Christ.

Violence, on the other hand, is a countersign to the "unity of the whole human race" and obscures the identity of the Church as a sacrament of Christ. The claim that the Church is the Body of Christ should not license boasting of the Church's virtue, but rather serve to highlight the scandal of the Church's violence.

---

158 Hilary M. Carey 2013. *God's empire: Religion and colonialism in the British world, c.1801-1908.* Cambridge: Cambridge University Press, 2013; Carole Blackburn. 2000. *Harvest of souls: The Jesuit missions and colonialism in North America, 1632-1650.* Montreal, Quebec: McGill-Queen's University Press.

159 Edward Andrews. 2010. "Christian Missions and Colonial Empires Reconsidered: A Black Evangelist in West Africa, 1766-1816." *Journal of* Church & State. 51 (4): 663-691.

160 Katharine Gerbner. 2018. *Christian slavery: Conversion and race in the Protestant Atlantic world.* Philadelphia: University of Pennsylvania Press.

161 Agbonkhianmeghe E. Orobator, "A Global Sign of Outward Grace: The Sacramentality of the World Church in the Era of Globalization." CSTA Proceedings 67 (2012), p. 19, accessed 16 May 2016 at https://ejournals.bc.edu/ojs/index.php/ctsa/article/download/2174/1939.

Writing about the Spanish Civil War, Dorothy Day invokes a reflection on the mystical body by Pope St. Clement of Rome: "Why do the Members of Christ tear one another; why do we rise up against our own body in such madness; have we forgotten that we are all members, one of another?"[162] Appealing to St. Augustine, Day affirms, "We are all members or potential members of the mystical body of Christ."[163] Therefore, it is not only violence against other explicit members of the visible Church that is a countersign to the Kingdom of God; all violence is an attack on Christ himself.

Religious roots of violence against women

Women are particularly affected by the pervasive use of sexual violence — rape and forced sexual enslavement — as both a tactic and consequence of male deification and domination. Even as wars end in defeat or negotiated settlement, even when institutions "stabilise" around male security, violence against women or others who are seen as lesser, weaker or more vulnerable often increases as the violence inherent in the institution is absorbed into the intimate spaces, homes, or the bodies of the more vulnerable. Even in contexts of apparent peace, a silent and often unseen war may play out on women's and girls' bodies as multiple forms of violence and exploitation, including sex trafficking and femicide, are driven by a rape culture rooted in women's perceived expendability, impurity or unworthiness.

Key actors have misused religion to generate cultural belief systems that are often complicit in shaping and legitimating a culture of violence against women, and these systems may be marshalled to stigmatise female survivors of violence, shunning them from communities of faith at a time when they most

162 Dorothy Day, "The Mystical Body and Spain," The Catholic Worker, August 1936.

163 William Cavanaugh, 221. Emphasis added. Cf: Dorothy Day, "The Mystical Body of Christ", The Catholic Worker, October 1939.

need spiritual and emotional support. Finally, subtle and overt perceptions of women's inferiority and gendered norms that prescribe the limits of their authority, often no further than the household, result in structural forms of injustice that harm women. Marginalised from religious, political and social leadership, their priorities and needs are often not addressed, so perpetuating cultures of gendered violence.

The ideological and ritual infrastructure provided by culture drives structural and direct violence against women and is a symptom of it, as these ideas are drawn on to defend or legitimate those forms of violence. When it comes to creating and sustaining cultures in which direct and structural violence against women and girls becomes entrenched, some religious actors play a key role. Through asserting particular beliefs and practices about women (and men) that imply a hierarchy (men as dominant and normative, women as subordinate and "other") or that present women as ritualistically impure, sexually suspect, or intellectually inferior, or central only for reasons of potential maternity, some actors misuse religious traditions around the world to construct and reinforce cultural violence against women.

For example, Christian theologians and Church leaders have sometimes counselled women to stay in violent marriages and/or to forgive their abusers. They have reinforced and even sanctified interpretations of scripture or other religious narratives and teachings that reinforce an idea that women's dignity is less important than men's. Sometimes the Church appears to be ambivalent about the moral authority of women. They have drawn on interpretations of religion to legitimate the exclusion of women from leadership — including political and religious leadership.

The endemic existence of sexual violence against women, men and children within the Catholic Church perpetrated by priests can be seen as both a symptom and driver of this culture, and of the particularly dangerous environment that can be created when religious belief and practice and forms of gender and sexual violence collude. In order to transform violence against women and girls, and sexual violence that affects those of all genders, the cultural and religious ideas, norms and practices that drive and embed a perception that women have less dignity or capacity than men must be addressed as part of nonviolent movements to build a just peace, and religious leaders and organisations have a particularly critical role to play in this - given their too common patterns of complicity in helping to build and sustain the ideological foundation for violence against women.

To assert the centrality of nonviolence to the mission of the Church, though, clearly does not imply that the Church is fully nonviolent. Indeed, as William Cavanaugh puts it:

"Clearly the claim of Israel, and later the Church, to have a special role in God's salvation of the world is not a claim of the moral superiority of God's people. The biblical writers emphasise the sinfulness of God's people in order to highlight the goodness and faithfulness of God. God loves the people unconditionally, contrary to anything the people deserve. The claim of a unique role for the people of God is not a claim based on human effort but on the forgiving love of God. The reason the biblical authors are able to name the people's sin so bluntly and so truthfully is that the truth has been revealed to them in the law and in the person of Jesus Christ. The only reason God's people can witness to the rest of the world — even by their own sinfulness and repentance — is that they have been enabled to name sin truthfully through the revelation of the living God. If it were not for their relationship with the God of Abraham, Isaac, Jacob and Jesus, they would not be able fully to recognise their sin as sin."[164]

---

164 William Cavanaugh, "Pilgrim People."

Confessing our moral amnesia, reclaiming our Christian memory

Gospel nonviolence has always been a feature of the life of the Church. A profound nonviolent tradition is foundational in Judeo-Christian history. Nonetheless, as evidenced above, the Church as an institution has at times forgotten, ignored or actively suppressed — by omission or commission — our core commitment to following the nonviolent Jesus.

This has led to our Church's complicity in and justification of violence over many centuries. Theologically and pastorally, the Church has often supported and contributed to systems and conditions of domination — ecclesial, political and social — that foster sin and are at odds with Jesus's call to nonviolent love.

In recent years, the Church has begun to acknowledge its own violence, which is only a first step in responding to and repairing the harm done.

Popes John Paul II, Benedict XVI and Francis have made a series of public apologies and sought forgiveness. In 1985 in Cameroon, Pope John Paul II apologised to black Africans for the involvement of white Christians in the slave trade.[165] In 1998, Pope John Paul II formally apologised for the Church failing to take decisive action to stop the Holocaust.[166] In 2015 at the World Meeting of Popular Movements in Bolivia, Pope Francis apologised for the Church's role in colonialism and its devastating impact on Indigenous nations, saying, "I humbly ask forgiveness, not only for the offence of the church herself, but also for crimes committed against the native peoples during the so-called conquest of America."[167] On the 20th anniversary of the Rwandan genocide, Pope Francis expressed his profound

---

165 "Pope Apologizes to Africans For Slavery," The New York Times, 14 August 1985. <https://www.nytimes.com/1985/08/14/world/pope-apologizes-to-africans-for-slavery.html>

166 "Vatican Gives Formal Apology for Inaction During the Holocaust," The Washington Post, 17 March 1998 <http://tech.mit.edu/V118/N13/bvatican.13w.html>

167 "In Bolivia, Pope Francis Apologizes for "Grave Sins'" The New York Times, 9 July 2015 <https://www.nytimes.com/2015/07/10/world/americas/pope-francis-bolivia-catholic-church-apology.html>

sadness, and that of the Holy See and of the Church, for the genocide against the Tutsis and implored "God's forgiveness for the sins and failings of the Church and its members", among whom priests and religious men and women who "succumbed to hatred and violence, betraying their own evangelical mission", stressing that the failings of that period "have disfigured the face of the Church" and expressing the hope that his gesture may "contribute to a 'purification of memory and may promote, in hope and renewed trust, a future of peace."[168] In 2016, Pope Francis offered a short, unscripted apology for the persecution of gay people as part of a more general apology, saying, "I believe that the Church not only should apologise to the person who is gay whom it has offended, but has to apologise to the poor, to exploited women, to children exploited for labour; it has to ask forgiveness for having blessed many weapons."[169] Since the 1980s, the endemic nature of clergy sexual violence has been revealed to the laity and public. While the Church has not yet addressed the roots of this culture of violence, Popes John Paul II, Benedict XVI and Francis have issued a series of apologies for clergy sexual abuse.[170]

The sheer number of apologies — and the wide-ranging forms of violence that they address — underscores the Church's own history of violence and the need for transformation and restorative justice. While often unprecedented, these public statements are only the initial steps towards grappling with the violence perpetrated by the Church. The sex abuse scandal involving Catholic clergy is a

---

168 "Pope: the genocide in Rwanda has disfigured the face of the Church" La Stampa, 20 March 2017 <https://www.lastampa.it/2017/03/20/vaticaninsider/pope-the-genocide-in-rwanda-has-disfigured-the-face-of-the-church-EKLfGFFlyjSJFTL3eK1OGK/pagina.html>

169 "Pope says Christians should apologize to gay people" <https://www.cnn.com/2016/06/26/world/pope-apologize-gays/index.html>

170 Apologies from popes on Catholic Church's sexual violence and cover up include: Pope sends first email apology < http://news.bbc.co.uk/2/hi/europe/1671540.stm>; Pope apologizes for "unspeakable crimes" of sexual abuse<http://blogs.reuters.com/faithworld/2010/09/18/pope-apologizes-for-unspeakable-crimes-of-sexual-abuse/>; After Pope's sexual abuse apology, critics clamor for reform <https://www.politico.com/story/2015/09/pope-francis-sexual-abuse-catholic-church-214123>; Pope Francis apologizes for Catholic Church's past 'crimes' in Ireland <https://globalnews.ca/news/4410364/pope-francis-apologizes-ireland/>;
Pope Francis' apology for abuse in Chile would once have been unthinkable < https://theconversation.com/pope-francis-apology-for-abuse-in-chile-would-once-have-been-unthinkable-94958>

case in point. Nonviolence requires much more, including restorative justice, new structures of accountability and formation in nonviolent ways. That recent popes have been compelled to make this series of public apologies illuminates how the Church has violated the way of Gospel nonviolence, particularly in its treatment of women, sexual minorities, Indigenous people and other religions or cultures. Apologies are recurring because those harmed have not seen substantive change in behaviours, systems, or institutions.

In this age of global violence, each one of us is impacted in a personal and intimate way. As we deepen our understanding of the centrality of nonviolence to the life and mission of Jesus and thus to the life and mission of the Church, we begin to re-centre our lives in the spirituality and practice of active nonviolence. From this deep healing springs an evangelical desire to spread and activate Jesus's powerful method to the world, to transform the present global culture of violence into a flowering culture of just peace.

Emerging insights into anthropocentric theology and ecological violence

In these times, our moral imagination and Christian discipleship is being challenged and invited to expand to include integral ecology, which naturally leads to integral peace, providing emerging insights into theological violence.[171] As Pope John Paul II said in his 1990 World Day of Peace message, "Peace, justice and the preservation of creation are three absolutely interconnected themes, which cannot be separated and treated individually without once again falling into reductionism." Our Trinitarian doctrine is the foundation for understanding our interconnectedness and communion with all of creation.

---

171 "Nonviolence and Creation Care/Climate Justice" by Amy Echeverria, Global Catholic CLimate Movement, excerpts www.nonviolencejustpeace.net.

Prior to the Renaissance and Enlightenment periods, when humans began to see themselves as the centre of knowing and being, there existed a cosmological theology in the Christian tradition. Ilia Delio, OSF, writes, "Cosmology was part of theology as long as the cosmos was believed to be God's creation, but as modern science began to understand the laws of the universe, there was no need for a doctrine of creation."[172] With the growing detachment of humans from the Divine as Creator of All, the Catholic Church began to develop a dominion interpretation of stewardship of humans over the non-human natural world. This anthropocentric theology, coupled with the Industrial Revolution and the dualistic split between science and religion that emerged out of 17th century philosophy, in which faith and mysticism were seen as incompatible with science, has led to a human-induced rupture of our covenant with God's non-human creation. Humans are only beginning to awaken to the depth and breadth of the brokenness that we have caused and are in need of theological, spiritual and scientific reorientation in order to begin the healing process. We are only beginning to return to a cosmological theology that is at the root of our Catholic Christian tradition.

It is here, in our human-centred theology and Catholic social teaching that we can identify the first root of human induced ecological violence. For when we theologically separate ourselves into a position of dominance over God's creation, we improperly remove God from the relationship and usurp God's role as Creator of All. While sacred scripture cultivates a sense of wonder and awe in relation to God's creation, the Church has interpreted scripture such that the non-human natural world is a resource meant ultimately to serve human beings as the pinnacle of all creation.

An anthropocentric hermeneutic of scripture, in which the intrinsic value of nature is ignored, has led to a utilitarian relationship with the non-human natural world, and in this commodification we have removed the sacredness of the Earth and its inclusion of our understanding of the One Body. When we empty the non-human natural world of its divine presence it becomes much easier to

---

172 Ilia Delio, OSF, *The Unbearable Wholeness of Being: God, Evolution, and the Power of Love*. Orbis, Maryknoll, NY, 2013. p.13

disconnect from our sense of responsibility to care, honour and respect creation. The absence of love, respect, care and protection make way not only for violence against creation but also violence between people in their struggle for access to resources which help sustain human life.

The last 100 years has seen a slow turning towards a cosmological theology which expands our experience of God to include the non-human natural world. Notable theologians from their perspectives as scientists, artists and missionaries who have helped shape a creation story that is expansive beyond humans include, but are not limited to Pierre Teilhard de Chardin, SJ; Thomas Berry CP; Ilia Delio, OSF; and Sean McDonagh, SSC. Rereading mystics with an ecological interpretation such as St. John of the Cross, who used creation-centred allegory of the dark night of twilight, midnight and dawn, helps us know that union with the Cosmic Christ is the union for which we long.

Glimpsing the Church's history of nonviolence [173]

Throughout the Christian tradition, Jesus's foundational theology of nonviolence has often been ignored, suppressed, or misinterpreted. Nevertheless, it has always been present. Despite the Church's history, which has at times legitimated violence, women and men of faith, and whole movements within the Church, have lived the discipleship of Jesus's nonviolence over the past two millennia.

"A culture of nonviolence is not an unattainable dream, but a path that has produced decisive results. The consistent practice of nonviolence has broken barriers, bound wounds, healed nations."— Pope Francis, April 4, 2017[174]

---

173 Ken Butigan and John Dear, adapted for *Choosing Peace* (Marie Dennis, Ed., 2018: Orbis Books) from "An Overview of Gospel Nonviolence in the Christian Tradition," www.nonviolencejustpeace.net. Written for the April 2016 Nonviolence and Just Peace conference.

174 Personal letter to Cardinal Blase Cupich, archbishop of Chicago, IL USA.

The practice of Gospel nonviolence in the Christian community over the centuries has not always been visible, yet the early Church resolutely placed nonviolence at the centre of community and individual discipleship. Many Catholics throughout the years have believed that to be a disciple of Jesus has meant being comprehensively nonviolent.[175] This section highlights some of the many examples of nonviolence as practised by the Catholic/Christian community.

It is important to note that nonviolent practices in Christian history have often reflected the gendered roles in society. Men's nonviolent practices often took place in the sphere of abstaining from bearing arms and from participation in war. Women's nonviolent practices more often took place in the sphere of family, community and religious orders as they resisted direct and structural gender violence and exploitation.

In the first centuries after Jesus, the Church nourished a culture of spiritually grounded nonviolence through the corporal works of mercy, the practice of forgiveness and reconciliation, resistance to the culture of violence, and by preparing its members to face the consequences of their nonviolent resistance, including persecution and martyrdom. The witness of early Christian martyrs was often recorded and recited when the community celebrated Eucharist together as a way to encourage one another in their Gospel nonviolence.

Moreover, feminist scholars studying early writings such as the Acts of Thekla are recognising that women's resistance even then had a form of its own:

"The Acts of Thekla are an outstanding document on women's resistance during early Christianity. Although they must be regarded as a novel-like story (similar to the other Apocryphal Acts of the Apostles) and not as historical reports, they are nevertheless not to be underestimated in their relevance to the reconstruction of historical reality ... Thekla is – so the story goes – a beautiful virgin from an upper-

---

175 See Chapter 4, *Choosing Peace*, "Jesus and Nonviolence: Scriptural Evidence."

class family in Iconium. She is engaged to Thamyris. From a neighbouring house, she hears Paul's sermon on abstinence and resurrection, which addresses women in particular. She refuses to marry Thamyris and is punished ... sentenced to death because her refusal to marry is seen as a threat to public order ...

"The Acts of Thekla are a unique document of the history of women's resistance. According to this text, women's resistance evolved by women refusing their role, which again and again is forced on them by agents of the patriarchal order."[176]

There is also the story of Christian apologist Justin Martyr who, in the second century, wrote, "We who were filled with war and mutual slaughter and all wickedness have each and all throughout the earth changed our instruments of war, our swords into ploughshares, and our spears into farm tools, and cultivate piety, justice, love of humankind, faith and the hope which we have from the Father through the Crucified One."[177] He was tried, convicted and beheaded for his teachings by a Roman official in 165.

Many other saints and writers condemned Christian participation in killing. Among them were Tatian, Athenagoras, Irenaeus, Clement of Alexandria, Cyprian, Minucius, Felix and Lactantius.[178]

Perhaps the most celebrated Christian in the first 1,000 years of the Church was St. Maximilian. In 295, this 21-year-old son of a Roman veteran refused conscription into the Roman army and was beheaded. At his trial he said, "I cannot serve in the army. I cannot engage in wrongdoing; I am a Christian."[179] His testimony was read as part of the Mass for centuries after his death.

176 Luise Schottroff, "Nonviolence and Women's Resistance in Early Christianity," in Harvey L. Dyck, editor, *The Pacifist Impulse in Historical Perspective* (Toronto: University of Toronto Press, 1966) 83 and 85.

177 Clive Barrett, *Peace Together: A Vision of Christian Pacifism* (James Clark & Co., 1987), pp. 29-30.

178 Ibid., pp. 30-31. See also: Michael G. Long, *Christian Peace and Nonviolence: A Documentary History* (Orbis Books, 2011), pp. 17-24.

179 Michael G. Long, *Christian Peace and Nonviolence: A Documentary History* (Orbis Books, 2011), p. 31.

When Christianity was legalised by Constantine in 313 CE and Christians, as Lisa Sowle Cahill has written, "gained access to and responsibility for government and political power", a just war tradition began to develop — even a "crusade ideology, in which violence was claimed to serve the Gospel itself."[180] Yet thousands of Christians over the centuries have followed the path of Gospel nonviolence. They have been a remnant Church, a small movement.[181]

In the centuries after Constantine, pockets of Christian men and women retreated to the deserts to keep the nonviolence of Jesus alive. Later, monasticism developed with communities created for worship and study, service to the local community, and the practice of peace and hospitality. (They were largely, but not universally, nonviolent. Bernard of Clairvaux, for example, is well known for having preached the Second Crusade.)

Other persons and movements have also pursued the path of Gospel nonviolence. An iconic example after the Constantinian shift is the witness of Saint Martin of Tours (316-397). Martin was an officer in the Roman army before his conversion to Christianity. After becoming a Christian he felt he could no longer remain a Roman soldier. Just before a battle in the Gallic provinces, Martin told his superior officer, "I am the soldier of Christ: it is not lawful for me to fight." The commander was furious. As the saint's contemporary biographer, Sulpicius Severus, recounted: "The tyrant stormed on hearing such words, declaring that, from fear of the battle, which was to take place on the morrow, and not from any religious feeling, Martin withdrew from the service. But Martin, full of courage ... exclaimed, 'If this conduct of mine is ascribed to cowardice, and not to faith, I will take my stand unarmed before the line of battle tomorrow, and in the name of the Lord Jesus, protected by the sign of the cross, and not by shield or helmet, I will safely penetrate

---

180 See Chapter 5, *Choosing Peace*, Lisa Sowle Cahill.

181 An excellent study of this tradition is *The Catholic Peace Tradition* by Ronald Musto, Orbis Books, 1986.

the ranks of the enemy.'"[182] Baffled by Martin's offer to stand unarmed in front of the battle line, the commander put him in prison and considered taking him up on his offer. Then the unexpected happened: "The following day the enemy sent ambassadors to treat about peace and surrendered both themselves and all their possessions." Severus connects this turn of events to Martin's nonviolent resistance: "In these circumstances who can doubt that this victory was due to the saintly man?" After leaving the army, Martin lived as a hermit, founded a monastery, was installed as a bishop in Gaul, and spent his life serving people, living in poverty.

In the fifth century Pope Leo the Great saved the city of Rome by nonviolent dialogue when Attila the Hun invaded Europe[183] and Saint Severin mediated between the Germanic tribes who were threatening populations of fortified cities. He successfully asked the inhabitants to enter into dialogue with the enemy, and war and destruction were avoided.

In the European Middle Ages, the Truce of God was instituted by the Church as a measure to suspend warfare, especially the many private wars, during certain days of the week and during Church festivals and Lent. The Peace of God was fostered by the Church and later by civil society to protect women, priests, pilgrims, merchants, other noncombatants and Church property from violence.

In the 13th century, Francis of Assisi was an icon of Gospel nonviolence. He reclaimed the nonviolence of Jesus, pointed Christians back to the Gospel, and almost single-handedly reimagined the Church. As an affluent youth fighting in his local military, he was imprisoned, experienced a profound conversion, embraced life at the margins of society and began to live a radically nonviolent life. He formed a community of practitioners of Gospel nonviolence who refused to take

182 Sulpicius Severus, *On the Life of St. Martin, From: A Select Library of Nicene And Post-Nicene Fathers of The Christian Church*, Second Series, Volume 11 (Buffalo: The Christian Literature Company, 1894).

183 Hildegard and Jean Goss-Mayr, "The Gospel and the Struggle for Justice and Peace: Training Seminar (The Swedish Ecumenical Council and the International Fellowship of Reconciliation, 1990), 20.

up arms. They lived in poverty, served the poor and greeted everyone with the phrase "Pace e Bene" ("Peace and Goodness"), often being attacked as a result. Within a few years, their movement began to spread. Thousands joined.

During the Fifth Crusade, Francis took bold action. He crossed contested territory and met the Sultan Malik al-Kamil, the leader of the "enemy", to make peace. Along with Clare of Assisi and her sisters, Francis and his early community offered a Christian witness of nonviolence that historians now believe helped end feudal violence.

A well-known story about Clare describes her decision to have the Blessed Sacrament placed on the walls of the convent when an attack by invading "Saracens" was imminent. To her sisters she said, "Don't be afraid. Trust in Jesus." The "Saracens" fled.[184]

Francis forbade any follower to own a weapon, support war or kill others. St. Francis is widely regarded as the greatest, most beloved saint in history, but he was first of all a practitioner of a deeply holistic and integral form of Gospel nonviolence.

In the centuries after Francis, religious orders and communities focusing on the works of mercy and charity proliferated. Moreover, after the Protestant Reformation and Counter-Reformation, small "peace Churches" blossomed which explicitly espoused the nonviolence of Jesus, including the Anabaptists, Brethren, Mennonites and the Society of Friends (Quakers). These peace Churches advocated nonviolent social change. Along with powerful Christian anti-slavery and anti-war leaders such as Sojourner Truth and Frederick Douglass, the "peace Churches" contributed vision and organisation to the abolition movement that led to the end of slavery in the US. Many of the most powerful and well-known suffragists were from these peace Churches, including Susan B. Anthony, Lucretia

---

184 Fr. Don Miller, OFM, "Saint Clare of Assisi," www.franciscanmedia.org

Mott and the Grimke sisters; their actions and writings have helped inspire and sustain other nonviolent social movements around the world.

At the beginning of World War I, the International Fellowship of Reconciliation was established as one expression of a renewed attention to Gospel nonviolence. As Hildegard Goss-Mayr writes, "It was the first organised and ecumenical expression of Christians who, in following Jesus Christ, are not only saying 'no' to the use of violence as a means of conquering injustices and resolving conflicts, but at the same time are rediscovering the creative force of the nonviolence of God."[185]

In the United States, Ben Salmon from Denver, Colorado, gained notoriety as a Catholic conscientious objector during World War I. Ben, who was married with four young children, believed that the war was immoral and an abuse of political power. "The Germans," he said, "are my brothers. I will not train to kill them." He was arrested, tried in a military court, though he was not in the military, and convicted of treason. Sentenced to death and then to a reduced sentence of 25 years of hard labour, Salmon was sent to seven different federal prisons where he was often paraded in chains and kept in solitary confinement. In prison he was refused access to the sacraments, was eventually ruled insane, and was sent to St. Elizabeth's Hospital in Washington, D.C. Two years after the war ended, thanks to pressure from the newly established American Civil Liberties Union and Fr. John Ryan, a professor at Catholic University, Salmon was released.[186] In Great Britain, at least 100 Catholic men refused to serve in the military during World War I; many were imprisoned.[187]

Also in the United States, Dorothy Day founded the Catholic Worker movement, a network of houses of hospitality, now present in many countries, where Catholics

185 Hildegard and Jean Goss-Mayr, "The Gospel and the Struggle for Justice and Peace: Training Seminar," The Swedish Ecumenical Council and the International Fellowship of Reconciliation (1990): 20.

186 Jack Gilroy, "Imprisoned War Resistor Rooted in Catholic Faith," National Catholic Reporter, July 16, 2016.

187 Valerie Flessati, "For King and Country … and conscience," The Tablet, 7 November 2018, https://www.thetablet.co.uk/features/2/14875/for-king-and-country-and-conscience

welcome the poor and the homeless to live with them, and where they also publicly denounce and resist war and preparations for war in obedience to the nonviolent Jesus. Day engaged many times in nonviolent civil disobedience for peace and justice.

During World War II, Blessed Franz Jägerstätter of St. Radegund, Austria was another powerful, faithful witness for nonviolence. A Catholic, Jägerstätter was ordered to join the Nazi military in 1943 but refused on the grounds that this would disobey Jesus's teachings in the Sermon on the Mount. He was arrested, brought to Berlin, tried and beheaded. After the war his action and writings became known and have influenced thousands of people around the world; many who have become involved in grassroots movements for peace have cited his witness as a motivation. Jägerstätter was beatified by the Catholic Church on 26 October 2007.

When German troops occupied northern Italy in 1943, Italian men were conscripted into Hitler's army in violation of international conventions. Among them was a young man, Blessed Josef Mayr-Nusser, who was enlisted into the SS in September 1944. Deeply influenced by Saint Thomas More's letters from prison and the challenge of taking a stand based on conscience, he, at the end of his training, refused to take the oath of loyalty to Hitler. He was arrested, imprisoned and condemned to death for undermining military morale. Severely weakened by prison starvation and dysentery, he died on 24 February 1945 in the cattle wagon on his way to Dachau, where he was to be shot. Josef was beatified on 18 March 2017.[188]

As World War II drew to an end, in March 1945, Pax Christi, a Catholic movement for reconciliation between the French and the Germans, was founded in France by a Catholic lay woman, Marthe Dortel Claudot, and the bishop of Montauban, Pierre Marie Théas. Bishop Théas had just returned from the detention camp at Compiègne after being arrested by the Gestapo for speaking out against the persecution of Jews. The Pax Christi movement spread quickly in post-war Europe

---

188 Pax Christi UK, "Martyr for nonviolence Josef Mayr-Nusser to be beatified on 18 March," www.nonviolencejustpeace.net.

and later throughout the world, promoting reconciliation and active nonviolence, demilitarisation, social justice and human rights.

With the atomic destruction of Hiroshima and Nagasaki by the United States during World War II, the threat of global nuclear annihilation became a possibility. Through the development of grassroots movements and the widespread legacy of Gandhi, millions of people began to awaken to the teachings and methodologies of nonviolence, helping to build a global movement that succeeded in making possible nuclear arms control agreements, including the 1962 Partial Test Ban Treaty, the 1968 Treaty on the Non-Proliferation of Nuclear Weapons and the 1993 Comprehensive Test Ban Treaty signed by 183 nations that ended most nuclear testing worldwide.

Thomas Merton, the celebrated Trappist monk and author, called for the abolition of war and nuclear weapons. His book, *Peace in a Post-Christian Era*,[189] which was banned by the Abbot General of his Trappist community and finally published by Orbis Books over 40 years later in 2004, was (in mimeographed form) an important influence on the Second Vatican Council. Jim Forest's foreword to the Orbis edition gives an excellent account of the impact of Merton's writing on millions of people around the world. The presence and efforts of peacemakers from PAX and the Catholic Worker at debates during Vatican II led to an explicit condemnation of nuclear war and provision for conscientious objection.

Following the Second Vatican Council, many Catholics, including laity, clergy and religious communities became more deeply involved in political activism for social justice and peace. For example, "while the Catholic Church as an institution never played a leading role in the civil rights movement, those black and white Catholics who participated in demonstrations and spoke out concerning Catholic social teachings helped promote the cause of equality."[190]

189 Thomas Merton (Patricia A. Burton), *Peace in a Post Christian Era* (Maryknoll, NY: Orbis Books, 2004).

190 Catholic University of America, The Civil Rights Movement, online history of the American Catholic experience. http://libraries.cua.edu/.

Encouraged by encyclicals such as *Pacem in Terris* (1963), Vatican Council documents such as *Gaudium et Spes* and other Church documents, including the 1971 Synod of Bishops' statement, *Justice in the World*, many Catholic religious communities of women and men made corporate commitments to nonviolence, peace and social justice and implemented those commitments through community action.

Dolores Huerta and Cesar Chavez, co-founders of the United Farm Workers, led carefully orchestrated nonviolent campaigns in the United States for farmworker justice, including the Delano Grape Strike of 1965. The farmworkers' approach reflected the dominance of the Catholic tradition among the workers and fully integrated symbols of the faith and liturgical expression into the heart of most actions.

In many Latin American countries where assassinations and disappearances in the 1970s and 1980s were a frequent occurrence, the mothers of the disappeared – the CoMadres in El Salvador, the Mothers of the Plaza de Mayo in Argentina, the Mothers and Relatives of the Kidnapped and Disappeared in Nicaragua, the Grupo Apoyo Mutuo (GAM) in Guatemala — led powerful, persistent, public acts of resistance to brutal violence.

During the same period, the leadership of Fr. Miguel D'Escoto, MM as foreign minister of Nicaragua decidedly emphasised nonviolence, which he considered to be the "essence of the Gospel". During Lent in 1985, as the war between the Contras and the Sandinistas intensified, he initiated a month-long fast, which he called an "evangelical insurrection". Then he led a 200 mile, two-week-long Via Crucis (Way of the Cross) across Nicaragua to promote reconciliation and an end to the violence.[191]

---

191 Paul Wehr, Heidi Burgess, Guy Burgess, editors. *Justice Without Violence* (Boulder: Lynne Rienner Publishers, 1994), 90.

In El Salvador and around the world, the example of Saint Archbishop Oscar Romero inspired a new generation of Catholic peacemakers. He was assassinated on 24 March 1980, the day after he preached that Christians were forbidden to kill and that members of the military and death squads should disobey orders to kill, quit their positions and stop the repression in his country.[192] Catholic religious and lay people around the world, with justice and peace departments, commissions and committees in bishops' conferences, dioceses and parishes were involved in nonviolent efforts to end the Vietnam War, the military dictatorships in South America, the extremely violent wars in Central America, apartheid in South Africa. Catholics led the Solidarity movement in Poland, were involved in the peace communities in Colombia and peace zones in Mindanao, Philippines. Julius Nyerere, a Catholic, was the first president of Tanzania, where his vision cemented a peaceful identity for a new nation. Followers of Jesus in Northern Ireland, including Nobel Peace Prize laureates Mairead Corrigan Maguire and Betty Williams, finally brought the "troubles" to an end. Catholics in East Timor, including Bishop Carlos Belo, recipient with Jose Ramos-Horta of the 1996 Nobel Peace Prize, weathered a vicious occupation by Indonesian forces and denounced horrific human rights abuses until East Timor achieved full sovereignty in 2002.

Just as the global anti-nuclear movement has applied nonviolence to the struggle for a world without weapons of mass destruction, thousands of other movements involving followers of Jesus have proliferated for more democratic societies, human rights, economic justice and environmental sustainability over the past half-century, using the power and methods of nonviolence for effective change. Forming broad coalitions with people of many traditions and faiths, they have successfully banned anti-personnel landmines and cluster munitions, and generated significant international efforts to cancel unjust and unsustainable foreign debt, promote fair trade and end human trafficking and destructive mining practices.

---

192 Oscar Romero, Homily, March 23, 1980. <http://www.romerotrust.org.uk>

Nonviolence has also characterised the courageous and important movements working within the Church for an end to the violence of sexual abuse and thorough accountability for the abuse of power and violation of confidence pervading that horrific crime against children. Also courageous and creatively nonviolent are those many women and men in the Church who have been working against racism and for the full inclusion of women in the life and leadership of the Catholic community.

At the same time, followers of Jesus have played pivotal roles in developing positive, innovative approaches to addressing violence, injustice, human rights violations and war. These include restorative justice (Victim Offender Reconciliation Program; Peace Circles); forgiveness and reconciliation training; third-party intervention and unarmed civilian protection and accompaniment (Witness for Peace, Christian Peacemaker Teams, Nonviolent Peaceforce, Operation Dove); nonviolent communication; conflict transformation programming; trauma healing; anti-racism training; and innumerable initiatives for interfaith dialogue.

Also important in recent decades is a dramatic increase in academic degree programmes in peace studies in Catholic universities around the world, along with research on the core values of nonviolent change, including forgiveness, creativity, love, compassion and empathy, as well as nonviolent civil resistance, movement-building and the dynamics and infrastructure for a culture of peace and nonviolence.[193]

Gandhi, who read the Sermon on the Mount every day for 40 years, concluded that Jesus was the greatest person of nonviolence in history, and that everyone who followed him was called to be a person of nonviolence. Many Christian saints, martyrs and holy people for over 2,000 years have affirmed, like Gandhi, that Gospel nonviolence is the way of Jesus and have sustained a commitment to follow him in that way.

---

193 Lisa Sowle Cahill's reflections in Chapter 5 in *Choosing Peace* refer to the Catholic Peacebuilding Network formed by many of these universities.

The story of the people power movement in the Philippines is one clear example of when the official Catholic Church led the wider Catholic community to understand active nonviolence and to put the principles and practices learned into effective action at a critical time. Under the US-backed regime of Ferdinand Marcos there was much corruption, poverty, widespread human rights violations and a lack of democracy. Systematic violence by the government was aimed at destroying the opposition, including community-based organisations and movements working for change. There was little hope of social transformation. There was a growing armed struggle led by a group called The New People's Army. At the same time, however, the Catholic Church in this predominantly Catholic country was casting about for an alternative. Was there an alternative to passivity on the one hand and violence on the other?

Many people were not too sure. A bishop was quoted at the time as saying, "I used to believe in nonviolence, but Marcos is too cruel; only a bloody revolution will work against him."[194] When he was asked how long such a revolution would take, he said, "Ten years." The 1983 assassination of opposition leader Benigno Aquino seemed only to confirm the bishop's gloomy assessment.

Catholic sisters were pushing for greater nonviolent leadership from the Church. It was then that Cardinal Jaime Sin decided to see if an alternative was possible. He put the full weight of the Church behind an exploration of Gospel nonviolence and how it could be applied to change the situation in his country.

Ultimately, in Manila, over one million unarmed human beings joined the self-described People Power movement and demonstrated how nonviolent people power can trump tanks and circling bombers. There were many factors to its success, but two of those included a call from the Church to take nonviolent action, and the role of the Church in organising nonviolence training.

---

194 Ken Butigan, "The Philippines' People Power revolution wins new victory," WagingNonviolence.org, February 28, 2013.

Formation in nonviolence

To be nonviolent disciples of Christ does not come easily. To act as a Church as if the nonviolent imperatives of Jesus and the Kingdom should find expression in the here and now requires robust processes of lay and ordained formation. Reflecting on the Church as the locus of formation in Jesus's nonviolence, Fr. Donal Harrington from Ireland speaks of the Church as an educational community: "In learning nonviolence the Christian community is not learning some discrete item of knowledge. It is learning the Mystery of being Church, initiating itself into a very neglected dimension of what it means to imitate Christ and be his disciple."[195]

No one is "born" a Christian — no more than one is "born" a member of a political party, or possessing a national identity, or belonging to any other religious or cultural community. All of these are learned identities and perspectives: they are conveyed from persons already steeped in a given tradition or way of life, as apprentices learn a craft from a master in a given field. Language works much the same way — nobody invents their own language, no one is born speaking a language, and all language acquisition in some sense is acquired from someone else. You can innovate in it, make up new words, but first you have to internalise what it is like to think, dream, love and inhabit the world that language creates.

In some ways, Christianity is like a language that one learns from other skilled speakers. Just as languages are different in the realities they allow their speakers to express, so too different religious traditions equip their adherents to think, perceive, feel and act in ways different from persons who have not been "formed" or socialised within those traditions. According to the late Yale theologian George Lindbeck, an observer at Vatican II, "There are numberless thoughts we cannot think, sentiments we cannot have, and realities we cannot perceive, unless we learn to use the appropriate symbol systems."[196] Before people can act in the

---

195 Donal Harrington, "The spirituality of nonviolence," The Furrow, Vol. 42, No. 11, November 1991, p. 622.

196 George Lindbeck, The Nature of Doctrine (Westminster John Knox, 1984), p. 34.

world as "Christians" in any non-trivial sense, they must first be shaped by the narratives of Jesus and Israel, of the prophets and the saints and by the other stories of the faith.

While the role of apprenticing people into the faith has been performed variously by the family, the state and the culture, from the beginning of the Christian movement such formation has been the ineradicable obligation of the Church. The Church is the only "school of discipleship" where people learn — however incompletely or imperfectly — to make the priorities, dispositions and practices of Jesus their own. At its best the Church provides experiences (through liturgy, study, service and more) and time-intensive mentoring in which people come to inhabit practices and habits that help generate and deepen the ongoing conversion of mind, heart and action called for to be a pilgrim people in the world.

Such formation is always controversial, of course, and is always a matter of political struggle. For the Church is not the only social force seeking to form the attitudes, desires and dispositions of people — the formation of Christians is always a contested matter, usually in competition with that sponsored by states, nations, corporations, ideological movements and other powers that shape human cultures and futures. Forming nonviolent followers of Jesus comes into direct conflict with those institutions, ideologies and priorities for whom violence is a necessary feature of their identities and vocations. In this sense, among others, "becoming a Christian" remains an intrinsically countercultural matter even as Christianity lives and breathes inside the various cultures of the world.

There exists much literature about the "crisis of Christian formation" in many parts of the world. The breakdown of older ways of incorporating the young and new members into the Church, the incomplete or compromised versions of the faith that have come to dominate in certain places, and the strength of more powerful agents and processes of cultural formation — all of these and more have made questions of Christian formation and the forming of Christians a matter of urgency in many places worldwide. While no single solution, effective in all times and places, is likely to emerge, it remains true that without a revitalisation of more intentional and intensive processes of Christian formation, the nonviolent message of Christianity is fated to remain an abstract and generally ignored feature of the Christian life. Such renewed formation, whatever shape it takes, must not be limited to clergy or people in religious life — it must prioritise the laity.

A spirituality of nonviolence

The spirituality of nonviolence requires ongoing formation, conversion and transformation of individuals and the Church — to acknowledge one's violence and to grapple with it; to break the cycles of retaliatory violence; to pursue nonviolent options and justice for all with humility, compassion, openness and determination.

The spirituality of nonviolence seeks to engage and transform all that inhibits one's journey to God — all that keeps one from fully experiencing, feeling, embracing and grasping the depth of God's love. For each person, these inhibitors will be different: the hardened heart, spiritual paralysis, unhealthy attachments and habits, vanquished hopes, an unwillingness to face deep pain, grief and fears, a reluctance to be open to healing and transformation and an unwillingness to take responsibility for one's own growth.

Jesus transforms hearts of stone that prevent us from living fully, into the grace of transformation.[197] Through prayer, preaching, training, reflection, community-building, ministry and pastoral and prophetic engagement, we are called to plumb the spiritual depths of nonviolence. "Nonviolence is the Spirit of God that disarms our hearts," writes John Dear, "so that we can become God's instruments for the disarmament of the world. This nonviolent Spirit of God transforms us to

---

197 John Dear, *The God of Peace: Toward a Theology of Nonviolence*, Orbis, 1995; Wipf and Stock 2011.

transform the world. Spirituality … is the life of transformation from violence to nonviolence."[198]

Formation in the way of nonviolence might benefit from what Pope Francis has recommended as a kind of "evangelical discernment" on the part of Jesus's missionary disciples, an approach "nourished by the light and strength of the Holy Spirit" (EG 50, citing John Paul II, Post-Synodal Apostolic Exhortation *Pastores Dabo Vobis* (25 March 1992), 10: AAS 84 (1992), 673.) As he writes, "Let the grace of your baptism bear fruit in a path of holiness. Let everything be open to God; turn to him in every situation. Do not be dismayed, for the power of the Holy Spirit enables you to do this, and holiness, in the end, is the fruit of the Holy Spirit in your life (cf. *Gal* 5:22-23)" (Pope Francis, *Gaudete et Exsultate* 15).

The Beatitudes figure prominently in this formation process. Glen Stassen notes the direct parallel between the Beatitudes, Isaiah 61 and Jesus's first public preaching in Luke 4:18.[199] The presence of the Holy Spirit marks each passage, pointing to the qualities and virtues of discipleship Jesus is seeking to cultivate in his followers by enfleshing them himself. Anointed by the Spirit, Jesus brings good news to the poor, proclaims release from bondage, comforts those who mourn, heals the broken-hearted, upholds righteousness and perseveres joyfully in the face of persecution. In addition to a central virtue of nonviolent peacemaking, other key virtues of a spirituality of nonviolence would include mercy, compassion, empathy, humility, hospitality, solidarity and courage.[200]

The Beatitudes, Pope Francis noted in his 2017 World Day of Peace message, are a kind of manual for formation in nonviolence as a way of life. They "provide a portrait of the person we could describe as blessed, good and authentic" (para.6).

---

198 Ibid.

199 Glen Stassen, *Living the Sermon on the Mount: A Practical Hope for Grace and Deliverance* (Jossey-Bass, 206), 50.

200 Eli S. McCarthy, *Becoming Nonviolent Peacemakers: A Virtue Ethic for Catholic Social Teaching and U.S. Policy*, Wipf and Stock Pickwick Publishers: 2012.

Stassen emphasises that the Beatitudes "speak to disciples who are already being made participants in the presence of the Holy Spirit through Jesus Christ ..." (41) Through Jesus's life, death and resurrection, the Reign of God is already among us, and Jesus invites his disciples to live in the reality of that reign joyfully, guided by the Holy Spirit.

In the first and third Beatitudes, the Greek word *praeis* is used, and often it is translated as "meek". Stassen points out that wherever this word appears in the Bible, "it always points to peacefulness or peacemaking." The third Beatitude follows closely Psalm 37:11, "But the meek will inherit the land and enjoy great peace."[201]. The whole of Psalm 37 speaks to the qualities associated with the Reign of God that Jesus preaches, a reign characterised by Christ's gift of peace[202].

This connotation of peacemaking fits with another meaning that Clarence Jordan ascribed to the word *praeis*. He preferred to render it as "completely surrendered to the will of God".[203] Jesus models what it means to be completely surrendered to God, which is the true meaning of spiritual poverty, as Gustavo Gutiérrez notes (cf. "Preferential Option for the Poor").

In Galatians, Paul contrasts the fruits of fallen human nature with the fruits of the Holy Spirit: "What human nature does is quite plain.... People become enemies and they fight; they become jealous, angry and ambitious. They separate into parties and groups.... I warn you now as I have before: those who do these things will not possess the Kingdom of God. But the Spirit produces love, joy, peace, patience, kindness, goodness, faithfulness, humility and self-control" (Gal. 5:19-26).

Reflecting on this text, Raniero Cantalamessa notes, "Meekness (*prautes*) is placed by Paul among the fruits of the Spirit (Galatians 5:23), that is, among the

---

201 Stassen 50; cf. Benedict XVI, Jesus of Nazareth, 80-84.

202 Stassen, 50.

203 Stassen, 49, citing Jordan, 1974, 24-25.

qualities that the believer manifests in [her] life when [s]he receives the Spirit of Christ and makes an effort to correspond to the Spirit."[204]

A spirituality that seeks openness to God's will and peacefulness witnesses to the marks of nonviolence by preferring to bear suffering than to inflict it, placing trust in the persuasive power of the truth that we are all sisters and brothers, and realises that there is no "winning" in nonviolence, only the victory of reconciliation.[205] In all situations of conflict — personal, familial, corporate, political — a spirituality of nonviolence will seek to acknowledge the dignity of all persons involved, privileging a stance of care over a stance of control. It will naturally seek to build relationships across lines of difference, rather than participate in structures that tear down community, or that require protecting our interests through harmful means.[206]

The Sacraments

Building a reconciled, nonviolent community requires not heroic individuals but disciplines of formation that inscribe peace into the hearts and bones of sinful human beings. God has given us the sacraments as grace-filled conduits of such habits. Sacraments in general pay tribute to the goodness of creation and the reality of the incarnation, both of which are central to a theology of nonviolence. Sacraments proclaim that the Kingdom of God is not merely a future reality but is

204 Raniero Cantalamessa, 2nd Lenten sermon (3/18/07). See also Pope Francis, *Gaudete et Exsultate* 15: "73. Paul speaks of meekness as one of the fruits of the Holy Spirit (cf. Gal 5:23). He suggests that, if a wrongful action of one of our brothers or sisters troubles us, we should try to correct them, but "with a spirit of meekness", since "you too could be tempted" (Gal 6:1). Even when we defend our faith and convictions, we are to do so "with meekness" (cf. 1 Pet 3:16). Our enemies too are to be treated "with meekness" (2 Tim 2:25). In the Church we have often erred by not embracing this demand of God's word. 74. Meekness is yet another expression of the interior poverty of those who put their trust in God alone. Indeed, in the Bible the same word – anawim – usually refers both to the poor and to the meek. Someone might object: "If I am that meek, they will think that I am an idiot, a fool or a weakling." At times they may, but so be it. It is always better to be meek, for then our deepest desires will be fulfilled. The meek "shall inherit the earth", for they will see God's promises accomplished in their lives. In every situation, the meek put their hope in the Lord, and those who hope for him shall possess the land ... and enjoy the fullness of peace (cf. Ps 37:9.11). For his part, the Lord trusts in them: "This is the one to whom I will look, to the humble and contrite in spirit, who trembles at my word" (Is 66:2). Reacting with meekness and humility: that is holiness."

205 Donal Harrington, "The Spirituality of Nonviolence," The Furrow, Vol. 42, No. 11, November 1991, p. 619.

206 Michael Crosby, OFMCap, "The Spirituality of Nonviolence," CMSM Shalom Strategy (Washington, DC, 1991), pp. 29-38.

already among us in material form. In baptism, God overcomes divisions between Jew and Greek, slave and free, male and female (Gal. 3:27-28). All the violence-causing divisions of ethnicity, creed, class, gender, race, nation and so on are transcended by membership in the body of Christ conferred by baptism.

In the Eucharist, we remember the victim on the cross, we anticipate the future by calling down the heavenly banquet to the altar, and we are formed into the body of Christ by eating the body of Christ and drinking his blood. Christ's act of nonviolent self-sacrifice is made available to us in the Lord's Supper, incorporating us into Christ's reconciled and reconciling body.

In the sacrament of reconciliation or penance, we examine our own consciences and acknowledge the ways that we have failed to live into the future Kingdom. We ask for reconciliation with God and with our fellow human beings. If we are honest, we acknowledge that we share in the sinfulness that we would righteously try to correct in others through coercive means.

The reality of sacrament brings us back to a conviction that must underlie any attempt to live nonviolently: unless the Lord builds the house, the labourers labour in vain (Ps. 127:1). Nonviolence is not only a technique by which human beings can fix the world. Nonviolence is ultimately a recognition of the sacramental presence of God among us. God saves the world, not us. We merely try to conform ourselves to the God who is revealed to us.

The sign of peace

More than a mere symbol, the sign of peace is a reality-creating ritual that is ever ancient and ever new. It is ancient in that it originated in the gift of peace offered by Jesus to His disciples on the night before he died.[207] "Peace I bequeath

---

207 The following is taken from Michael J. Baxter, "The Sign of Peace: The Mission of the Church to the Nations," CTSA Proceedings 59 (2004): 21-2.

to you," Jesus says, "my own peace I give you, a peace which the world cannot give, this is my gift to you" (John 14:27). In using the first-person possessive — "my own peace," "my gift to you" — Jesus makes it clear that the peace on offer is not from "the world", which cannot give it. Rather it comes from Jesus in union with Abba God through "the Paraclete, the Holy Spirit, whom Abba God will send in my name", who "will teach you everything and remind you of all I have said to you" (John 14:26). The centrality of this gift of peace is made clear later in John's Gospel when Jesus appears to the disciples in the upper room and twice says to them, " Peace be with you," then commissions them with the words, "As the Abba God sent me, so I am sending you," after which He breathes on them, saying, "Receive the Holy Spirit. If you forgive anyone's sins, they are forgiven..." (John 20: 21-23). Jesus's breathing on the apostles recalls God's breathing into and giving life to Adam at the creation (Gen 2:7). In this pentecostal scene, therefore, the gift of peace is part of the new creation that becomes a reality as the disciples share in divine life with Abba God, the Beloved One, and through the Paraclete; the Father, Son and Holy Spirit.

This sharing in the divine life was enacted by Christians in antiquity through the practice of the holy kiss. The Apostle Paul urged his readers in Rome to "greet each other with a holy kiss" (Rom 16:16). A similar instruction can be found in several of Paul's other letters as well (1 Cor 16:20; 2 Cor 13:12; 1 Thess 5:26). This kiss was not only an expression of affection. It was seen as the deepest form of communication available to humanity, an exchange of the breath of the Holy Spirit. The profound meaning of the sign of peace was extended in many Christian liturgical contexts. It was part of the early initiation rites, when the presider offered a kiss to the newly baptised. In some places, it served as a ritual conclusion to the Liturgy of the Word. It was widely used to welcome back those who had broken away from the Church due to serious sin. Later, it was incorporated into liturgies conferring holy orders and it was a regular part of the entry rites into monastic communities. Eventually, it served a a pre-communion rite of reconciliation, in keeping with Jesus's exhortation to be reconciled with our brothers and sisters before bringing our offering to the altar (Matthew 5:23).

All these ritual forms of the sign of peace indicate its deeply rooted and central importance in the life of the Church.

The sign of peace is a venerable ritual that is, at the same time, ever new. Today, when members of the Church gather for the liturgy of the Eucharist, the presider recalls the gift of peace bestowed on the apostles and prays that this same gift of peace be given again, here and now, to the local assembly and the entire Church. After this, the presider, or deacon if present, issues the invitation, "Let us offer to one another the sign of peace" and then, as the rubrics in the sacramentary indicate, "All make an appropriate sign of peace according to local custom." Local customs vary greatly. Some ways of sharing the sign of peace are fast and formal, others are more expressive, as people shake hands, embrace, or kiss. In all cases, those present at the liturgy share, with visible gestures, the invisible grace that transforms those present into an assembly of unity and peace, a transformation completed in the Rite of Holy Communion as the members of the Body of Christ become what they receive.

The gift of peace given in the liturgy here and now underscores the Church's genuine catholicity, her presence throughout all the world, a unity that reaches every tribe, people and nation. Herein lies the full meaning of this ordinary, seemingly simple rite, for it signifies how at the Fall humanity became divided by rivalry and sin and now in Christ, the New Adam, we recover the original unity of all humanity, a unity to be fulfilled in the coming of Christ at the end of time. In this day and age, when humanity suffers from such deep divisions of rich and poor, along racial and ethnic lines, and by national interests and imperial designs, nothing is more urgent than for the Church to embody in and through her members the peace and unity enacted in the sign of peace. Let Christians everywhere throughout the world receive the gift given by Christ to the apostles in the upper room in Jerusalem, and given again as they gather at Eucharist. And may they bring this gift to every race and people, to all the nations, repeating the words of Christ to the apostles and to all humanity: "Peace be with You."

God's great vision for humanity is the nonviolent transformation of the world, a new creation where all are reconciled. Jesus incarnated this divine vision by proclaiming the Reign of God, a nonviolent order of justice and dignity for all. In Christ we see the love that sustains all things, that rescues all things from nothingness, *ex nihilo*. The cross and resurrection are not just events in history but reveal the nonviolent love that stands at the core of all being.

The Reign of God is both "here" and "not yet". But even in the "not yet" we are called to act *now*: to love our enemies, to put down our sword, to be compassionate as God is compassionate, to spread the good news of God's nonviolent reign.

Called to be a people of nonviolence, the Church exists for the sake of God's nonviolent reign. Beginning with the power of the Holy Spirit poured out at Pentecost, the Church emerged as a liberating and peaceable community of disciples.[208]

To speak of the Church's call to nonviolence, though, is not to imply that it has always responded faithfully to it. Indeed, "we confess that the people of God has betrayed this central message of the Gospel many times, participating in wars, persecution, oppression, exploitation and discrimination."[209] To affirm Gospel nonviolence is to confess our own violence and to perennially open ourselves, as people and as the Church, to conversion to the way of Jesus's nonviolence under the living guidance of the Holy Spirit.

Despite its violence and failings, the Church is called by the Holy Spirit in every age to respond prophetically to the challenges of its time. In an age that is undergoing what Pope Francis has named a "world war in instalments", we are called today to respond to global violence and injustice with decisive action in a spirit of nonviolent love throughout the Church and world.

----

208 Baxter, 44.

209 "An Appeal to the Catholic Church to Re-Commit to the Centrality of Gospel Nonviolence," final document, Nonviolence and Just Peace Conference, April 11-13, 2016, Rome, 2.

PART III: THE PRACTICE AND POWER OF NONVIOLENCE

Grounding nonviolence globally

Over the past century active nonviolence has spread all over the world.[210] From civil resistance to the Marcos dictatorship in the Philippines and the mostly peaceful dissolution of the Soviet bloc to contemporary movements in response to climate change and violence against women, successful nonviolent social and political change has demonstrated the efficacy of nonviolent action in addressing injustice and constraining evil.

In India in the 1920s, after Mohandas Gandhi returned from South Africa, he and his spiritual community, including Abdul Ghaffar Khan and his nonviolent peace army, began experimenting with approaches of refusing to co-operate with British rule. Through a constructive programme, as well as civil disobedience, boycotts and a deep grounding in prayer and the work of common people, they succeeded in loosening the colonial grip of the British Empire and set India on the path to self-determination. Gandhi wrote, "Mute prayer is my greatest weapon."

---

210 Peace researchers have compiled extensive databases of nonviolent action. See Nonviolent and Violent Campaigns and Outcomes Dataset (NAVCO) Data Project (University of Denver, USA); Global Nonviolent Action Database (Swarthmore, USA); Global Digital Activism Data Set (Ann Arbor, MI/USA: Inter-university Consortium for Political and Social Research); and the Conflict Data Program (Department of Peace and Conflict Research, Uppsala University, Sweden, and National Centre for Peace and Conflict Studies, University of Otago, New Zealand)

In spring 1940, the German army invaded Denmark. Danish leaders adopted a strategy of "resistance disguised as collaboration", and undermined German objectives through negotiations, delay and confusion. The Danish Lutheran Church issued a pastoral letter in 1943 condemning the arrests of Danish citizens— Christians and Jews. An underground resistance movement organised strikes and rescued nearly all of Denmark's Jewish citizens.

In the United States, Rev. Martin Luther King, Jr., a Baptist minister, and other African-American leaders travelled to India to study Gandhi's tactics.[211] In the 1960s, African-American college students in Nashville, Tennessee, took up the weapons of nonviolence against brutal discriminatory laws. Disciplined and strictly nonviolent, they successfully desegregated Nashville's lunch counters and launched the third phase of the civil rights movement.

In 1977, a quarter century after the Catholic Church in South Africa began campaigning against apartheid, Catholics embarked on a policy of civil disobedience to the government's apartheid laws. Led at first by Dominican sisters and priests, the Church authorised the admission of blacks to previously all-white schools, as well as hospitals, homes and orphanages. These moves were made in defiance of apartheid laws that required segregation in all institutions, public or private. Cardinal Owen McCann, Archbishop of Cape Town and head of the Church in South Africa, addressed an open letter to the government: "We see these upheavals as the result of a burning sense of injustice among those who are deprived of so many rights. Depriving a person of his rights as a human being is a kind of violence." Catholic leadership took crucial steps to end apartheid.[212]

In 1980, striking workers in Poland demanded independent unions. Using their leverage to negotiate unprecedented rights in a system where there was no power separate from the Communist Party, they created a union called "Solidarity". The

---

211 See Baltimore Archbishop William E. Lori's pastoral letter that elucidates these principles: "The Enduring Power of Martin Luther King Jr's Principles of Nonviolence," February 2018, https://www.archbalt.org/kingpastoral/.

212 "Catholic Defiance of Apartheid Is Stirring South Africa" by John F. Burns (The New York Times, Feb. 6, 1977).

martyred priest and nonviolence role model Jerzy Popiełuszko served as chaplain of the Polish freedom movement. Polish Catholic and union leader Lech Walesa was driven underground by a government crackdown in 1981, but Solidarity re-emerged in 1989 as Poland's governing political party with Lech Walesa as president.

In 1983, Chilean workers initiated a wave of nonviolent protests against the military dictatorship of General Augusto Pinochet. Severe repression failed to stop the protests and violent opposition failed to dislodge the dictatorship — until the democratic opposition organised to defeat Pinochet.

More recently around the globe, mass nonviolent protests have been demanding that national leaders step down. People are rising up against their governments in places as varied as Puerto Rico, Sudan, Algeria, Chile, Lebanon, Ecuador, Argentina, Hong Kong, Iraq and Britain. We may be in the midst of the largest wave of nonviolent mass movements in world history.

The experiences of these and the other nonviolent movements teach many lessons. Mobilising and sustaining a popular movement geared to nonviolent action goes hand in hand with forming a civil society, building strong communities, promoting human dignity and sustaining democracy. The true rhythm of nonviolent action is less spontaneous outbursts than it is spiritually rooted, sustained and intentional.

Perhaps the greatest misconception about conflict is that violence is the ultimate form of power, surpassing other methods of advancing a just cause or defeating injustice.[213] But Indians, Danes, Poles, South Africans, Chileans, African Americans and many others have proved the efficacy of nonviolent action, which, as nonviolence scholar Gene Sharp has written, "is capable of wielding great power even against ruthless rulers and military regimes, because it attacks the most vulnerable characteristic of all hierarchical institutions and governments: dependence on the governed".

213 Jack DuVall and Peter Ackerman, *A Force More Powerful: A Century of Nonviolent Conflict*, St, Martin's Griffin, 2000.

Catholics have always been part of these nonviolent movements, bringing spiritual grounding, prayer, courage, strategy and organisation, along with healing, restorative justice, trauma-care, pastoral presence and solidarity.

When St. Pope John Paul II visited India in 1986, he paid homage to Gandhi, "the apostle of nonviolence". "It is entirely fitting that this pilgrimage should begin here," the pope said of the Gandhi memorial on the bank of the Jumna River. "Today we hear him still pleading with the world: 'Conquer hate by love, untruth by truth, violence by suffering.'"

1. The Transformational Impact of Nonviolence

Erica Chenoweth, reflecting on several case studies collected by the Catholic Nonviolence Initiative, said, "The stories about nonviolent action are often untold or subjugated to stories about violence. Nonviolent responses must address different dimensions of structural violence. Finally, people are using an infinite number of creative and innovative nonviolent methods to pursue justice and change."

The depth of change brought through nonviolent action, and the place of faith and spirituality in work to challenge violence, are often neglected in traditional social science measurements or analysis, yet are clearly powerful elements in the lives of Catholics. They describe practices and change at personal, communal and political levels.

For many Catholic leaders in nonviolence, engagement in nonviolent change and action has been a life-choice. Elizabeth Kanini Kimau (Kenya) puts it this way: "My experience of using nonviolence myself and then with communities at war with each other, has motivated me to gain deeper understanding. The language of nonviolence helped me transform myself and empowered me to be able to live and work in hostile environments."

Nonviolent Christian practices also require self-knowledge. Merwyn DeMello (Afghanistan) said, "I began to see beyond my own rhetoric of categorising people, and the importance of nonviolent communication. ... I recognised the art and skill of setting aside bias. ... Some of my responses to people were from a bias of self-righteousness rather than a quest for righteous justice."

Florington Aseervatham (South Sudan) described the approach of the Nonviolent Peaceforce with which he works: "Teams of unarmed civilian peacekeepers live within the communities they serve. As a result, they are extremely sensitive to the specific dynamics at play within a community, and can respond quickly and effectively to counter threats as they arise".

Of his experiences in the war-zones Pietro Ameglio (Mexico) said, "All of us have changed our lives, our inner and outer reflection, the way we think about nonviolent action in the midst of situations of war as those experienced in Mexico."

Relationships formed with victims of violence both motivate and transform, as Martha Ines Romero (Colombia) related: "The most important hopefulness comes from those most affected by violence because they resist, and build trust with us, in a humble and persistent way. ... The Bojaya community expressed their call for the need to reconstruct the social fabric, to hope, to rediscover trust, to look forward to the future, to look ahead with the goal of building a society that is able with its relationships to keep Colombians healing from atrocities of the past."

Mel Duncan, Nonviolent Peaceforce co-founder, commented: "The real transformation lies in the individual. More of us are transcending the illusion of separation and embodying the unity required for our survival. There are more peacebuilders, mediators, conflict resolvers, trauma healers, unarmed civilian protectors and civil resisters on the planet today than any other time in history. Everything that is needed to build a culture of peace and nonviolence already exists in each of us."

Faith as a Guide and Motivator to Nonviolent Action

Faith is what impels many Catholic nonviolent peacebuilders, expressed in phrases such as seeing all as created in God's image; in re-affirming the precious nature of life; and spiritual practices of prayer, fasting and taking time out have nurtured and grounded people in their work.

For Ana Raffai (Croatia) building the connection between peace and faith was important: "We started slowly, seeking miraculous incentives from our faith.... For more than 10 years we have deepened our knowledge of the peace potential of faith and also increased our self-criticism with regard to the patriarchal activity of religious institutions."

Natalia Chan, who works with the Sudan Council of Churches, said, "Faith is critical to counter the despair, to give people hope. Prayer and deep reflection are what led to this Church-led vision of peace. The Church leaders have acknowledged themselves that their Churches have also been deeply affected at a personal level, and humility and spiritual guidance are at the heart of their response." Faith leaders can sometimes take risks because of who they are.

Jamila Raqib reflected: "What came through very clearly is that in each of the cases I looked at, the Church and spiritual communities acted as connectors and facilitators in environments where there was a weak civil society because it had been eroded due to conflict or for other reasons. ... As a global institution with a deep and diverse network, the Church connected local struggles with global movements."

Empowering Communities to Act Without Violence

Many Catholic nonviolence leaders emphasised the importance of building relationships of trust that supported communities in creating new relationships and resisting violence with nonviolence. Martha Ines Romero (Colombia) wrote: "In our project we saw a new style of leadership in confronting violence – a collective way to nonviolently confront perpetrators and the Colombian government in order to protect civilians. ... The bishop actually carried a hidden camera on his body that documented the army and paramilitary actions in the area. This was a big example to the people of a bishop willing to sacrifice and risk."

One of the most poignant statements in these case studies, said Erica Chenoweth, was Sarah Thompson Nahar's observation that "the faithful must get to the frontlines themselves". It certainly seems plausible – based on both historical cases (e.g. Archbishop Oscar Romero in El Salvador) and contemporary cases (e.g. Rev. William Barber in North Carolina) – that active participation in grassroots contentious mobilisation by faith-based communities would have a profound effect on the individuals as well as the political power of such movements. Communities of faith can provide inspiration, moral imagination, stamina, spiritual nourishment, spaces for collective grieving, celebration, discernment, preparation, training and mobilisation, and various other essential capacities.

In many places, Catholics are on the right course in putting the skills, tools, techniques and a spirituality of nonviolence into action. Individuals, communities and movements around the world are engaged as part of the nonviolent peace corps, the nonviolent army, the disarmed forward base of the Church – some within Church-based structures, others beyond them. Guided by Pope Francis, the Catholic Church as an institution is also moving in the right direction. It is good to recognise and affirm this and encourage our Church to do and be more. For example, these Catholic nonviolence leaders encouraged the Church to:

• Communicate and proclaim that nonviolence is active, positive, normal.
• Affirm the ministries of nonviolence and just peace practitioners.
• Train, nurture, support champions of nonviolence and just peace.
• Offer spiritual guidance, encouragement and clarity of teaching on Catholic nonviolence.

Mel Duncan is co-founder of the Nonviolent Peaceforce, the largest unarmed civilian accompaniment model currently in operation. He sees great potential within the institutional Catholic Church.

Mel said, "Local churches are well placed to support localised approaches and provide bases for the ongoing reflections required to adapt nonviolent approaches. Churches can also provide the venues for training. And they can play an important role in mobilising the resources for trauma treatment. An encyclical on nonviolence by Pope Francis is required to set the direction for churches and to emphasise the scale of the violence that is engulfing the world. The case studies illustrated instances where the Church played a positive role, but others where the Church was an impediment. Without strong papal leadership, churches will continue to play mixed and confused roles. Clergy will have to take militant, Romero-like stances, not only in conflict-affected countries but also in the seats of the empire, following the example of Jesus's entry into Jerusalem."

Maciej Bartkowski, senior researcher for the International Center for Nonviolent Conflict, provided a critical look at the role of the Catholic Church and mass civil resistance. Mac said, "I support a call for a civil resistance mindset to be integrated into development of civic programmes by the local and national Catholic churches and the Vatican. External actors, including the Catholic Church, must be able to identify a civil resistance movement when it happens. Some yardsticks to use: 1) Is it genuinely grassroots? 2) Is people's participation voluntary? 3) Is it inclusive and representative of the community/society? 4) Does it display a strong nonviolent discipline? 5) Is it united around goals and means? 6) Does it practise nondiscrimination, non-exploitation and non-repression while resisting injustice? 7) Is it able to advance communal solidarity through mutual aid? 8) Does it use diverse nonviolent disruptive/obstructive, constructive and symbolic resistance methods? Once it is able to look for and identify important attributes of a civil resistance movement, the Catholic Church on the local, national and transnational levels can develop different approaches to assist people in their struggles."

Through its teachings, advocacy and support for peacebuilding and social justice endeavours globally, the Catholic Church offers manifold moral and material resources to promote a world without violence.

Providing support for those around the world engaged in nonviolent resistance to advance rights, peace and dignity — doctrinally, through Catholic teaching, education and formation, through the policy-influencing arms of the Church, and through field-based programmes, is a concrete and powerful way to counter violence globally. Increasing solidarity and material support to those nonviolent change agents around the world is a specific way to reduce the huge loss of life that inevitably follows when people take up arms or governments drop bombs.

Fortunately, there is an ever-expanding living library of resources. A growing number of capacity-building organisations around the world specialise in helping conflict-affected communities organise nonviolently for change. The US Institute of Peace, Rhize, the International Center on Nonviolent Conflict, Nonviolent Peaceforce, the American Friends Service Committee, Operation Dove and Christian Peacemakers Teams are only a few such organisations.

Together with remarkably active and effective organisations such as Pax Christi International, Mercy Corps, Caritas International and Catholic Relief Services, expanding and deepening partnerships and synergies focused on improving knowledge and skills related to nonviolent action could help prevent and mitigate violent conflict around the world.

At a policy level, the Church's first response to conflict could be firm overt support for nonviolent practices and embrace of the nonviolent warriors resisting injustice on the front lines of nonviolent change; profound pastoral sadness and public identification of our corporate failure when violence is chosen; and a clear, principled rejection of war. This would be a significant step in realising Pope Francis's vision of a world in which conflicts are transformed without violence.

Nonviolence is not "one size fits all". It must grow in the context for which it is needed, drawing on the culture, arts, history, traditions of the people closest to the conflict. Nonviolence includes a broad spectrum of approaches, from diplomacy to trauma healing, from restorative justice to unarmed accompaniment, from peace education to research and policy advocacy. For the vision of Catholic nonviolence to take root, the whole Church must take to heart the words of Elizabeth Kanini Kimau in Kenya: "Nonviolence is a crop that can feed the whole world — but the farmer must know her own soil."

2. Differing Techniques of Active Nonviolence

In each of these cases above, unarmed civilians used nonviolent direct action, or what nonviolent action scholar Gene Sharp described as techniques outside institutionalised behaviour for social change that challenge an unjust power dynamic, using methods of protest and persuasion, non-co-operation and intervention without the use or threat of injurious force. The theoretical underpinnings of nonviolent resistance, articulated by Sharp and by earlier scholars including German philosopher Hannah Arendt, hold that power is fluid and ultimately grounded in the consent and co-operation of ordinary people, who can decide to restrict or withhold that support.

Sharp identified six key sources of political power, which are present to varying degrees in any society: authority, human resources, material resources, skills and knowledge, intangible factors and sanctions. Ultimately, these sources of power are grounded in organisations and institutions, made up of people, known as "pillars of support". When large numbers of people from various pillars of support (bureaucracies, trade and labour unions, state media, educational institutions, religious institutions, security forces etc.) use various nonviolent tactics to strategically withhold consent and co-operation from regimes or other power-holders in an organised fashion, this can shift power from the oppressor to the oppressed without bombs or bullets.

What are the factors that make a nonviolent campaign successful? Heavily influenced by military strategists, Sharp emphasises that strategic planning is an essential element of successful nonviolent movements. He argues that the development of strategy and long-term goals before planning tactics is of critical importance, and that an oft-repeated mistake made by leaders of popular struggles is that they emphasise tactics at the expense of long-term strategy. Very often in social and political movements, the individuals and groups involved recognise that they need to plan how they are to act, but do so only on a very limited, short-term or tactical basis. They do not attempt to formulate a broader, longer-term or strategic plan of action. The result of such failures is that the chances of success are drastically reduced and at times eliminated. One's strength is dissipated. One's actions are ineffective. Sacrifices are wasted and one's cause is not well served. The failure to plan strategically is likely to result in the failure to achieve one's objectives.

Sharp identified 198 methods of nonviolent action, which included peaceful marches, vigils, social and consumer boycotts, stay-aways, sit-ins, street theatre, humour and the creation of parallel structures and institutions (included in what Gandhi referred to as the "constructive programme", which focused on social uplift for the poor and marginalised).

The rise of social media technologies, including Facebook, Twitter, WhatsApp and Instagram, has offered new avenues for communication, mobilisation and peer learning across borders (to both positive and nefarious effect) and has expanded the universe of nonviolent tactics even further. Successful movements have integrated both on- and offline forms of mobilisation, organisation and direct action — online activism is never a substitute for nuts-and-bolts offline organising.

Nonviolent struggle draws on courage, strategic planning and, for many people involved in nonviolent resistance, spiritual discipline and motivation. In many of the most iconic historical nonviolent movements, Catholic and Christian faith communities and institutions played pivotal roles in exposing injustices, encouraging global solidarity, providing organisational strength and offering spiritual nourishment for activists and nonviolent change agents.

Despite these successes, deep economic disparities, institutionalised racism and discrimination, protracted intra-state wars and the rise of extremist groups continue to wreak havoc on lives and livelihoods around the world. The civil war in Syria, which began as a nonviolent uprising against the Bashar al Assad dictatorship in 2011, has now claimed over 250,000 lives. The Islamic State of Iraq and Syria (ISIS) has used brutal tactics to take over territory in an attempt to create an Islamist totalitarian state. In Uganda, which boasts the largest per capita youth population in Africa, the 30-year autocracy of Yoweri Museveni was recently extended another five years after elections marred by fraud, violence and intimidation. In the United States, structural injustices and police violence continue to adversely target African Americans, while politicians mobilise fear, xenophobia and hatred as part of a strategy to take and maintain power.

Nonviolent Resistance is More Effective than Violent Resistance

Despite the prevalence of these and other injustices around the world, there is reason for great hope. Catholic teachings focus on the need to avoid war and prevent violent conflict by peaceful means. Fortunately, empirical data reveal that there is a force more powerful than violence to achieve social justice, which Pope Paul VI called the basis of peace.

In recent years, a wide range of social scientists have recognised how unarmed civil resistance movements, with increasing frequency, have been able to succeed where strategic alliances, armed guerrillas and intergovernmental organisations have often failed, including bringing down some of the most entrenched dictatorships on the planet. The study of nonviolent struggle has become part of the international studies curriculum only recently, but world events have led an increasing number of scholars to recognise the importance of the application of such non-conventional social action, leading to a dramatic increase in the scholarly literature over the past four decades.

According to research conducted by Maria J. Stephan and Erica Chenoweth, which culminated in their 2011 book, *Why Civil Resistance Works: The Strategic Logic of Nonviolent Conflict,* nonviolent resistance against formidable opponents, including those with predominant military power, has been twice as successful as armed struggle. They examined 323 violent and nonviolent campaigns against incumbent regimes and foreign military occupations from 1900-2006 and found that the nonviolent campaigns succeeded, in terms of stated political objectives, about 54 percent of the time, compared to 27 percent for violent campaigns.

In addition, their study concluded that nonviolent campaigns were associated with both democratic and peaceful societies. Armed rebel victories almost never produce democratic societies (less than four percent resulted in democracy); worse, they are often followed by relapses into civil war. The data clearly show that the means by which peoples challenge injustices and oppression strongly influence the character of the societies that follow. For a Catholic faith community that places a premium on the avoidance of war and the protection of human life as the moral foundation of society, these are significant findings.

Nonviolent civil resistance has proven to be more successful than violence in part because it allows for much broader participation. Stephan and Chenoweth found that the average nonviolent campaign attracted *11 times* the level of participants compared with armed campaigns. The physical, moral, informational and commitment barriers to participation in nonviolent campaigns are much lower compared with violent campaigns, which means that young and old people, men and women, rich and poor, disabled and able-bodied, peasants and professionals can all participate in nonviolent activism.

The range of nonviolent tactics is vast, facilitating participation: Sharp's list of nonviolent methods has greatly expanded with the rise of social media and new tactics invented by creative nonviolent resisters around the world. When large numbers of people from diverse societal groups engage in acts of protest, non-co-operation and nonviolent defiance, their actions create social, political, economic and moral pressure for change. When violence is used against disciplined nonviolent protesters, the chances that the violence will backfire against the perpetrator, causing them to lose legitimacy and power, is much greater than when violence is used against armed resisters.

Although nonviolent movements contain elements of spontaneity and artistry, the chance of success increases significantly if participants adhere to basic principles of strategy[214]. Those include achieving unity around achievable goals and nonviolent methods, building capacity to maintain nonviolent discipline, focusing on expanding the diversity of participation and innovating tactically.

The strategic dimensions of nonviolent resistance were first articulated by Peter Ackerman and Christopher Kruegler in *Strategic Principles of Nonviolent Action* and by retired U.S. Army colonel Robert Helvey in *On Strategic Nonviolent Conflict*. In *Why Civil Resistance Works*, Stephan and Chenoweth, building on writings by sociologist Brian Martin and others, discussed why state violence targeting nonviolent movements (versus armed resisters) was more likely to backfire against the perpetrator, leading to greater support for the movement. They highlight the strategic importance of innovating tactically and alternating between methods of concentration (e.g. street demonstrations, sit-ins) and methods of dispersion (e.g. consumer boycotts, go-slow actions) to reinforce movement resilience and effectiveness.

Helvey makes the case that to maximise its effectiveness, civilian-based unarmed resistance should be based on a "strategic estimate" that identifies the strengths

---

214 "Strategy" and "tactics" are used intentionally in this section, which is focused on the utilitarian use of nonviolence and the work of Peter Ackerman, Christopher Kruegler and others who introduced the value of strategic approaches to nonviolent action.

and weaknesses of the resisting population and the opponent. Drawing from military planning methodologies, Helvey lays out a schema of questions (a "strategic estimate") that should be answered by nonviolent movements as they engage in strategic planning. For example: What is the mission? Who or what is the opponent? What are the opponents' and protagonists' pillars of support? Who are natural allies? What are the strengths of the protagonists? How does communication function? What are pressure points? What does a successful outcome look like? Is it a sustainable outcome? Developing a strategic estimate is essential to any nonviolent campaign.

The techniques-based approach to nonviolent action described by Sharp, Ackerman and others focuses on the pragmatic, utilitarian use of nonviolent action, which is detached from religious or ideological underpinnings. This approach is distinguished from "principled nonviolence", whose adherents reject violence on moral or religious grounds and include pacifists. An advantage of the technique-based approach is that it does not create a barrier to participation for those who are not pacifists (i.e. most people around the world). It is possible to convince those living under profound oppression, who might otherwise take up arms or who have taken up arms, that there is a more effective way to challenge injustice — without having to first convince them that violence is always wrong.

On the other hand, there is tremendous value in the principled nonviolence approach, which provides moral, religious and philosophical anchors to remaining nonviolent when the going gets tough (as it often does) and the temptation to use violence is high. And nonviolence offers a long-term vision for societies and the world writ large that is built on nonviolent communications, peaceful co-existence, processes of restorative justice and reconciliation.

In practice, the line is not so stark between the principled and pragmatic nonviolence traditions. Spiritual belief and religious organisations and institutions have often played critical roles in nonviolent movements. Gandhi referred to Jesus as nonviolence *par excellence*.

On the most practical level, it is extremely difficult for a nonviolent movement challenging entrenched and long-standing injustices to maintain morale and to sustain active participation over an extended period of time — especially without the support of their religious and moral leaders. Activists burn out. Sustained resistance becomes burdensome. In such circumstances, activists and movement leaders need to be able to draw on resources that will inspire, encourage and nourish. Their strength and resilience depend on it.

Faith communities and institutions can provide that sense of community solidarity, spiritual nourishment and the cultivation of virtuous habits. It is difficult to imagine the US freedom movement sustaining its vibrancy and effectiveness without the spiritual and organisational power provided by the Black Churches. The iconic images of the Filipino nuns, rosaries in hand and kneeling in prayer in front of dictator Ferdinand Marcos's soldiers, together with declarations by Cardinal Jaime Sin imploring justice over Radio Veritas, helped galvanise the popular nonviolent struggle for a democratic Philippines in 1986. Archbishop Desmond Tutu of South Africa drew on faith-based beliefs grounded in justice and reconciliation in his insistence that the struggle for a free South Africa be nonviolent and that forgiveness be the guiding principle of the post-apartheid state. In East Timor, Catholic priests and religious sisters from around the country spoke out against the atrocities committed by Indonesian forces and provided protection and material support to those youths and others who were fighting nonviolently for self-determination. In Liberia, a group of women of faith came together and organised a remarkable nonviolent direct action campaign that pressured the warring parties to sign a peace agreement in 2003. Peace vigils, sex strikes and social pressure were a few of their tactics. In Guatemala, a broad-based coalition involving peasants, students, lawyers and religious leaders used boycotts, strikes and protests to challenge entrenched government corruption, forcing a kleptocratic president to step down without violence in 2015.

Nonviolence works first because of the way it increasingly withdraws co-operation and builds nonviolent people-power for an alternative. Based on the theory of power that says "power rises", the ones who have the biggest guns and who are able to threaten people with violence and cause great fear are not really powerful at all. They only appear powerful because those underneath them go along. If those with the real power stop co-operating, the ones with apparent power fold like inflated paper bags that have lost their air. (Gandhi asked, "Why do 100,000 British people rule us, a country of 250,000,000? The answer: because we let them.")

The first step in a successful nonviolent campaign is to call everyone's attention to the problem — those experiencing the injustice or the violence, those who are supporting the perpetrators of the injustice and those who are the perpetrators. This first step is accomplished through an unlimited array of potential approaches — marches, demonstrations, plays, exposés, lawsuits, reports in the media. Once the problem has been, as Dr. King often said, "dramatised", then it is time to approach the ones in charge and ask if they are ready to negotiate, to sit down together and figure out a way to solve the problem. That is what nonviolence always aims to have happen — to change the adversary from an opponent to a friend who is willing to work together to find a peaceful resolution.

If dramatising the problem is not enough, the next step in a nonviolent campaign is to withdraw co-operation from the ones who are committing the injustice or the violence. Gandhi's resistance to the occupying British is an example. He had done much to alert the countryside to the injustices perpetrated on India by the Raj. He had dramatised the problem but found the Viceroy deaf to his entreaties. So his next step was to ask all the lawyers who worked in the legal system of the Raj to withdraw their participation, the teachers in the school system of the Raj to resign their positions and start their own schools, all the headmen in the villages who worked with the system to solve local problems and collect taxes to resign their positions. The Raj's system began to sway in the wind. He asked the people to stop buying alcohol from the government shops, to stop buying imported cloth, to stop paying unfair land taxes. The Raj's revenue from India began to plummet. Gandhi then asked the Viceroy if he was ready to negotiate. The response came back — "Never."

So Gandhi moved to the next strategy — civil resistance. Gandhi chose a particularly egregious, unfair law to violate — the law against manufacturing salt. Britain had a monopoly on salt. Salt is a vital necessity. Britain had a tax on salt. Even the poorest of the poor had to pay the tax to secure a handful of salt. Gandhi had a great sense for powerful symbols. He began a 200-mile march with 100 well-trained satyagrahi from his ashram to the sea coast town of Dandi. As he marched, dozens, then hundreds, then thousands accompanied him. By the time he reached into the ocean and grasped a handful of salt, hundreds of reporters from all over the world had gathered to report the story. The British arrested Gandhi and his supporters. The country was aflame with resistance. The Raj filled the jails with thousands of resisters. When they could not get the people all around the country to obey, they ordered the native police to beat them with steel-tipped lathis. When they still could not get them to obey, they began to fire live ammunition at the gathering, resisting crowds. As a result the British had revealed themselves for what they were — violent imperialists. The whole country, middle class, upper class, the poor in the villages united as never before as the veil of disguise dropped from the so-called beneficent Raj. People from all over the world followed the story of the violence. Britain experienced great loss of prestige around the world. Even at home the British people were sickened by the stories of violence inflicted on a nonviolent population. Gandhi approached the Viceroy and asked if he was ready to negotiate. The Viceroy responded, "Mr. Gandhi, will you come to London to participate in the Round Table Conference?" Nonviolence works because of the coercive force it can generate and the way it can undercut the opposition's pillars of support.

The second way that nonviolence works is in the way that it employs self-suffering. Gandhi called it *tapasya*. Gandhi knew that real change does not happen by reaching peoples' heads, it is necessary to reach their hearts. Self-suffering is not masochism. Self-suffering works because instead of inflicting harm on another it willingly takes the suffering on oneself, with the hope and intention of reaching the heart or the better nature of the one inflicting the suffering.

Richard Gregg describes the "three mirrors of strength" embodied in the practice of *tapasya*, or self- suffering. The first mirror is in the face of the one who is experiencing the suffering as he or she is perceived by the one inflicting the suffering, the violence, the injustice. The pain is too obvious. As the perpetrator looks at himself or herself in the mirror subsequently, the face in the mirror is the face of a violent, abusive person. It does not usually jibe with the person's self-identity. A doubt, a pang of uncertainty creeps in. "How can I be the person who is inflicting suffering on another human being?" The second mirror is the observing faces of the bystanders, the witnesses, even supporters of the one committing the violence, the force of public opinion. Consider some examples, in addition to what happened to the British after their explosion of violence on the Indian people. Many people witnessed on television Sheriff Bull Connor unleashing the snarling police dogs on the children marching peacefully in Birmingham, Alabama and then commanding the firemen to aim their fire hoses at the children, knocking them into the air and back five feet to the ground. Many people that day were so shocked at what they saw they began to see with much greater clarity just how evil was the Jim Crow system. The third mirror is the face of the one suffering looking at the perpetrator with love and positive regard even through the suffering. That can be powerful, and Jesus of course knew and practised the power of self-suffering.

Hearing the Song of the Earth [215]

It would be easy to despair when looking at the landscape of ecological violence. But there are signs of hope that ecological conversion and active nonviolence are taking hold in people's lives and in global policies when considering matters of the environment. Peace is mentioned at least 39 times in *Laudato Si'*, which has

---

215 "Nonviolence and Creation Care/Climate Justice" by Amy Echeverria, Global Catholic Climate Movement, excerpts www.nonviolencejustpeace.net.

been a huge light of hope added to the body of Catholic Social Teaching. Other faith responses that inspire include the birth of major international networks such as Global Catholic Climate Movement (GCCM)[216], Ecclesial Network for the Pan Amazon (REPAM)[217] and the Ecclesial Network for the Congo Basin (REBAC)[218]. Still other global processes and proposals, such as divestment from fossil fuels and carbon neutrality, liturgical reform to include a Season of Creation, and the Catholic Nonviolence Initiative are all nonviolent expressions of the Spirit breathing life and hope into the world. Creation itself and its natural regenerative process, threatened and under attack as it is, reminds us of our pascal faith that life does overcome death.

On Ash Wednesday 2015, during Pope Francis's visit to the Philippines and just months before the release of the Church's first encyclical that deeply addresses the world's environmental crisis and our relationship with the earth, the Global Catholic Climate Movement was born. Since then, GCCM has worked to animate the grassroots as well as Church leadership in bringing *Laudato Si'* to life. Its three areas of focus include: ecological conversion, lifestyle change and public sphere advocacy, which when woven together take individuals, communities and the world on a journey towards restoring right relationship with all who share God's common home. GCCM's campaign to keep rising temperatures below 1.5 degrees Celsius is just one nonviolent response to an ongoing human-induced violent conflict with Earth. Calling the Church to energy reduction, efficiency and carbon neutrality in our parishes, schools, hospitals, religious houses, seminaries and formation centres is yet another systematic response that will bring us into a healing and restorative relationship with each other, creation and God.

Born of a deep desire to bring healing, peace and justice to the Amazon and

216 Global Catholic Climate Movement (https://catholicclimatemovement.global)

217 Ecclesial Network for the Pan Amazon (http://redamazonica.org)

218 Ecclesial Network for the Congo Basin (https://rebaccongobassin.org)

Congo Basin, REPAM and REBAC have emphasised a territorial approach by creating space for local communities and Indigenous leaders to be protagonists in defending the rights of the people and the land. Locally led processes for education, formation and prayer about human and environmental rights, coupled with international advocacy in places such as the United Nations, U.S. Congress and the Inter-American Commission on Human Rights, are all ways that people and the earth are working in communion to bring nonviolent action and change to the Amazon region known as the "lungs of the planet".

A growing number of Catholic institutions, parishes and dioceses — such as the Archdiocese of Manila — are celebrating the Season of Creation (1 September - 4 October), an example of how the Church is taking up a systematic approach to bringing care for creation into liturgical and sacramental spaces. In doing so the Catholic Church is beginning to recognise, in deep theological and pastoral ways, that care for creation is not an optional dimension of our faith, but integral to our Christian discipleship.

Another important response is the growing Catholic institutional commitment to divestment from fossil fuels and promotion of positive-impact investing. In a divestment toolkit[219] prepared collaboratively between GCCM and Trocaire, the Irish member of Caritas Internationalis, a new set of criteria is proposed to measure ethical investments. According to the toolkit, "In the light of climate change, a more robust investment framework would apply four ethical tests to prospective investments:

- Does the activity in question contribute to observable, grave or large-scale harm?
- Does the organisation or sector contribute to a denial of the truth about harm, whether through misleading information campaigns or other means, intended to delay a response, thus leading to intractable resistance?

219 Full divestment toolkit here: https://catholicclimatemovement.global/wp-content/uploads/2017/11/GCCM_Tr%C3%B3caire-Catholic-Toolkit.pdf

- Does withdrawing investments from this sector have a symbolic, prophetic impact, contributing towards redefining society's moral code?
- Does redirecting investments enable pragmatic and productive investments in essential clean energy development and job creation?"

We can see how these practices can and need to be applied in contexts where violence and conflict occur, both among peoples in relation to the environment and to the environment itself. Networks such as REPAM and REBAC in the Amazon and Africa are doing just that. In the Philippines for example, the Save Sierra Madre Network[220] brings together Indigenous communities and the Church for education, advocacy and prayer. In the United States, many Catholics and Catholic organisations have stood in solidarity at the Standing Rock Sioux protest site against the Dakota Access Pipeline, while others have joined the years-long protests against the Keystone XL pipeline. In his book *They Will Inherit the Earth*, John Dear gives an account of Standing Rock and many other examples of where ecology and peace intersect. Of Standing Rock and the witness that can be seen there he writes, "They call themselves 'protectors' not protestors, 'pray-ers' not disrupters, 'peacemakers' not troublemakers. It's that kind of creative nonviolence that has attracted the interest and sympathy of people around the country and the world."[221] Embracing a spirituality and world view grounded in this kind of active nonviolence towards creation, which we so often see in Original Peoples, is not incompatible with our Catholic tradition but rather deeply rooted in the gospel of nonviolence and communion.

Finally, we have only to observe nature's inherent balance and harmony as a model for peace among humans and with all of creation. For billions of years, life, death and rebirth in the earth's ecosystems were sustained in a healthy rhythm that honoured time, space and relationship. We cannot diminish the role of creation itself in reminding us to practise sufficiency, patience, sacrifice, service and solidarity.

---

220 Save Sierra Madre Network (https://savesierramadre.page.tl/)

221 John Dear, They Will Inherit the Earth, Orbis Books, 2018, 67-68.

Women, Faith and Nonviolent Action to Transform Violence[222]

Nonviolent action in today's world must be cognizant of and seek to transform explicit and more subtle forms of overt, cultural and structural violence against girls and women as a central component of its agenda for peace, so as to produce a culture affirming the dignity of all genders. Moreover, central leaders in nonviolent movements can and must be women of faith (and no faith). Indeed, many women of faith around the world already actively mobilise as *de facto* leaders of local, national and transnational nonviolent movements in ways that are impactful and transformative. These women bring particular priorities to nonviolent movements based on their experience. They use tactics that are often unique and that leverage their authority as women — as faith leaders, scholars, journalists, activists, survivors, mothers, sisters, daughters, social and political leaders, and so much more — to advance their nonviolent cause. In so doing, they stand on the shoulders of women from their historic faith traditions who similarly and creatively leveraged their relationships, resources and power to advocate nonviolently for the dignity of all and for a culture of peace.

Despite the multiple forms of violence targeting women and girls, they have mobilised powerfully and creatively in nonviolent action for the cause of peace. This includes both women who are mobilising as part of secular-oriented organisations and institutions, as well as women who ground their work in faith-inspired organisations and religious institutions. Women's efforts to organise and lead nonviolent movements have often not been fully acknowledged or appreciated by outside observers. Rather, the oft-heralded leaders of successful movements of nonviolent resistance have tended to be men: Gandhi, Martin Luther King, Jr, or Abdul Ghaffar Khan. But the reality is that critical nonviolent movements throughout history and throughout the world in the contemporary moment are being galvanised and led by women. This is not surprising, upon consideration. Given women's marginalisation from the spaces in which decisions about, and

---

222 "Following Her Lead" by Rev. Susan Hayward, U.S. Institute of Peace excerpts www.nonviolencejustpeace.net

leadership of, armed political movements are made, it makes a certain sense that women have tended to choose the avenue of unarmed resistance movements in order to address injustice and wage nonviolent conflict.

History provides many examples of women leading movements of creative nonviolent resistance to advance the cause of just peace, including that of Harriet Tubman in the United States who helped organise the escape of enslaved Africans. In the play *Lysistrata*, the ancient Greek playwright Aristophanes tells of a sex strike imposed by Athenian women in order to pressure men to bring about an end to war. This method has been used successfully by women throughout history, including by Iroquois women in 1600 or Liberian women led by Leymah Gbowee in 2003.[223] Women across the world have used creative processes of nonviolent resistance in their efforts to advance gender equality and reduce violence targeting girls and women. This can be seen in the myriad movements worldwide for women's right to vote throughout the 20th century, which often took the form of boycotts, street marches, hunger strikes and popular campaigns with transnational connections in places such as China, Turkey, Egypt and the United States.[224] In the First Intifada, Palestinian women played critical roles in organising committees and nonviolent actions in response to Israeli repression.[225] During the Arab Spring in 2011, women were central leaders of nonviolent movements against authoritarianism. Tawakkol Karman, known as the "Mother of the Yemeni Revolution", who won the 2011 Nobel Peace Prize alongside Leymah Gbowee, led the efforts in Yemen on behalf of not only women's rights, but the rights of all Yemenis oppressed by President Ali Abdullah Saleh. Noting the preponderance of women participating in resistance movements against his oppressive rule, President Saleh sought to mobilise opposition to them by religious and other leaders, arguing that their involvement in political activities in public went against cultural and religious

---

223 Codur and King, "Women in Civil Resistance" in Kurtz and Kurtz. Women, War and Violence.

224 Ibid.

225 Maria A. Principe, Women in Nonviolent Movements (2016), 6.

norms.[226] In Egypt, women such as Asmaa Mahfouz used the internet to organise and spark the nonviolent revolution centred on Tahrir Square.

Let us turn our focus in particular to religious women's leadership in nonviolent movements for just peace. One example from Colombia is the Ecumenical Women's Peacebuilding Network, comprising entirely women who are leaders in their churches and communities, and who do extraordinary work for peace on the front lines of violence: supporting victims, confronting armed actors to create zones of peace, facilitating hard reconciliation conversations in local communities — as combatants return home to communities they previously terrorised — advocating national peace processes (and advocating for more women to be included in the peace processes), insisting that the needs of victims and women be taken into account in the negotiations … and so much more. In Honduras, Catholic sisters and lay women joined forces with Indigenous leaders, women of other faiths and none and Afro-descendants in order to protest against the 2009 coup and the violence associated with it. In so doing, they sometimes defied their own (male) religious leadership.[227] The aforementioned Leymah Gbowee of Liberia mobilised women through Christian organisations, partnering with Muslim women's organisations and drawing on powerful religious and cultural practices — including song and prayer — to build a nonviolent movement that helped bring an end to a brutal civil war marked by extensive forms of violence targeting civilian women and girls.

Women's ability to mobilise powerful nonviolent movements can be attributed in part to the perception of them as less threatening, apolitical, or because they are less visible and so able to operate "under the radar" to access critical spaces and organise powerful resistance movements undetected and unchallenged until too late by those who might seek to disrupt their efforts. Security forces and other

---

226 Susan Hayward and Katherine Marshall, *Women, Religion, and Peacebuilding: Illuminating the Unseen* (2015), 73.

227 Ibid., chapter 11.

armed actors may be less inclined to respond violently to women activists at the front lines of resistance movements, given the kind of backlash it might spark and because they are seen as less dangerous than a group of men might appear, for social-psychological reasons.[228] Women will often use their invisibility and non-threatening status in subversive ways to their advantage in waging nonviolent conflict, documenting abuses and engaging in provocative acts of defiance against authoritarian leaders.[229]

Women's propensity to lead nonviolent movements should not necessarily be ascribed to some aspect of her essential nature. In fact, history and contemporary times provide us with examples of women's involvement in armed campaigns or in cajoling men into armed battle. However, women's social and political position and experiences are probably more determinative of their selection of these forms of action than is their biological nature.

Nonviolent movements seeking to create and sustain a just peace must be gender-aware and inclusive. They must take into account forms of violence that affect women and girls, seeing these as just as critical to address as the political forms of violence more often acknowledged, especially in wartime. They must acknowledge and support the critical leadership of women and incorporate women's priorities into their movements' objectives. Without so doing, they are unlikely to be successful. Moreover, without careful attention and conscious steps taken to this end, these nonviolent movements may unintentionally reinforce forms of violence — especially structural and cultural — that affect women and girls in particular.

But the need is more than a pragmatic one. It is a moral one, rooted in the call of the Christian tradition and the example of Jesus to affirm the dignity of women. More attention is needed from Christian theologians and ethicists to the ongoing

228 Codur and King, 434.

229 Maria A. Principe, *Women in Nonviolent Movements* (2016), 5.

and extraordinary problem of violence against women and girls, and of sexual violence (that affects women and girls in particularly pervasive ways, but also men and boys). As noted above, this problem has not been tackled adequately by the Christian tradition, despite the witness of Jesus, who confronted violence against women head on. Attention to violence against girls and women that is direct, structural and cultural must be named and addressed as sins that are personal, relational and social, causing harm to individuals, to relationships built on trust and mutual care, and by infecting societies with structures of dominance that destroy community. Only by doing this can a holistic transformation of these death-dealing forms of violence result. Nonviolent resistance remains the most effective and ethical means by which to transform these varieties of violence, and as demonstrated, women of faith have a great deal to offer in creating effective processes of nonviolent resistance.

PART IV: EMBRACING NONVIOLENCE

1. A New Moral Framework for Catholic Theology

Flowing from the Church's recommitment to the nonviolence of Jesus, this section suggests a new moral framework in response to the violence and injustice of our time – a moral framework of "active nonviolence and just peace".

The mission of the Church is to draw people to a loving relationship with God by illuminating God's way in the person of Jesus and inviting the community to live in the presence of the Holy Spirit. This calls the Church to be a sacrament of our ultimate unity as children of God and with all creation. In doing so, the Church reads the "signs of the times" (*Gaudium et Spes*, 4), situating its narrative in both time and space, recognising human evolution and the different contexts of an incarnated and inter-inculturated Church, and validating its unfolding tradition and teaching through the lived experience of the people.

Consistent with Vatican II's call to "undertake an evaluation of war with an entirely new attitude" (*Gaudium et Spes*, 80), the reflection that follows seeks to identify essential characteristics of a renewed moral framework for responding to the violence and injustice of our times – one that nurtures a worldview, a spirituality and a practice of nonviolence. This framework should help the institutional Catholic Church devote its considerable moral, ecclesial, structural, political and financial resources to end the practice of violent conflict and other forms of social or environmental violence, as part of the process of fostering nonviolence and shifting to an integral or just peace approach. We recognise that this framework must be capable of being expressed, understood and implemented flexibly in different cultures and contexts.

We hope to refocus the evangelising energy of the Church on nonviolence and just peace. We attempt to do so in a pastoral manner that listens to the experiences and voices of people on the ground in conflict situations, in multiple cultural and societal conflicts that may understand words and concepts differently, respecting and centring the unique voices of women and the experiences and wisdom of those on the margins, learning from them and creating a conversation which draws from the riches of all these sources. And we attempt to do so reflecting on the signs of the times.

Too often, the Church's rich teaching on peace and nonviolence is obscured by a reactive approach to particular conflicts in which "just war" is at the centre — and is often misused by the state to provide religious justification for military action or by religious leaders to support the state in military action, in other words to "justify" the need for violent action, rather than oppose or severely restrict resort to lethal force. Some argue that a Church teaching that is highly restrictive of "just war" compels one to find nonviolent alternatives to resolve conflicts. Others argue that a moral framework focused on whether violence is morally legitimate, even in a restricted form, has led to and will continue to lead to significant spiritual and material energy on war preparation and violence, rather than adequately investing in spiritual and material resources to transform violent conflict into integral peace. For example, Cardinal Peter Turkson said, "It [just war theory] can undermine efforts to develop alternative capacities and tools for conflict to be overcome and transformed."[230] There are additional issues and concerns raised with the just war ethic.[231]

---

230 Cardinal Turkson quoted in Christopher Lamb, "Pope urged to abolish creed of 'just war'," in Sunday Times, 24 April 2016. In addition, Bishop Robert McElroy stated that the Church must "recognize the increasing incapacity of the just war tradition to be an effective constraint on warfare in the modern age." Quoted in article by Joshua McElwee, "Pope Condemns Possession of Nuclear Weapons," National Catholic Reporter, 10 Nov. 2017.

231 For example, the just war ethic does little to help us and may even distract us from transforming conflict by

At the same time, even as it emphasises the urgent need to promote an ethic of nonviolence and just peace, this renewed moral framework draws insights from all Catholic ethical traditions related to peace and conflict.

Hopefully, the moral framework articulated here will provide an invitation to ongoing dialogue among those with a range of positions on traditional just war principles, especially by situating such dialogue and related moral discernment within a larger set of superseding and constant moral commitments and norms that make violence much less likely and strenuously promote the elimination of war. The core emphasis here is on expanding and reinforcing the growing importance of nonviolence and peacebuilding in Catholic teaching, including redoubling efforts to scale up nonviolent approaches for the prevention of violent conflict, protection of lives amid violent conflict and conflict transformation.

A renewed moral framework would enable the language of the institutional Church as a moral authority to be more consistent with the nonviolent creativity of the Gospel, while its programming, pedagogy – including the scriptural passages chosen for liturgies – and witness would better reflect Jesus's method of socially creative transforming initiatives that break vicious cycles of violence. In turn, a moral framework built on nonviolence and just peace would better illuminate the sacred dignity of all people and creation.

---

addressing the personal, relational, structural and cultural dimensions. It often enables the cultivation of the structural violence of massive preparations for war and the arms race, which also divert needed resources; as well as contributing to a cultural violence to support or limit resistance to such preparations for a possible "just war". Further, even when wars may appear "just" this ethic often gets us stuck in vicious cycles of violence. This ethic has failed to adequately form us as peacemakers. For example, we spend little if any time trying to imagine how to humanise or illuminate the dignity of our enemies. By signalling war may be just, this ethic can obstruct the movement towards outlawing war. This ethic does little to help us build sustainable peace. "Just war" is also of little resemblance if not directly contradictory to Jesus's call to love the way he loved us, and thus can distract or even obstruct missionary discipleship. For some of these points, see Gerald Schlabach, "Just War? Enough Already," in Commonweal, 31 May 2017, and "Letters: More Just War," in Commonweal, 20 Sept. 2017. Also see Eli McCarthy, "The Gospels Draw us Further: A Just Peace Ethic," in Ethics in Focus, 2018, 80-102, https://expositions.journals. villanova.edu/article/view/2322/2227; "Just Peace Ethic and Gospel Nonviolence" at "The Catholic Church Moves Toward Nonviolence? Just Peace and Just War in Dialogue" conference with military representatives at the University of San Diego, 6-7 Oct. 2017, pp. 5-6, http://www.sandiego.edu/cctc/events/past-events/just-peace-just-war.php.

Renewing the Narrative for an Ethic of Nonviolence and Just Peace

Our goal is a just peace, consisting in political co-operation for the common good, respect for the dignity of all persons and the natural world, pre-empting violence before it begins and the transformation of violent conflict by nonviolent approaches.

Based on a strong commitment to peace and a realistic understanding of the nature of war, we propose an ethic of nonviolence and just peace that includes a set of contextually relevant practices for preventing destructive conflict and violence, protecting vulnerable people and promoting sustainable peace founded on equal dignity, respect for life and nature, universal human rights, economic justice and a culture of peace and reconciliation. A narrative of nonviolence and just peace does not negate the reality of past narratives but rather reads the signs of the times and advances Catholic teaching. The movement from just war to nonviolence and just peace is not a rejection of the intent of earlier teachings, but a recognition that we have advanced to a stage where we can see that nonviolent approaches are better able to achieve just peace. The Church recognises that knowledge grows and evolves. Tools and technology have developed to an extent that no war could be considered "just". A new narrative is essential, even as we learn from the past.

This renewed narrative promotes a just and sustainable peace, and is based on a contemporary appropriation of Jesus's ministry, embodied in a community of self-emptying love, tender-heartedness, that takes action for those in distress and restores right relationships, love, mercy and forgiveness. This transforms conflict and excludes violence, yet not only permits but demands active nonviolent resistance to injustice. Called to be the sacrament of salvation and human unity (*Lumen Gentium*, 1; *Gaudium et Spes*, 45), the Church fulfils that calling when it faithfully lives as just such a community. Nonviolence is both a way of life and a set of actions. This commitment to nonviolent love is expressed by Pope Francis when he says, "May charity and nonviolence govern how we treat each other as individuals, within society and in international life," as well as "To be true followers of Jesus today also includes embracing his teaching about nonviolence" (World Day of Peace message, 2017).

We affirm and call for a return to the practice of active nonviolence at the heart of the Catholic Church, in order to align the institutional Church with the worldwide effort by the People of God to end all forms of violence — armed, direct, structural, cultural, ecological — and war as a human institution, and together to generate effective nonviolent practices that serve both as alternatives to lethal force and build integral peace. We commit to becoming more nonviolent ourselves and to using nonviolent approaches for responding to injustice, developing societies and transforming conflict. As John Paul II proclaimed at Drogheda, Ireland in 1979, "Violence destroys what it claims to defend: the dignity, the life, the freedom of human beings. Violence is a crime against humanity, for it destroys the very fabric of society" (No. 9). This is why, in his 2017 World Day of Peace message, Pope Francis called for nonviolence as "a style of politics for peace".

Positive and active peace

The just peace we seek is a positive and active peace, which Jesus Christ, the Prince and Author of Peace, taught and practised. "Peace I bequeath to you, my own peace I give you, a peace which the world cannot give." (John 14:27). Peace is not the absence of conflict but the presence of creative processes by which human communities become ever more skilful and habituated at working through their conflicts without recourse to violence and without demeaning one another's dignity. Christians, who by their baptism follow Christ as disciples, are called to be — and are blessed when they are — peacemakers, for this is a constitutive part of being "called children of God" (Matthew 5:9). For we are called "not to return evil for evil, or insult for insult, but instead to give blessing" (1 Peter 3:19). Just peace is not merely the absence of destructive conflict, violence and war. Nor is it achieved through passive withdrawal or abdication of moral responsibility.

The Sermon on the Mount grounds and guides the Church's public engagement on the difficult path to peace in a troubled world, as Pope Francis has affirmed by calling it the Church's "manual" for peacemaking at every level of human society (World Day of Peace, 2017). While affirming the people's *traditional righteousness* as far as it went, Jesus consistently diagnosed the vicious cycles of violence from which it could not free them and which it too often perpetuated, and thus Jesus graciously offered *transforming initiatives* to empower the people to take creative nonviolent risks to strengthen human solidarity.

Nonviolence is not only the (negative) refusal to do harm. It is (positive) reverence for life anchored in the absolute, innate dignity of every human person and all creation. It is more than the absence of violence; it is the interjection of a transformative force into circumstances of violence. It is the power of love in action, the path to fuller truth, a spirituality, a distinct virtue, a way of life, an effective methodology for challenging all forms of direct, structural and cultural violence, as well as for protecting all people and the earth. It is a set of tools, methods and norms for preventing violence, actively making peace and advancing post-conflict reconciliation, reconstruction and sustainable peace. This more adequate and fuller understanding of nonviolence goes beyond pacifism — which rather than being understood as a vibrant ethic for peace is often misused by states and individuals to abdicate responsibility to the vulnerable, or by the religious to preserve individual piety, or more crudely adhered to as a lifeless rule — by challenging us to become more human as individuals and societies in engaging conflict. A more robust understanding of nonviolence helps us steer clear of a simplistic "rule against violence" by challenging us to become more human, to "become the children of God" (John 1:12).

Transforming Initiatives and Sustaining Integral Peace

Recognising the interconnected roots of violence, social and economic injustice, poverty and ecological destruction, as well as the critical need for systemic and structural transformation, Catholic social teaching describes a nonviolent way of life that leads to a renewable, sustainable dynamic of just peace — *integral peace*. Following the example of Jesus, the Catholic Church is well placed to promote the understanding and development of effective nonviolent approaches — *transforming initiatives* — for preventing violence, protecting vulnerable people and promoting cultures of just peace. Pope Francis's insistence that "time is greater than space" and that "unity prevails over conflict" implies that we should take time to imagine the best possible ways to transform a given conflict oriented by, and consistent with, a just peace. As Christians, we also recognise the eternal aspect of time. This helps clarify the role of the Church. It also helps determine our action choices and how we measure both the fruit and costs of action.

Given the reality of violence, including extreme violence, the Catholic Church calls the global community to an immediate and long-term commitment to *sustaining* peace — to applying on a consistent basis in every country the lessons we have learned about what makes for enduring peace. This includes preventative measures that address the root causes of conflict, support for those who challenge injustices nonviolently and active approaches for de-escalating destructive conflict, cultivating reconciliation, transforming patterns of perception and behaviour and cultivating conversion.

The Catholic Church's Approach to Difficult Ethical Decisions

We recognise that moral ambiguities and difficult compromises will be involved as we attempt to address complex, violent, sinful situations, and that there may not be a single template which covers all eventualities. We are challenged to consider a kind of realism without militarism based on Pope Francis's insistence that realities are more important than ideas. While differences exist about how best to promote flourishing human communities as part of a well-ordered creation and defend them against violence, we have a common commitment to significantly scaling-up nonviolent practices, institutions and cultures, as well as a recognition that the Church can make a significant contribution to those ends.

In approaching ethical decisions on conflict, war and peace, the Church would:

- *humbly recognise its own complicity in a violent world*, seeking forgiveness for its participation in Crusade and Conquest, for the Doctrine of Discovery, for the institutionalised violence of patriarchy, the marginalisation of women, frequent indifference to domestic and gender-based violence, the violence of sexual abuse and its cover-up and for failing too often to denounce repression and militarism, direct and institutionalised violence.

- *accompany persons who are poor, powerless and marginalised*, protecting and acting in solidarity with the most vulnerable communities and transforming the unjust institutions which make them vulnerable into just institutions recognising their dignity. Accompaniment must be a two-way process, not a dynamic of the "privileged/developed" accompanying the "under-privileged/under-developed".

- *employ diplomatic power and legislative influence* to provide an ethical framework to engage governments or world powers; suggesting procedures for limiting and ending war and violence at whatever level; encouraging just, integral peace and nonviolence; and discouraging war as a tool of statecraft in favour of effective nonviolent alternatives.

- *be pastoral*, not letting a concern with abstract moral principles alone obscure the fundamental importance of witness; questioning and naming unjust or violent public policies and practices without condemning persons; recognising that active nonviolence, ranging from skilful dialogue to nonviolent civil resistance and just peace practices, offers powerful alternatives to violence, increasingly realisable and consistent with the Gospel.

- *offer normative guidelines* for transforming conflict; preventing war and other expressions of violence; and defusing existing violence — guidelines crucial to the moral framework we are attempting to articulate. In addition, a renewed moral framework should include norms that would seek to reduce or outlaw the production and distribution of weapons, weapon systems and ammunition and shift investments to nonviolent approaches and technologies.

We call on the whole Church to share this focus and energy, to no longer speak of wars as "just", and to dedicate resources anew to creative, nonviolent approaches to transforming conflict; preventing or stopping many types of violence in our world; and promoting cultures of just peace.

A moral framework for nonviolence and just peace

The focus of this renewed moral framework should be on the potential for a given strategy to be conducive to building just and sustainable peace. Thus, in adopting a just peace moral framework inspired by the virtues and transformative practices in the Gospels, the Church could promote moral guidelines for public action that extend Catholic social teaching and its vision of human thriving through reconciling relationship. The Church could draw on the growing body of knowledge about what actually makes for just and integral peace; on the rich diversity of nonviolence and just peace experiences found in different cultures and societies; and on norms that Catholic thinkers and diplomats have helped to embed into international human rights and humanitarian law.

A just peace moral framework will in many ways recapitulate Catholic social teaching as a whole, while emphasising active, intentional, nonviolent approaches, which include, but are not limited to, both nonviolent civil resistance and peacebuilding. As such it will inevitably be more expansive than either pacifism or the just war tradition, the two major traditions of Christian discernment that have sought to resist and restrict war and violence through many centuries.

Moral philosophers and theologians note that negative moral norms are easier to delineate with precision than positive moral norms, because they mark the outer boundaries of what a community may permit. Both pacifism and the just war tradition, each in its own way, mostly name negative norms and thus, as delimiting ethics, can summarise their criteria succinctly. In contrast, positive norms are virtually infinite and thus require generalisation, for they guide and point to all the activities by which all members of the human community build healthy lives and relationships, according to their concept of the good. While including negative norms, in order to rule out acts that always undermine human thriving, a just peace framework will place far more emphasis on positive norms, which require countless positive actions to create the conditions for peace.

Although a just peace framework is necessarily expansive, wide reflection by Christians about the social conditions and priority practices that nurture just, integral peace — informed by findings from the maturing fields of peace studies and peacebuilding — yields an emerging set of patterns amenable to summary.

In continuity with Jesus's teaching of transforming initiatives in the Sermon on the Mount, we propose three categories of just peace norms for: (1) preparing for and working through the inevitable conflicts in human societies (*jus in conflictione*); (2) abandoning vicious cycles of violence (*jus ex bello*); and (3) building sustainable peace (*jus ad pacem*). Threading through and uniting all three categories is a set of assumptions that strengthen each other like a braid:

- Just, integral peace expects human beings to thrive when ends and means are closely integrated, such that the means chosen in the pursuit of ends are consonant with or reflect those ends (the "principle of reflexivity"). The very term "just peace" responds to this principle: a social order will be truly peaceful only to the degree that it is just; the pursuit of justice will sow new seeds of injustice unless done through peaceful means.

- Achieving a just, integral, sustaining peace requires constant attention to the root causes of violent discord and to the social conditions that make for peace. Insofar as a nonviolence and just peace framework addresses the root causes of war and social injustice, while recognising the interconnectivity of all creatures (as Pope Francis emphasises) and "attending to the requirements of relationship" (as Cardinal Turkson has defined justice), it is simply being realistic in rejecting simplistic solutions that make violence deceptively tempting. Chief among the root causes of violence in the modern world are the pathologies of poverty, inequality, oppression, domination, environmental degradation, alienation and marginalisation, often facilitated through power structures shaped by cultures of patriarchy and the dehumanisation of marginal groups.

• While the category of *jus ex bello* names explicit approaches for escaping vicious cycles, all just peace practices benefit from diagnosing these cycles, and can be understood as transforming initiatives. They are transformative precisely because they resist the temptation to counter the root causes of injustice through incongruent means, and instead seek to "overcome evil through good" (Rom. 12:21).

• A powerful contribution of these norms is that they apply at all stages of conflict. The categories can also overlap in time and space.[232]

Among the many positive human actions that constitute "the things that make for peace" (Luke 19:42), a "nonviolence and just peace moral framework" will insist that the following practices are morally normative. In other words, while a diversity of gifts, talents and vocations may lead different people to prioritise their own practices and approaches of action according to their differing historical contexts, they should choose actions that consistently enhance and never obstruct the moral norms that these embody.[233]

---

232 "El todo es superior a las partes. La unidad es superior al conflicto. El tiempo es superior al espacio. La realidad es superior a las ideas." Pope Francis has identified this formula as a guide for building social peace (Lumen Fidei, 57; Evangelii Gaudium, 222, 223; Laudato Si', 178).

233 See: Just Peace ethic handout, created for April 2019 "Path of nonviolence, towards a culture of peace" workshop, https://nonviolencejustpeace.net/resources/#justpeace

Jus in conflictione

1. Jus in conflictione *(preparing for and working through the inevitable conflicts in human societies):* As believers, citizens and communities, develop the virtues and skill sets to be able to transform conflict and work for integral peace:

- Nurture spiritual practices of prayer, contemplation, study of nonviolence and Eucharistic participation to sustain nonviolence as a spirituality and way of life.

- Cultivate virtuous dispositions and habits of mercy, compassion, empathy, forgiveness, humility, hospitality, solidarity, courage, transparency, integrity, truth-telling, justice and nonviolent peacemaking.

- Control rumours as an antidote to fear and to the lies of violence and war.

- Develop participatory processes for discernment and decision-making at every level, from family to community to social movements and institutions to body politic, giving particular attention to those most affected by violence and in need of empowerment, such as women, youth, those with special physical needs and minorities.

- Deepen skills in social analysis of the root causes of violence. Re-conceptualise "strength" and "security" to decouple them from armed or military strength.

- Begin developing personal and communal understanding and skill sets for nonviolent action and conflict transformation as vocational priorities long before destructive conflict is immediate or acute.

- Build nonviolent peacemaking communities, institutions and cultures of just peace.

Note that these norms preserve and deepen the traditional criterion of right intention associated with the just war tradition, by requiring deliberate formation of habituated intention and the skill sets needed to carry out right intention effectively.

Jus ex bello

2. Jus ex bello *(escaping vicious cycles of violence)*: With courage and creativity, seek every opportunity to practise transforming initiatives that break cycles of destructive conflict or violence, through approaches that "overcome evil with good" by aligning means with ends:

- Prioritise local nonviolent approaches that already exist and are rooted in local cultures, and work within local contexts with humility and respect for these practices.

- Engage in skilful dialogue, diplomacy, mediation and negotiation.

- Utilise nonviolent direct action, especially civil resistance, protecting vulnerable communities through unarmed civilian protection and early warning systems; and work to expand nonviolent civilian-based defence to national and international levels.

- Use methods of conflict transformation to address both immediate and root causes of destructive violence, confronting and engaging with adversaries and drawing them towards partnership.

- Take independent initiatives that cultivate trust by doing first what one wishes one's adversaries would do, step by step.

- Acknowledge responsibility for harms and injustices committed by one's own side, and courageously ask for forgiveness.

- Re-humanise rhetoric and narratives about all whom violence has de-humanised, either as victims or perpetrators of violence.

- Encourage processes of integral disarmament to reduce the fuel of weapons and the arms trade that make violent conflicts easier to start and harder to stop.

- Institute trauma awareness and restorative justice processes, such as truth and reconciliation, the healing of memories and transitional justice, that allow societies to confront historic wrongs and break cycles of violence while requiring accountability, reparation and redress for victims in situations of historical and systematic human rights violations that normal judicial processes cannot handle.

Note that these norms continue to draw upon and transform traditional criteria associated with the just-war tradition, by requiring just-peace practitioners to determine appropriate approaches and calibrate their campaigns. The practitioners do this by ensuring but going beyond noncombatant (i.e. bystander) immunity, proportionality and probability of success, seeking to defend human dignity and restore, build and sustain healthy relationships.

Jus ad pacem

3. Jus ad pacem *(building sustainable peace)*: Steadfastly commit to the long-term, ongoing work of sustaining peace, which the United Nations defines as "activities aimed at preventing the outbreak, escalation, continuation and recurrence of conflict, addressing root causes, assisting parties to conflict to end hostilities, ensuring national reconciliation, and moving towards recovery, reconstruction, and development" (Security Council Resolution 2282, April 2016):

- Address the root causes of violence by recognising institutional and systemic forms of violence, which are often hidden, and seeking to transform them.

- Promote relationality, gender justice and reconciliation that includes theological understanding of reconciliation, but also has themes of justice, truth, forgiveness and repentance.

- Strengthen inclusive political participation and a robust civil society.

- Promote environmental sustainability and ecological justice.

- Foster respect for the human dignity and rights of all, including adversaries.

- Cultivate cultures that celebrate, respect, accept and appreciate the rich diversity of our world's cultures.

- Promote just and sustainable economies, with a focus on eliminating poverty, ensuring racial justice, reducing inequality and serving marginalised people.

- Support just and effective governance based on the just rule of law at international, national and subnational levels.

Note that these norms underscore and transform the traditional criteria of just cause and right intention concerning ends, while focusing the criteria of proportionality and legitimate authority on the institutions, cultures and relationships that sustain the long-term well-being of all people within environmentally healthy ecosystems. They also embody the goals of the newer *jus post bellum* category in just war theory.

As the institutional Church and the people of God, we are especially called to accompany those who are subject to direct or structural violence and to search with them for effective nonviolent methods of defence, end the violence, address root causes of violent conflict and build a just, sustainable peace. The work of trauma-awareness and healing, restorative justice, reconciliation, and the long-term task of sustaining peace, after all, are intrinsic to the identity of the Church as a "field hospital" and "sacrament of human salvation". The virtues, policies and practices above are the very ones that research on armed conflict shows are associated with dramatic reductions in the instance of warfare. Central to a new moral framework is working to spread, deepen and institutionalise these virtues, policies and practices until the Church's vision of a world without war becomes a reality.

We invite the institutional Church to consider the norms of this renewed moral framework as serving the purposes identified in Pope Francis's 2017 World Day of Peace message.

"Peacebuilding through active nonviolence is the natural and necessary complement to the Church's continuing efforts to limit the use of force by the application of moral norms; she does so by her participation in the work of international institutions and through the competent contribution made by so many Christians to the drafting of legislation at all levels. Jesus himself offers a 'manual' for this strategy of peacemaking in the Sermon on the Mount" (Pope Francis, 2017 World Day of Peace message).

While this vision and commitment to ending war itself should become a more central focus, the reality of armed conflicts that still exist, especially in those areas of the world with chronic cycles of war, challenges the Church to ask difficult questions.

Just and Effective Governance: Embedding Norms of Nonviolence

A new moral framework working toward just, sustainable, integral peace in a world "freed from the age-old slavery of war" (*Gaudium et Spes*, 81) incorporates

Catholic social teaching's long-standing commitment to more just and effective governance. A key part of building peace is building just political, social and economic institutions – ones embedding norms of nonviolence, equity, dignity and participation – at the international, national and local levels. Such institutions are better able to end existing violence or armed conflicts and avoid relapses, as well as to address the underlying causes of direct violence and new wars– preventing them from starting in the first place, and creating conditions within and among countries where violence and war become increasingly inconceivable.

At the international level, this requires strengthening and deepening an overlapping web of intergovernmental organisations, non-governmental organisations, treaty regimes, ecumenical and interfaith bodies and civil society groups. Such institutions are able to cultivate interdependence and co-operation, norms against war, alternative dispute resolution mechanisms and sustained diplomacy. Their influence helps build the greater global governance the Church consistently calls for, and they have proven successful in mediating existing armed conflicts and helping administer post-conflict agreements that create an enduring peace.

International actors can also help support local women and men in working for just and effective institutional governance at the national and local levels. Nonviolent movements to "replace corrupt, dictatorial and authoritarian forms of government by democratic and participatory ones" are crucial (John Paul II, *Sollicitudo rei Socialis*, 44) and multiple studies have shown that civil resistance is a key driver of democratisation. Just governance includes responsive, accountable and fair public officials and political institutions that uphold the rule of law, provide space for a vibrant, multi-cultural civil society and protect basic human rights, especially for women, girls and those with special needs. Sustainable and equitable economic development, along with preventing corruption and ending the influence of powerful special interests who benefit from violence and war, can also contribute to dramatic decreases in the risk of violence and war.

This new moral framework, rooted in the experience of those who have lived in contexts of war, destructive conflict and violence, and reinforced by evidence of effective nonviolent alternatives, highlights the moral responsibility of the institutional Church and its members to end war and other forms of violence, transform conflicts and promote nonviolent approaches for ending oppression and addressing direct and structural violence. The Catholic Church as an institution should encourage its followers to develop and promote strong, effective nonviolent alternatives to military force to protect vulnerable people, enhance inclusive security and promote integral and inclusive peace. To be authentic and have any credibility, the Church must also confront its own contributions to violence.

As a witness to the in-breaking reign of God, the Church is called to urge humanity towards a reality — a just, sustaining peace — that enables the transformation and flourishing of each person and the whole earth community. Stirring the creative imagination of a human community that is mired in repeating cycles of violence with profoundly destructive consequences, the Church must become a community defined by its lived commitment to nonviolent means of transforming the social order in the light of the Gospel. "I pray that the image and likeness of God in each person will enable us to acknowledge one another as sacred gifts endowed with immense dignity. Especially in situations of conflict, let us respect this, our 'deepest dignity,' and make active nonviolence our way of life" (Pope Francis, World Day of Peace, 2017).

2. A New Moral Framework Applied

The following brief case studies applying the new moral just peace framework to immigration at the US/Mexico border, gang violence in El Salvador, civil war in South Sudan, the civil war in Syria and ISIS in Iraq.

Migration: US/Mexico border [234]

The phenomenon of immigration to and in the US is fundamentally marked by direct and institutionalised violence. In turn, a framework of just peace provides a more capacious approach for the Church's discernment of its responsibility to accompany and protect people whose life is threatened by deportation. Through a close look at the socio-historical context, the just peace ethic begins by seeing clearly the root causes such as direct violence, social instability and political repression.

The just-peace-ethic category of virtues and skills to engage conflict constructively suggests the importance of cultivating the virtue of active nonviolence and the spiritual discipline of discernment about the possibility of the Church offering sanctuary. Such ecclesial discernment calls forth the just peace norm of participatory processes. With the just peace category of breaking cycles of violence, we can see that sanctuary is a form of nonviolent direct action and unarmed civilian protection. There is a need for civil initiative, i.e. the actualisation of the just peace norm of enhancing a robust civil society, and the Church ought to play this transformative role. Such a commitment will also call forth virtues of solidarity, hospitality and courage.

These norms have a greater chance of becoming an integral part of our ecclesial imaginary and discourse because of the way in which a just peace ethic merges them with the Christian tradition. As long as violence in Central America continues to threaten the lives and humanity of people there, they will continue to seek life outside their countries, even in "unauthorised" ways. Those that flee to the United States and successfully enter, present the Church with a responsibility to protect that entails risking our security for theirs in order to resist the legalised violence of our government. Envisioning and practising "Church as sanctuary" is an initiative that begins to form and transform a people — the Church — into a people of nonviolence and peace.

---

234 Excerpt from Leo Guardado's "Just Peace, Just Sanctuary: Immigration and Ecclesial Nonviolence," in *Just Peace Ethic Primer: Building Sustainable Peace and Breaking Cycles of Violence*, (Georgetown University Press, 2020).

Gang violence: El Salvador [235]

Although the Salvadoran civil war officially ended in 1992, violent deaths have become part of the ordinary post-conflict landscape. Indeed, based on the number of homicides, there have been more deaths in the post-war period than in the 12 years of civil strife.[236] Most of the deaths have been attributed to gang members; however, although it looks straightforward, the numbers hide the complexity of gang violence in the country and the state's preference for repressive responses. Such repression helps strengthen gang structures and operations, as well as increase levels of violence and create cycles of violence and retaliation. Root causes also include the increasing economic inequity, drug/arms trafficking and state corruption.

The just peace norms of participatory processes, sustainability and economic justice would orient us to new mechanisms of sustainable, inclusive social and economic development to stop vicious circles of poverty and violence. For instance, such mechanisms would include vocational training and accompaniment of young people returned to the country via deportation. With the norms of nonviolent skill training and conflict transformation, this ethic draws us towards more violence prevention skills, unarmed protection and trauma-healing. We see some examples of this through Catholic Relief Services programmes such as YouthBuild, or the Cure Violence programme, such as hiring unarmed credible messengers to function as violence interrupters.

This ethic can challenge the repressive state approach by shifting more toward restorative justice mechanisms and the re-humanisation of gang members through the language and representations within the social imaginary. Dialogue must always be on the table as a possibility in this multi-pronged approach, otherwise

---

235 Excerpt from José Henríquez Leiva's "Envisioning a Just Peace approach to address gang violence in El Salvador" in *Just Peace Ethic Primer: Building Sustainable Peace and Breaking Cycles of Violence*, (Georgetown University Press, 2020).

236 According to the International Crisis Group (ICG), there were 93,000 murders between 1993-2016, while civil war deaths were 75,000. See ICG (2017), El Salvador's Politics of Perpetual Violence, Latin America Report N° 64, p. 1.

violence becomes entrenched. The norms of acknowledging responsibility for harm and just governance, which respects human rights and robust civil society, are also key in this context. They would enable the society to move in a more constructive direction along the path of reconciliation.

Civil war: South Sudan[237]

After 22 years of civil war in Sudan, the 2005 agreement suggested a brighter future. However, once South Sudan was created in 2011, the habits of violence re-ignited shortly thereafter into another civil war. Following a common pattern found in other cultures, the apparent "just war" for independence perpetuated conditions and habits for ongoing violence.[238]

The just-peace-ethic category of breaking cycles of violence is particularly helpful in such situations. Within this category is the norm of nonviolent direct action, particularly the key practice of unarmed civilian protection (UCP). It calls us to scale up this present practice in South Sudan, such as embodied by the Nonviolent Peaceforce. They are invited by and live in the struggling communities, and also hire both locals and internationals. They have prevented sexual assault and rape by accompanying women on long walks to get firewood or water. They have accompanied and convened dialogues with local chiefs afraid to cross certain territories. They directly saved fourteen women and children during an armed militia attack at a UN compound by refusing to leave them and concede to the demands of the armed militia. They help local communities set up early warning/response systems. They provide protection to humanitarian aid organisations trying to get into dangerous rural areas. They train local people to

---

237 Excerpt from John Ashworth and Mel Duncan's "Reflecting with a Just Peace Ethic in South Sudan" in *Just Peace Ethic Primer: Building Sustainable Peace and Breaking Cycles of Violence*, (Georgetown University Press, 2020).

238 Many of the characteristics of a violent liberation struggle - centralised authority, hierarchy, lack of democracy, secrecy, lack of transparency, rigid structures and chains of commands, subjugation of everyone and everything to the cause, intolerance of dissent, militarisation of society and of course violence itself - may be perceived as essential to the success of the struggle, but are in direct counterpoint to the needs of the post-struggle community. Successful violent struggle by its very nature often contains the seeds of its ultimate failure in terms of building a post-struggle society.

become UCPs and have developed 44 South Sudanese women peace teams, who engage in protection of civilians as well as direct advocacy towards local armed groups.

The just-peace norm of re-humanisation is also actualised by this practice, since Nonviolent Peaceforce sets up lines of communication with all actors involved. Further, they cultivate key virtues for the community to engage conflict more constructively, which is the first category of just-peace norms. These include empathy, humility, active nonviolence, solidarity, hospitality, justice and courage. The Catholic Church has been engaging in some forms of accompaniment and building relationships across divides, as illustrated by Bishop Taban's Peace Village. To help amplify and scale up these practices, a just-peace ethic offers norms such as cultivating peacemaking communities, a more robust civil society, economic justice, relationality, reflexivity (ensuring means consistent with ends), integral disarmament, acknowledging responsibility for harm and conflict transformation, which includes the practice of identifying human needs along with trauma-healing.

Civil and proxy war: Syria and Iraq[239]

Considering the circumstances in 2016, a just-peace approach would clarify the root causes of the conflict and might suggest some of the following transformative initiatives to break the cycles of violence. Being attentive to the virtue of active nonviolence, which calls us to humanise all parties, we would exercise humanising rhetoric towards all and reduce cultural marginalisation in order to defuse the violence and see more clearly the path towards just peace. In accord with the norm of participatory processes, we would focus on inclusive diplomacy which attempts to include all, not just some key stakeholders, both armed and unarmed, both elite and civil society.

---

239 Eli McCarthy, "A Virtue-Based Just Peace Ethic," in Journal of Moral Theology, v.7 no.2 (2018). See earlier articulations "Religious Leaders Urge a JustPeace Response to ISIS" in Huffington Post, Sept. 19, 2014.

We would increase funding for peacebuilding, such as building up local, nonviolent civil society organisations, particularly led by women, and offer creative forms of trauma-healing and nonviolent civil resistance. For example, Jesuit Refugee Services offers trauma-healing, which prevents young men from joining the civil war.[240] Trauma-healing is not just vital for youth, but especially for those who influence people in political negotiations or those directly involved in such negotiations, as well as armed actors. Examples of nonviolent resistance against ISIS include: Muslim leaders encircled a sacred site in Mosul which prevented ISIS from destroying it; a Muslim woman marched to ISIS headquarters thirty straight days demanding release of political prisoners as they put a gun to her head and spat on her, yet many joined her and they got some prisoners released in Raqqa; local businesses went on strike in Aleppo, slowed down the operations of ISIS and got electricity restored.[241] In Mosul, over 80 percent of residents participated in some form of nonviolent resistance, such as refusing to pay taxes, withdrawing from ISIS schools, not following their legal institutions, dragging their feet while working.[242]

Economic pressure would be applied on all armed actors fuelling the flames of war, such as those buying oil from ISIS. Rather than ad hoc attempts, a co-ordinated strategy would be developed for using credible messengers to entice defections from armed groups such as ISIS.[243] Further, the integral disarmament norm would orient us more to promoting a significant reduction in the flow of arms. It is notable that 92 percent of civilians in Syria who lived in ISIS territory opposed the U.S.-led bombing and 56 percent opposed it in

240 Jesuit Refugee Services, "Syria: Finding Community at the Alberto Hurtado Centre," en.jrs.net/campaign_detail?T-N=PROJECT-20170317103615.

241 Maria Stephan, "Resisting ISIS," Sojourners, sojo.net/magazine/april-2015/resisting-isis and Alia Braley, "This Talk is Not About ISIS," TEDxTV, www.tedxtv.blogspot.com/2017/04/this-talk-is-not-about-isis-alia-braley.html.

242 "How Ordinary Iraqis Resisted the Islamic State" in Washington Post, March 22, 2019.

243 Srdja Popovic and Raphael Mimoun, "How to Beat the Islamic State through Nonviolence", Foreign Policy, foreignpolicy.com/2016/03/14/how-to-beat-the-islamic-state-through-non-violence/.

244 Paul Shinkman, "Poll: Syrians, Iraqis Believe U.S. Created ISIS, Don't Support War", U.S. News and World Report, www.usnews.com/news/articles/2015-12-18/poll-majority-of-syrians-iraqis-dont-support-obamas-anti-isis-war-believe-us-created-extremists.

Iraq.[244] Reportedly, the U.S. killed at least 9,000 civilians in the "liberation" bombing of Mosul.[245] The norm of just governance would focus us on ensuring human rights, a robust civil society and accountability through restorative justice mechanisms.

The issue of policing

In affirming the role of just governance in creating the conditions of peace, a Catholic moral framework in turn recognises the human needs that just law enforcement or policing mechanisms with their best intentions seek to meet. In other words, it recognises the just exercise of those enforcement mechanisms that any community needs in order to protect all life, especially the vulnerable, ensure accountability for inhumane behaviour and facilitate the just rule of shared community guidelines or law. At the same time, the Church must recognise the reality that in too many communities around the world, the concepts of "law" and "police" are met with deep suspicion, as they are seen merely as part of the apparatus of oppression, brutality, corruption, injustice and gender violence. The word "policing" conjures fear, and it would take a lot of convincing that just policing can be a positive aspiration.

As Catholics reflect the need to protect all life, we might envision healthy protection mechanisms through the lens of the Eucharist. The Eucharist is God's expression through Jesus of nonviolent love, risking and offering life for others without killing. Jesus risks his life to save and protect us from the ultimate death of being disconnected from God. When we participate in the Eucharist, we are empowered and called to embody this kind of risking of life for others. This represents Jesus's saving work to the world and thus draws us all further into the way of salvation, which is authentic protection of our lives and illumination of our sacred dignity. "In the silence of the Cross, the uproar

---

245 Associated Press, "Freedom from IS in Mosul Costs Lives of 9,000 Plus Civilians", The Washington Post, www.wtop.com/middle-east/2017/12/9000-plus-dead-in-mosul-cost-to-oust-islamic-state-group/.

of weapons ceases and the language of reconciliation, forgiveness, dialogue and peace is spoken. "[246] With this emphasis on such risking of life, the primary orientation for any law enforcement mechanism becomes to save every life.

In this context, we recognise, value and support the scaling-up of both existing and emerging models of alternative policing, such as the use of mostly unarmed policing units in some countries (e.g. Britain, Norway, Ireland, New Zealand, Iceland and most of the Pacific Island nations). These unarmed policing units build trust, empower the community and reduce crime - in part because of their increased willingness to actively risk their lives to save others.

Unarmed civilian protection (UCP) initiatives have protected people and saved lives in war zones and large-scale conflicts. UCP has been practised by organisations such as the Nonviolent Peaceforce in areas of violent conflict around the world including South Sudan, the Philippines, Kurdistan, Palestine, Kenya, Colombia and the United States. Another form of UCP is the age-old Church practice of "sanctuary"; in South Sudan, tens of thousands of people have sought protection in Church compounds. Multiple independent evaluations have shown that these unarmed approaches build better trust with all stakeholders; enable nonviolent resistance capacity; cause local people to feel safer and more secure; significantly reduce shootings and killings; build sustainable peace; increase participation and local ownership in peace processes; and improve relationships between armed actors. Multiple high-level documents at the United Nations have called for scaling up these unarmed protection approaches.

Another effective unarmed civilian protection mechanism for local communities uses a public health approach, which recognises that violence or killing mimics a contagious disease. It clusters and is transmitted through observation, experience and trauma. Thus "credible messengers" who enjoy

---

246 Pope Francis, Vigil of Prayer for Peace, no. 3 (7 September 2013)
    http://w2.vatican.va/content/francesco/en/homilies/2013/documents/papa-francesco_20130907_veglia-pace.html

trust in the community are deployed to interrupt the transmission, in order to prevent such violence and its contagion. The approach also creates initiatives to change local cultural norms which legitimate violence. Research has shown this public health approach to reduce shootings and homicides on average from 40-75 percent. The neighbourhoods they work in Honduras have shown 88 percent reductions.

Traditionally, many communities have had ways to maintain order – elders, women, clan members, age sets, spiritual leaders – but these mechanisms have now largely been eroded except in very traditional areas (e.g. South Sudan, Swaziland, and among some pastoralist and semi-nomadic peoples). Modern developments of these informal or semi-formal approaches emphasise the community taking responsibility and include *Nyumba kumi* ("10 households") in Tanzania and Kenya. The people get to know their neighbours who are within reach. Another development is "community policing", whereby trusted people are chosen by the local community to prevent crime and violence, to protect the community, to mediate conflicts, to investigate crimes, to retrieve stolen property etc. They are unarmed and non-uniformed, and are "owned" by the community, not by any government organs. As employed in a number of countries in the Global North, the term "community policing" has a somewhat different meaning, for it describes uniformed official police officers assigned to work closely with the local community.

In many parts of the world, including in many minority communities in the Global North, anyone wearing a uniform and associated with the state will be automatically distrusted. "Community policing" is perceived as extending police presence and surveillance into everyday life. However, there are also many "neighbourhood watch" schemes where local communities do look out for each other. At its best, "community policing" in the Global North can be affirmed as an attempt to demilitarise official police forces and recover the community-embedded and accountable practices that are still evident in more traditional societies in the Global South.

Admittedly, "policing" of any sort is easily discredited whenever police forces are militarised or made to serve narrow interests rather than the common good. It becomes especially difficult to advocate or even imagine just policing in communities and regions that have perpetually experienced "the police" as an occupying military force. But this makes it all the more incumbent to distinguish policing proper from war-making. Good policing draws upon training for conflict mediation and other skills needed to defuse social tensions nonviolently. It aims to apprehend alleged criminals who will then be tried by an independent judiciary; it does not project overwhelming force in order to pacify civilian populations and control territory; it is "policing by consent". Unlike militaries that are designed to be expeditionary, policing is embedded in the communities and societies that it serves. Ideally, police are thus more likely to avoid "we/them relationships" with local populations and instead remember that "they-are-we". In turn, police forces can be more closely tethered to the just rule of law than are military forces. As compared with military operations, therefore, it ought to be far less likely, if at all, that police operations would resort to armed and potentially lethal use of force.

This then offers an opportunity to work in continuity with, and also to develop for our times, the Church's inherited moral wisdom. To recognise these emerging and creative types of unarmed policing, as well as to recognise the essential differences between war and policing, contributes to affirming the best intentions of the Church's tradition, even while re-centring the tradition in Gospel nonviolence.

The issue of Responsibility to Protect

Papal teaching stresses nonviolence yet affirms not only the right but also the duty of intervention for humanitarian purposes. In 1993 John Paul II warned, regarding Bosnia, that when "populations are succumbing to the attacks of an unjust aggressor, States no longer have a 'right to indifference'. It seems clear that their duty is to disarm this aggressor, if all other means have proved ineffective."[247] But how do we disarm the aggressor? In 2014 Pope Francis clearly stated regarding ISIS that the international community should "stop the aggression but not make war or bomb". In 2005, the United Nations ratified the nascent principle of the "Responsibility to Protect" (R2P), marking an important development in nonviolent protection and the just war tradition by qualifying the absolute rights of national sovereignty and national self-defence. The principle of protecting the vulnerable from genocide, war crimes, ethnic cleansing or crimes against humanity coheres with the Gospel responsibility to serve the neighbour and "the least of these".

However, from a Christian standpoint, the use of armed force to do so is much more controversial, especially in view of the clear Gospel and papal priority of nonviolence and the understanding that violence almost always leads to a cycle of more violence. That is why, even while initially endorsing the Responsibility to Protect, the Holy See has emphasised the priority it gives to prevention and juridical, diplomatic and other nonviolent means of intervention (Pope Benedict XVI, *Address to UN General Assembly*, 18 April 2008; Pope Francis, *"Vigil of Prayer for Peace"* [in Syria], 7 September 2013; Pope Francis 2014 conversation with press, on return flight from Korea). Further, the World Council of Churches (WCC) has called resort to armed force in these situations a "sign of a serious failure and obstacle in the Way of Just Peace". Acknowledging the role of international law, the WCC states: "As Christians we feel obliged to go further" and challenge "any justification for use of military power."

There is a danger that, just as the just war tradition has often been misused to legitimise war rather than prevent it, the R2P doctrine may lead to similar uses of armed force. The Church must recognise the reality that in many parts of the world, particularly the Global South, the concept of "R2P" is met with deep suspicion, as it is seen merely as part of an apparatus and logic of neo-colonialism, oppression, racism, injustice and even widening the reasons for

---

247 Pope John Paul II, Address to the Diplomatic Corps, 18 January; cf. 2002 World Day of Peace message, no. 11).

war. The Holy See became more critical of the Responsibility to Protect norm in September 2008 in a statement by Msgr. Celestino Migliore to the 63rd Session of the General Assembly of the United Nations. He said, "In the past, the language of 'protection' was too often a pretext for expansion and aggression ... [T]his same understanding and practice tragically continues today. This principle is still being invoked as a pretext for the arbitrary use of military might. The use of violence to resolve disagreements is always a failure of vision and a failure of humanity." In 2014, Pope Francis continued to express this concern: "We need to remember how many times, using this excuse of stopping an unjust aggressor, the powerful nations have dominated other peoples and made a real war of conquest."

While R2P is a principle that does not dictate any specific actions or tactics, the invocation of R2P to justify military intervention in Libya, resulting in the violent overthrow of Muammar Gaddafi in 2011, has been criticised for leading to further violence and remains at minimum controversial. In the case of Syria, the UN has referenced R2P in multiple resolutions, but the international community – in part because of the deep partisan involvement of the five permanent members of the UN Security Council and other powerful countries in the conflict – has repeatedly failed to identify effective ways to act together in defence of Syrian communities without escalating the violence.

The use of military intervention on R2P grounds will remain a highly contested course of action.[248] At the same time, military force was never intended to be the main tool of the R2P doctrine. The main pillars of the doctrine, which tend to be de-emphasised, highlight the key importance of preventative measures. Nonviolent collective action and civilian protection have been shown to be

---

248 The Responsibility to Protect (RtoP) was developed as a doctrine to prevent mass atrocities. Offering an important exception to the principle of nonintervention, it relies on the UN Security Council to authorize its most aggressive provisions such as armed intervention. A decade of practice has revealed that RtoP can easily be curtailed by the objections of UN member states. With the aim of reducing risk factors such as civil war, arguments are now made for a new normative framework called The Right to Assist (RtoA), which would strengthen international coordination and support for nonviolent civil resistance campaigns demanding rights, freedom and justice against non-democratic rule. See "Preventing Mass Atrocities: From a Responsibility to Protect (RtoP) to a Right to Assist (RtoA) Campaigns of Civil Resistance" by Peter Ackerman and Hardy Merriman (ICNC Press, May 2019) and "Should There Be a 'Right to Assist' Campaigns of Civil Resistance?" by Stewart M. Patrick (World Politics Review, 21 October 2019).

effective, even in cases of mass atrocities.[249] Empowering and accompanying local communities, a special role of the Church, is key to defusing such violence and to long-term peace. Supporting women's participation in decision-making processes in matters of peace and security is especially crucial, for they are both frequent targets of gender-based violence, and courageous and creative builders of peace.

3. Integrating Nonviolence Throughout the Catholic Church

In this Kairos moment, we urge the Church to bring nonviolence from the periphery of Catholic thought to the centre — mainstreaming nonviolence as a spirituality, a lifestyle, a programme of societal action and a transformative universal ethic. Toward this end, we respectfully invite Pope Francis to share with the Church and the world a new teaching on nonviolence and just peace recommitting the Church to the centrality of Jesus's nonviolence and calling on all people in the Church and throughout the world to take concrete steps on the path of nonviolent transformation for peace, justice and reconciliation.

As part of this historic shift, we call on the Church:

- To integrate Gospel nonviolence at every level of the Church — dioceses, parishes, religious orders, seminaries, universities and schools — through education, formation, preaching, pastoral life, and advocacy.

- To articulate a new moral framework for Catholic teaching on violence and war based on a nonviolent just peace ethic, including by making this teaching clear in the Catechism.

---

249 "Nonviolent Resistance and Prevention of Mass Killings During Popular Uprisings" by Evan Perkoski and Erica Chenoweth (International Center on Nonviolent Conflict, Vol. 2, April 2018). Finds that "nonviolent resistance is generally less threatening to the physical well-being of regime elites, lowering the odds of mass killings. This is true even though these campaigns may take place in repressive contexts, demand that political leaders share power or step aside, and are historically quite successful at toppling brutal regimes".

- To create an office/portfolio in the Dicastery for Promoting Integral Human Development and in each diocese around the world focused on nonviolence and just peace.

- To advocate both inside and outside the Church increased investment in key nonviolent practices such as restorative justice, nonviolent communication, unarmed civilian protection, trauma-healing, nonviolent resistance and nonviolent civilian-based defence.

- To initiate a global conversation on nonviolence within the Church, with people of other faiths and with the larger world, to respond to the monumental crises of our time with the vision and strategies of nonviolence.

We invite the Church to envision practical and concrete steps that all Catholics could take to meet these goals. What if the institutional Catholic Church encouraged Catholics worldwide to study nonviolence and to engage energetically in the development of more and more effective nonviolent practices for protecting vulnerable communities, preventing violent conflict, transforming structures of violence and promoting cultures of integral peace? What if:

- Catholics were formed from the beginning of their lives to understand and appreciate the power of active nonviolence and the connection of nonviolence to the heart of the Gospel — trained to understand the real-life implications of "love your enemies"?

- Every Catholic parish integrated Gospel nonviolence throughout the life of the church — in its preaching, sacraments, ministries, spirituality, formation process and its work to foster just peace in its neighbourhood, community and society?

- All Catholics in the world were alert to signs of impending violence wherever and at whatever scale — and were trained to transform the conflict and prevent violence?

- Catholics everywhere were encouraged to study and consciously join, even organise nonviolent campaigns to achieve the just and peaceful world and the healthy planet for which we all long?

- Catholics advocated actively for less spending on military and more, for example, on diplomacy, unarmed civilian protection, early warning systems, trauma healing, trauma-informed programmes and training in conflict transformation, as well as on just and sustainable development, education, environmental healing — efforts that we know can make a difference.

A recommitment to Gospel nonviolence invites the Church to integrate the study and application of nonviolent practice explicitly into Church life and work through dioceses, parishes, schools, universities, seminaries, religious orders, voluntary associations, agencies and ministries throughout the world.

Effective nonviolent approaches require certain key elements to be successful: 1) Discipline and self-sacrifice; 2) spiritual groundedness; 3) a common goal and a higher purpose; 4) creativity and careful thinking; 5) access to all levels of the society; and 6) an ability to negotiate.[250] The Catholic Church excels in all of these key elements.

This section provides a few examples of how the Church could develop, teach and spread the theology, spirituality and catechesis of Jesus's nonviolence throughout the global Church.

---

250 Erica Chenoweth and Maria J. Stephan. *Why Civil Resistance Works: The Strategic Logic of Nonviolent Conflict* (New York, NY: Columbia University Press, 2011).

Pastoral Implications

For the Church to focus on nonviolence and just peace has deep pastoral implications.

Nonviolence is a way of life. If we recognise that all human beings are created in the image and likeness of God and, with St. Francis of Assisi, that all creation is related as brothers and sisters, that we are called to love others as we love ourselves, and that we are One Body in Christ, then it is impossible to imagine harming any part of that Body. To harm others is to harm myself. Nonviolence is the very essence of our being as Christians; it represents our deepest values. In that respect it is a spirituality, and, as such, it needs to be nurtured by the pastoral ministry of the Church.

As Church we are called to follow the way of Jesus and to help form the conscience of our community. A Church committed to Gospel nonviolence and just peace would be a confessional Church, acknowledging its own historical and contemporary complicity with war and violence, including the intimate violence of sexual abuse; would act as a "bridge-builder" linking different sectors of society in transformative dialogue (*Laudato Si'* C.5), a particular expression of the just peace norm of relationality; might enliven the minds and spirits of Catholic youth with creativity and courage; would generate a deeper discernment about vocations; would consistently join with oppressed and violated people to identify and address the root causes of violence; and would unfailingly nurture cultures of nonviolence and just, integral peace.

The Church would continue to provide moral guidance, encouraging Church leaders, elected officials and ordinary citizens, political decision-makers, members of the military or armed forces, people working in the security sector, and all those addressing difficult, violent, or potentially violent situations, to follow just peace norms consistently; to develop, support, pilot and employ effective unarmed methods of resistance, defence and protection; to commit explicitly to disarmament, demilitarisation, ending war and preventing violence, including in our neighbourhoods; to nurture right relationships within the Church and beyond, and to invite adversaries to become future partners.

The Church would encourage states to dissolve their militaries. The experiences of Costa Rica, which continues to reap social dividends from abolishing its military in 1948, and Mauritius, which has one of the strongest economies in Africa, are good examples.

The Church would foster and support as examples groups that provide unarmed civilian protection in violent conflict zones, such as Operation Dove, Christian Peacemaker Teams, Nonviolent Peaceforce and other explicit illustrations of just peace norms practically applied. It would support those engaged in nonviolent collective action to change the unjust policies and practices that fuel violence. The Church also would model and encourage a spirit of acknowledgment, repentance and reconciliation for the harm done by war and by local, structural and systemic violence.

Nonviolence should not be considered an option only for individuals and social movements but should be the first and consistent response of the Church — and hopefully of governments and international institutions — to violence, repression and injustice. Nonviolence and peacebuilding should become a core element of Catholic identity, culture and way of life. Governments should take seriously their obligation to develop institutions, approaches and means of nonviolent conflict transformation (*The Harvest of Justice Is Sown in Peace*, 5). This would also reinforce the Church's long-term vision of strengthening international law, international institutions and the means of conflict transformation.

Finally, the leadership of women in peacebuilding and the practice of active nonviolence is well documented. To integrate the spirituality and practice of Gospel nonviolence more completely into the life of our Church, it is important to recognise the challenges faced in both Church and society that prevent full gender equality. The contributions of women religious to peacebuilding while serving in war zones and areas of extreme violence are inspiring. At the same time, grassroots movements for peace that employ active nonviolence are often led by laywomen who courageously challenge the status quo of gender inequality.

Opportunities for Discernment

Universal Church

- Identify and expand existing Catholic-affiliated unarmed civilian protection programmes, giving them special recognition and support.

- Revitalise or institute a lay order dedicated to nonviolence that takes a vow of nonviolence.

- Consider integrating this with a more robust encouragement to conscientious objection to military service for Catholics.

- Consider a lay youth movement that takes a vow of nonviolence.

- Create a Nonviolence and Just Peace Commission under the auspices of the Dicastery for Promoting Integral Human Development to support and build on the work of nonviolence practitioners, researchers, theologians, non-governmental agencies and grassroots leaders.

- Institute a non-parochial Archdiocese for Nonviolent Unarmed Peacemakers to provide the Catholic Church's full range of pastoral ministries and spiritual services to those representing the Catholic Church on the front lines of violent conflict.

- Advocate funding, research, models and legislation for nonviolent civilian-based defence in national and international settings.

- Develop and promote nonviolent programmes, approaches and practices throughout the Church (e.g. nonviolent resistance, restorative justice, trauma healing, unarmed civilian protection, conflict transformation and peacebuilding approaches).

- Consider how Article V of the Catechism of the Catholic Church could re-centre nonviolence and just peace as the normative frame for all Catholics.

- Establish a nonviolence news service that reports on nonviolence, teaches about nonviolence and develops radio spots on related topics. Establish a robust social media presence with this news service.

- Review Church-related investments at all levels to screen out revenue from military-related products and services or weapons manufacturing. Support positive shareowner action to address the underlying problems that lead to armed conflict, and target investments to address conflict triggers and build positive peace.

Bishops and episcopal conferences

Bishops and episcopal conferences would play a key role as Gospel nonviolence is more fully integrated into the life of the Church. We celebrate the leadership of many bishops, who have witnessed and taught about the power of Gospel nonviolence. Their deep connections with grassroots people, who suffer the most during violence or who go to war, are essential to maintain. In addition, bishops and episcopal conferences could:

- Encourage the Secretariat of State to host a conference on nonviolent civilian protection for its diplomatic corps, with expert practitioners from global conflict zones.

- Urge the Pontifical Council for Promoting the New Evangelisation to include the spirituality of Gospel nonviolence as a topic for its Catechetical Congress and explore ways diocesan evangelisation campaigns could include nonviolence in their toolkit.

- Establish and fund a national Catholic nonviolence and just peace commission (or adapt an existing social justice commission to centralise nonviolence and just peace).

- Host diocesan or regional conferences on Gospel nonviolence based on the model of the April 2016 Rome conference on nonviolence and just peace.

- Many national bishops' conferences offer an annual social justice statement and it would be helpful to encourage and expect this in every region, accompanied by a "nonviolence and just peace" audit for the region. Rather than providing theme-based statements, an assessment tool measuring structural, commercial and militarised violence could be used to measure changes in human dignity, social health and the common good - published annually and monitored through a national commission on Nonviolence, Just Peace and Integral Creation.

- Engage in morally responsible investment, develop clear screening criteria in relation to war and violence, and prepare for dialogue and then divestment where necessary.

- Maintain independence from political and economic power in order to have the space to speak out prophetically about injustice or threats to society, especially to better reduce military spending and avoid legitimating violent responses.

- Integrate courses on active nonviolence in diocesan educational systems, including universities, schools, seminaries, catechesis, etc.

- Hold seminars on Christian nonviolence for the clergy and lay leaders serving in the diocese.

- Promote restorative justice, arbitration and mediation at the diocesan level to show that conflicts can be transformed in a nonviolent way. Appropriately transparent conflict transformation processes should be normalised within all Church institutions and organisations.

- Building upon Pope Francis's Christmas address to the Roman Curia (21 December 2017), the bishops' visits *Ad Limina Apostolorum* that also involve meetings with the various dicasteries could include on their agenda an exchange on practices promoting nonviolence and just peace. This may apply in particular to the meetings with representatives of the Secretariat of State and the Dicastery for Promoting Integral Human Development.

- Issue statements that include not only clear Catholic teaching, but also examples of nonviolent practices already practised in local communities and actions the Church will take to implement nonviolent transformation of the given conflict.

- When dehumanising rhetoric is used as a tool to advance ideologies or military action, Church representatives can model human dignity, civility, nonviolent communication and public acts of respect, and clearly indicate that respecting the dignity of the other can accompany difference in beliefs — respect is a precondition for transformation, even as it doesn't guarantee it.

- Talk with and join Catholics and others involved in frontline nonviolent campaigns, especially be more willing to promote obstructive tactics such as strikes, boycotts, civil disobedience.

Families and parishes

"It is fundamental that nonviolence be practised before all else within families ... The family is the indispensable crucible in which spouses, parents and children, brothers and sisters, learn to communicate and to show generous concern for one another, and in which frictions and even conflicts have to be resolved not by force but by dialogue, respect, concern for the good of the other, mercy and forgiveness. From within families, the joy of love spills out into the world and radiates to the whole of society" (Pope Francis, 2017 World Day of Peace, 5).

Families and the extended "family" that comprises Catholic parishes are the building blocks of a peaceful world that transforms conflicts nonviolently. Families and Catholic parishes committed to active nonviolence would:

- Emphasise at all stages and venues of family and parish life the necessity of living Gospel nonviolence, of promoting justice, peace and reconciliation. Nurture the spirituality of nonviolence. Support the development of right relationships within the family, the parish, the larger community, with the Earth and with the self.

- Prioritise peace education in the spirit of Gospel nonviolence. Equip families to learn together how to communicate and live nonviolently.

- Support training in parenting skills dealing with social media and discipline in the home.

- Provide information about the Church's teachings on nonviolence and just peace.

- Elevate the language of nonviolence within the Church and in Church teachings, as Pope Francis has done, particularly in the 2017 World Day of Peace message.

- Always include in intercessory prayers victim and perpetrator, those in unarmed civilian accompaniment and people building peace in dangerous situations.

- Lift up nonviolent peacemakers as heroes, heroines and saints of the Church.

- Organise forums, community-based training and popular education programmes on nonviolence as a spirituality, a way of life and an effective approach to conflict transformation. Build nonviolent peacemaking skills in the parish and local community.

- Collaborate locally to create peace teams which can deploy unarmed civilian protection units to situations of hostile conflict or violence.[251]

- Create an information hub on local, national and international nonviolent actions for just peace where knowledge and information can be shared quickly about successful civic organising in different contexts.

- Offer safe meeting spaces for people to come together, begin organising, exchange ideas, conduct fundraising and come up with approaches for civil resistance actions.

- Make people aware of the advantages of civil resistance in situations when resignation/passivity, violence, or even methods of conflict transformation alone are unlikely to be effective or may be counterproductive for the safety and long-term well-being of a group.

Sacraments and liturgy

At the heart of the life of the Church, liturgical celebrations can be a powerful expression of the way to peace, following the nonviolent example of Jesus:

- In the lectionary, the celebration of the Eucharist and other sacraments and prayers of the Church, give witness to the centrality of the teaching and actions of Jesus as a nonviolent leader. In homilies, written reflections and

---

251 For example, see the Shenti Sena Network in the U.S. or the Catholic model of Operation Dove.

study groups, highlight examples of nonviolence in the Gospels and in other scriptural passages.

- Develop the sacrament of reconciliation to include a wider development of examination of conscience and communal acts that celebrate this sacrament.

- Allow more freedom in the composition of liturgical texts and Eucharistic prayers, especially examples with more direct mention of Jesus's love of enemies and rejection of violence.

- Encourage liturgists, musicians and authors to reference nonviolence in prayers and songs and to share their creative work with parishes, dioceses, religious communities and others.

- Contribute the power of prayer, liturgical and sacramental witness to nonviolent actions in support of Gospel values and Catholic social teaching.

Education, seminary and religious life formation

Essential to the paradigm shift envisioned by the Catholic Nonviolence Initiative would be to infuse all forms and levels of Catholic education — from seminaries and universities to secondary and primary schools as well as in catechesis and the formation of religious — with explicit training in the spirituality and practice of Gospel nonviolence.

- With the guidance of the Congregation for Catholic Education, encourage Catholic schools and educational associations in various countries to make peace and nonviolence education a major thrust, beginning with the rediscovery of and recommitment to Jesus's nonviolence and including Catholic teaching on just, integral peace. Encourage all Catholic educational institutions to include programmes on nonviolence in their basic curriculum and required courses and to model nonviolent practices in their institutional life. Sample courses include Nonviolent Theory and Practice, Conflict Transformation, Unarmed Civilian Protection and Restorative Justice.[252]

- Develop a Just Peace Leadership Corps at universities and secondary schools. These would include both academic and nonviolent skill-training, such as nonviolent communication, bystander intervention, restorative circles, unarmed civilian protection and nonviolent resistance.

- Include formation in Gospel nonviolence for priests, deacons, sisters or other ministers so that they in turn form congregations and communities, especially the young, with the nonviolent Jesus at the heart of their faith, a just peace ethic to shape moral reasoning and effective nonviolence skills, practices, habits and approaches for transforming conflict.

- In Catholic moral theology and ethics courses de-emphasise and move away from just war thinking, theology, principles, ethics and practices in favour of promoting active nonviolence and just peace.

- Organise a global conference on peace and nonviolence education or request global educational organisations such as the International Federation of Catholic Universities to make this the theme for their global conferences.

- Look for close collaboration with the most influential Catholic organisations in the field of education, discussing with them the best methods to implement nonviolence in the life and work of Catholic educational institutions. For higher education and research it could be: IFCU (International Federation of Catholic Universities), ACCU (Association of Catholic Colleges and Universities in the US) and the international network of Jesuit universities and colleges. For secondary (and primary) education: JECSE (Jesuit European Committee for Secondary and

---

252 See www.nonviolencejustpeace.net/resources for sample resources.

Primary Education), the National Catholic Educational Association in the US and its counterparts in other countries.

- Give social media more importance as a tool for nonviolence education; use it to promote tolerance and nonviolence.[253]

- Encourage academic research and dialogue about different nonviolent methods. For example, how peace-building, conflict transformation and civil resistance approaches could be merged together in different phases of violent conflict (in covert structural violence situations, in overt violent conflict, during the settlement and post-settlement phases of conflict) to help an aggrieved group organise nonviolently, empower its members through different actions, including civil resistance, and lead to a more just and peaceful environment. Provide funding for research on nonviolent civilian-based defence mechanisms.

- Offer skills-based training in nonviolence and conflict transformation for the broader community — religious and secular. Publicise the results of this training using radio, TV, newspapers and social media so that the whole community can utilise nonviolent language, alternative dispute resolution, and develop a working knowledge and vocabulary in nonviolence and just peace.

- Catholic aid and development agencies, such as Caritas, Catholic Relief Services and Jesuit Relief Service, working with others, could develop and implement a nonviolent peacebuilding curriculum that includes conflict transformation, peace education, working with diversity and strengthening community relationships, trauma healing, alternative dispute resolution and restorative justice, with an emphasis on integrating peace into social and economic development work.

---

253 See "Social Media and Conflict Prevention" by Sheldon Himelfarb (US Institute of Peace, 20 December 2012) and "Making Peace in a Powder Keg" by Julienne Gage (Sojourners, June 2016).

- Promote peace journalism (reported stories for different platforms that cover active nonviolence).[254]

Religious communities and lay movements

Religious communities and lay movements have tremendous transformative potential in promoting Gospel nonviolence in the life of the Church. With their global reach and the depth of their networks they touch the lives of the faithful in significant and formative ways.

- Integrate nonviolence into formation and ongoing formation programmes.

- Encourage members and affiliates living in areas of conflict and/or violence to share their stories of effective nonviolent efforts to transform conflict, and to generate conversations locally about ways to strengthen the impact of nonviolence as a way of life and powerful strategy for transforming conflict or stopping violence.

- Prioritise Gospel nonviolence in outreach and promotional materials being sent to prospective members and benefactors.

- Endorse the appeal to the Catholic Church to recommit to the centrality of Gospel nonviolence.

- Advocate consistently nonviolent approaches in the local, national and international spheres. Mainstream the just peace norms, especially in foreign policy frameworks and at the UN.

---

254 See "How Peace Journalism can de-escalate conflict in the age of Trump and North Korea" by Michael Greenwell (29 November 2017), Centre for Broadcasting and Journalism, Nottingham Trent University.

- Be present / take part in community acts of resistance and nonviolent witness, offering solidarity and accepting the consequences of such actions.

Ecumenical and interfaith action and dialogue

Ecumenical and interreligious solidarity is critical to building strong societies and to responding in situations of violence. Building trust with other faith representatives, showing publicly that it is possible to respect and walk together, is a critical component to peacebuilding and a necessary component of nonviolence in times of violent conflict. The Church in South Sudan provides a model for empathetic approach to advocacy as well as speaking regularly, clearly and with unity in a manner that is led by what the churches on the ground feel is important. Building interreligious centres for training in nonviolence and just peace, such as the St. Francis Peace Center in Gangjeong, Korea, highlights the critical importance of this work to the whole community when space and resources are dedicated and multiple religious groups are involved. Religious leaders can continue to offer spiritual guidance and comfort for one another and for church workers in times of extreme difficulty.

In John 17, Jesus prays that we might all be one, as he and Abba God are one, "that the world may believe", indicating both how the scandal of division amongst Christians mitigates against our witness to our nonviolent God of love and peace, as well as pointing the way towards hope. At Vatican II, our Church embraced a new era of dialogue with peoples of other faiths and with the world.

We are now further blessed with a pope who has chosen the very name of Francis, desiring "a poor Church for the poor", seeing in St. Francis one who also "loves and protects creation"... a "man of peace" in contrast to a violent world at war. We embrace our deep and organic bonds with other Christians and peoples of other faiths, in this common pursuit of a lasting world peace through active nonviolence. To integrate nonviolence into ecumenical and interfaith spaces, the Church could:

- Provide more support for ecumenical and interfaith grassroots initiatives and projects in the field, such as developing Interfaith Peace Teams.

- Make nonviolence a regular agenda point at ecumenical and interfaith encounters at ecclesiastical and Vatican levels.

- Encourage Catholic schools and religious formation programmes to adopt ecumenical and interfaith competence training to reduce and eliminate prejudice towards the religious "other".

- Stress the values and principles that we share in common with other faith groups.

- Make the goal of interfaith action that of working together and co-operating for the common good, recognising that our global problems are shared and affect us all regardless of faith or religion.

- Foster and strengthen local ties ("dialogue of life" and "dialogue of action") between the Catholic faithful, in their respective dioceses and nations, ecumenical and interfaith organisations, and in their efforts for justice, active nonviolence and peace.

- Ask where the recentring and revitalisation of Gospel nonviolence — spirituality, practice and pedagogy — can meet a similarly robust revitalisation in Judaism and Islam.[255]

Policymakers, diplomats and United Nations

Policymakers, diplomats and activists in the public sphere who advocate justice, peace and the integrity of creation are key protagonists in showing the

---

255 See "Abrahamic Alternatives to War. Jewish, Christian, and Muslim Perspectives on Just Peacemaking," by Susan Thistlethwaite and Glen Stassen (US Institute of Peace, Special Report 214, October 2008).

effectiveness of active nonviolence and peacebuilding in resolving conflicts. The leadership of the Church, in promoting dialogue, negotiation and conflict transformation, is critical to building a more peaceful world. Here the role of the bishops and the pope, as well as of the diplomatic corps of the Holy See and Catholic NGOs advocating at the UN and with national governments, is essential to promoting a just peace.

- Integrate into the formation and the training of Vatican diplomats a stronger emphasis on nonviolence.

- Create spaces for and engage in genuine dialogue bringing together policymakers, Church actors, academia and broader civil society at and across all levels and sectors (local, regional, global). Utilise the 2017 World Day of Peace message "Nonviolence: A Style of Politics for Peace" by sharing it with key leaders and generating formal dialogues about it.

- Church representatives can continue to support peace processes, negotiations and diplomatic exchanges while always standing clearly and publicly in solidarity with the most vulnerable victims of violence, as well as illuminating the dignity of all actors in a conflict. Rather than condemning acts of violence, Church representatives can describe violence as a failure of leadership and propose independent obstructive and constructive nonviolent actions that can be taken by all people at every level of society.

- Church representatives can focus on mainstreaming the just peace norms, especially in national foreign policy frameworks and at the UN. Using case studies as examples can be particularly effective.

- Church representatives and others can advocate specifically the promotion and support of unarmed civilian protection (e.g. Peace Teams, NGOs, police, military, UN), restorative justice (e.g. in schools, criminal justice systems, violent conflicts), trauma-healing and nonviolent civilian-based defence. These are each gaining traction and could make a particularly significant contribution to a sustainable peace.

- Strengthen the capacity and role of the Holy See in the field of negotiation and conflict mediation.

- Enhance the link between the Church hierarchy/global Church and the local Church/grassroots movements. The Church's position should be communicated in a more effective manner so the message will reach Catholics in parishes and communities.

- As creation itself unravels under climate collapse, Church representatives can lead and act in concert with obstructive and constructive nonviolent movements to protect creation and her communities, as illustrated in *Laudato Si'*. As climate collapse contributes to violence, so climate care contributes to peace.

- Church representatives and others are encouraged to advocate specifically significant reductions in military spending and the arms trade. This should especially include national Church representatives as we seek "integral disarmament".

Pope Francis and the Catholic Church have taken a strong stand against guns and light weapons and their manufacture and trade. This work can be done at the level of the UN and multilateral organisations as well as continent by continent. For example, the African Union has set a goal to "silence the guns in Africa by the year 2020". The Church can call for creative public support for these initiatives and clearly identify independent action the Church is taking in support and invite all to participate.

Deliberation for the Internal Life of the Universal Church

Sensitive concerns

The Synod of Bishops in 1971 said, "... Anyone who ventures to speak to people about justice must first be just in their eyes. Hence we must undertake an examination of the modes of acting and of the possessions and lifestyle found within the Church herself" (40). Similarly, for the Church to recommit to the centrality of Gospel nonviolence will require an examination of the Church's own ways and an internal commitment to nonviolence.

A deep commitment to active nonviolence could also help Church representatives to effectively address sexual violence by clergy. Sexual abuse is often an extreme form of violence that is a spiritual, psychological or physical force exerted "for the purpose of threatening, injuring, damaging, abusing". Or it may be patterns of behaviour intended to establish and maintain coercive domination over an individual, intimate partners, family, household members, colleagues or congregants. Violence and abuse are used to establish and maintain power and control over another person or group, and often reflect an imbalance of power between the victim and the abuser. Maintaining control and power is one of the hallmarks of clericalism.

Within nonviolence and Catholic Social Teaching there lies the foundation for dismantling abusive systems of power and for promoting accountability among Church leaders and other decision-makers.

- Encourage all national bishops' conferences to initiate a Truth, Justice and Healing national commission with independent commissioners.

- Urge the Pontifical Commission for the Protection of Minors to use programmes and practices of nonviolence, including restorative justice and transparency tools, to work with trauma survivors and perpetrators, and to root out internal corruption using proven anti-corruption models.

By failing to fully recognise women's sacramental roles and/or have women as key public spokespersons and in positions of leadership and authority, the Church undermines its ability to truly model the peace of Christ and fails to perceive the alternate power models that women bring to situations of injustice created by systemic domination. By its decision to not even discuss the sacramental leadership of women and gender-non-conforming people, the Church decreases its capacity for understanding human dignity, expanding the believer's image of God, and acknowledging spiritual leaders of all shapes, sizes and genders. There needs to be greater inclusivity in Church structures, especially toward equity for women and minorities. Re-opening the diaconate to women will be a strong step forward.

4. Conclusion: Moving Forward as a People of God

At this critical moment, let us move forward as a Church and a world facing the great challenges of violence by neither retreating from them, nor accommodating them, nor relying on violence to fight violence. Instead, let us learn the ways of active nonviolence and build our capacity for nonviolent transformation at every level of the Church, and invite the entire world to do the same.

As we have seen in this document, active nonviolence is a powerful way to effectively confront violence and injustice, a way of life and a spiritual path, and a means of building the just peace for which people everywhere long.

Violence is a powerful, systemic reality that has long-term consequences. At the same time, nonviolence denotes a paradigm of the fullness of life that challenges this systemic violence — including all forms of injustice — and actively works for the well-being of all. Nonviolence is quantitatively twice as effective as violence, particularly in terms of a social movement's short-term political objectives,[256] a

256 Erica Chenoweth and Maria J. Stephan, *Why Civil Resistance Works: The Strategic Logic of Nonviolent Conflict*, Columbia University Press, 2011.

finding that is also borne out in the stories of nonviolence featured in this text from many places around the world facing acute violence.

We have also seen clearly that nonviolence is at the core of the life and mission of Jesus, rooted in a vision of God who longs for humanity to live nonviolently with one another. While the Church has often forgotten, ignored or suppressed this call to the spirituality and practice of nonviolence — something that recent popes have begun to address by publicly apologising for specific ways it has engaged in violence — it also possesses an illustrious history of people and communities who have sought to live the way of Gospel nonviolence, from St. Martin of Tours to Sts. Francis and Clare of Assisi; and from Dorothy Day to Saint Oścar Romero.

We stand at a powerful moment in which the Church can bring into sharper focus the theology of nonviolence, including a theology of creation, anthropology, Christology, pneumatology and ecclesiology. We have begun to envision a new moral framework based on nonviolence and just peace — and many practical proposals for integrating nonviolence at every level of the Church.

We invite the entire Church to imagine a shift "to institutionalise and internationalise nonviolence",[257] and invite Pope Francis to encourage this shift by sharing with the Church and the world an encyclical on nonviolence.

The size and scale of the Catholic Church is a factor in this effort to promote such a shift. The Catholic Church is like a large, sea-going vessel. It may take a lot to turn it, but once it does turn, a new direction with far-ranging outcomes is possible. Catholics make up 18 percent of the world population, with 1.3 billion people; the Catholic Church is the largest nonprofit organisation in the world; the Church runs nearly 100,000 elementary schools and 50,000 secondary schools; it operates 5,000 hospitals and 10,000 orphanages; the Vatican has a diplomatic presence in nearly every country in the world, as well as in major multilateral

---

257 Kazu Haga, Healing Resistance: A Radical Different Response to Harm (unpublished manuscript, 2018).

institutions such as the United Nations; and it has an organised, cohesive structure that allows information to flow independently from the margins to the centre and back out again without passing through government censors or captive media agencies.

By deliberately recommitting to the core Gospel value of nonviolence and taking concrete steps to bring it alive throughout the world, the Church could help the entire global community to step back from the brink of catastrophic violence and begin to take a more just and peaceful direction.

The good news about nonviolence is that it has proved effective in reducing violence and advancing a sustaining peace, and it can be effectively implemented at the scale of social movements or at the level of the individual.

For the Catholic Church today to serve effectively as a "field hospital" — as Pope Francis has termed it — the "trauma team" must be well trained in the spirituality and effective practices of a robust nonviolent faith. Together we step forward as a nonviolent people and nonviolent Church towards a nonviolent world.

Faced with the challenges of this age, let us be transformed. Let us become nonviolent people, a nonviolent Church, and a nonviolent world dedicated to faithfully healing our planet and honouring the infinite worth of every being.

Contributors

Contributors and participants are from or work in Afghanistan, Australia, Austria, Bangladesh, Belgium, Brazil, Cameroon, Central African Republic, Colombia, Croatia, Ecuador, El Salvador, Germany, Guatemala, India, Ireland, Italy, Japan, Kenya, Korea, Lebanon, Mexico, Netherlands, New Zealand, Nicaragua, Pakistan, Palestine, Philippines, Poland, South Africa, South Sudan, Sri Lanka, Syria, Tanzania, Uganda, United Kingdom, United States, Zambia, and Zimbabwe. Inclusion on this list does not indicate endorsement.

Pauline Silver Acayo	Juan Vicente Chopin	Aseervatham Florington
Manuel Acosta	Drew Christiansen	Anna Franklin
Pietro Ameglio	David Cochran	Pat Gaffney
Jane Andanje Ashworth	David Cortright	Jasmin Nario Galace
Margaret Angucia	John Dominic Crossan	Federico Gandolfi
Carmen Artigas	Pat Cunningham	Maria Teresa Gaston
John Ashworth	Héctor Dada Hirezi	Annemarie Gielen
Nate Bacon	MT Davila	Hildegard Goss-Mayr
Tom Bamat	Francisco José De Roux	Luke Hansen
Michael Baxter	Rengifo	Jo Hanssens
Rose Marie Berger	John Dear	Susan Hayward
Maria Clara Bingemer	Merwyn DeMello	José Henriquez
Michael Budde	Marie Dennis	Juan Hernandez
Gill Burrows	Aronette Diaz	Filo Hirota
Ken Butigan	Kevin Dowling	Sara Ianovitz
Lisa Sowle Cahill	Dina Dubon	Richard Jackson
Nora Carmi	Mel Duncan	John Katunga
Peter Casarella	Amy Woolam Echeverria	David Kaulem
Loreta Castro	Jef Felix	Elizabeth Kanini Kimau
Bill Cavanaugh	Valerie Flessati	Sheila Kinsey
Natalia Chan	Rosa Ines Floriana	Katarina Kruhonja
Erica Chenoweth	Carrera	Paul Lansu

Antonio Ledesma
Gerry Lee
Myla Leguro
Loes Lijnders
Cory Lockhart
Maryann Cusimano Love
Armando Marquez Ochoa
Anne McCarthy
Eli McCarthy
Boniface Mendes
Eva Menjívar
Marek Misak
Peter Basaliza Mubunga
Rania Murra
Felix Mushobozi
Ched Myers
Sarah Thompson Nahar
Elias Omondi Opongo
Anita Ortiz

Rosa Noemí Ortiz
Matthew Pagan
Wolfgang Palaver
Peter-John Pearson
Jan Peters
Margaret Pfeil
Nico Plooijer
Sarah Prime
Ana Raffai
Jamila Raqib
Lynette Rodrigues
Jeanette Rodriguez
Paul Rogers
Martha Ines Romero
Terrence Rynne
Eduardo Sancho
Gerald Schlabach
Robert Schreiter
Vincent Sekhar

Stefan Silber
Jon Sobrino
Maria Stephan
Jean Stokan
Eric Stoner
Paride Taban
Jean Baptiste Talla
José María Tojeira
AHMV (Fred) van Iersel
Miguel Ventura
Teresia Wamuyu Wachira
Stefanie Wahl
Nomfundo Walaza
Tobias Winwright
Scott Wright
Rubén Zamora

APPENDICES

Appendix 1:
An *"Appeal to the Catholic Church to Re-commit to the Centrality of Gospel Nonviolence"*, a statement endorsed by participants in the 2016 Nonviolence and Just Peace conference

Appendix 2:
"Nonviolence nurtures hope, can renew the Church", a statement from the Path of Nonviolence Toward a Culture of Peace workshop, April 2019

Appendix 3:
Ten elements of nonviolence

Appendix 1

An Appeal to the Catholic Church to re-commit to the centrality of Gospel nonviolence

The following statement, crafted in a consensus process, was released at the end of the Nonviolence and Just Peace conference in Rome, April 2016. Endorsements from individuals and organisations are welcome – go to https:// nonviolencejustpeace.net/final-statement-an-appeal-to-the-catholic- church-to-re-commit-to-the-centrality-of-gospel-nonviolence/ to sign.

As Christians committed to a more just and peaceful world we are called to take a clear stand for creative and active nonviolence and against all forms of violence. With this conviction, and in recognition of the Jubilee Year of Mercy declared by Pope Francis, people from many countries gathered at the Nonviolence and Just Peace Conference sponsored by the Pontifical Council for Justice and Peace and Pax Christi International on April 11-13, 2016 in Rome.

Our assembly, people of God from Africa, the Americas, Asia, Europe, the Middle East and Oceania, included lay people, theologians, members of religious congregations, priests and bishops. Many of us live in communities experiencing violence and oppression. All of us are practitioners of justice and peace. We are grateful for the message to our conference from Pope Francis: "your thoughts on revitalizing the tools of nonviolence, and of active nonviolence in particular, will be a needed and positive contribution".

Looking at our world today

We live in a time of tremendous suffering, widespread trauma and fear linked to militarization, economic injustice, climate change, and a myriad of other specific forms of violence. In this context of normalized and systemic violence, those of us who stand in the Christian tradition are called to recognize the centrality of active nonviolence to the vision and message of Jesus; to the life and practice of the Catholic Church; and to our long-term vocation of healing and reconciling both people and the planet.

We rejoice in the rich concrete experiences of people engaged in work for peace around the world, many of whose stories we heard during this conference. Participants shared their experiences of courageous negotiations with armed actors in Uganda and Colombia; working to protect the Article 9, the peace clause in the Japanese Constitution; accompaniment in Palestine; and countrywide peace education in the Philippines. They illuminate the creativity and power of nonviolent practices in many different situations of potential or actual violent conflict. Recent academic research, in fact, has confirmed that nonviolent resistance strategies are twice as effective as violent ones.

The time has come for our Church to be a living witness and to invest far greater human and financial resources in promoting a spirituality and practice of active nonviolence and in forming and training our Catholic communities in effective nonviolent practices. In all of this, Jesus is our inspiration and model.

Jesus and nonviolence

In his own times, rife with structural violence, Jesus proclaimed a new, nonviolent order rooted in the unconditional love of God. Jesus called his disciples to love their enemies (Matthew 5: 44), which includes respecting the image of God in all persons; to offer no violent resistance to one who does evil (Matthew 5: 39); to become peacemakers; to forgive and repent; and to be abundantly merciful (Matthew 5-7). Jesus embodied nonviolence by actively resisting systemic dehumanization, as when he defied the Sabbath laws to heal the man with the withered hand (Mark 3: 1-6); when he confronted the powerful at the Temple and purified it (John 2: 13-22); when he peacefully but determinedly challenged the men accusing a woman of adultery (John 8: 1-11); when on the night before he died he asked Peter to put down his sword (Matthew 26: 52).

Neither passive nor weak, Jesus's nonviolence was the power of love in action. In vision and deed, he is the revelation and embodiment of the Nonviolent God, a truth especially illuminated in the Cross and Resurrection. He calls us to develop the virtue of nonviolent peacemaking.

Clearly, the Word of God, the witness of Jesus, should never be used to justify violence, injustice or war. We confess that the people of God have betrayed this central message of the Gospel many times, participating in wars, persecution, oppression, exploitation and discrimination.

We believe that there is no "just war". Too often the "just war theory" has been used to endorse rather than prevent or limit war. Suggesting that a "just war" is possible also undermines the moral imperative to develop tools and capacities for nonviolent transformation of conflict.

We need a new framework that is consistent with Gospel nonviolence. A different path is clearly unfolding in recent Catholic social teaching. Pope John XXIII wrote that war is not a suitable way to restore rights; Pope Paul VI linked peace and development, and told the UN "no more war"; Pope John Paul II said that "war belongs to the tragic past, to history"; Pope Benedict XVI said that "loving the enemy is the nucleus of the Christian revolution"; and Pope Francis said "the true strength of the Christian is the power of truth and love, which leads to the renunciation of all violence. Faith and violence are incompatible". He has also urged the "abolition of war".

We propose that the Catholic Church develop and consider shifting to a Just Peace approach based on Gospel nonviolence. A Just Peace approach offers a vision and an ethic to build peace as well as to prevent, defuse and heal the damage of violent conflict. This ethic includes a commitment to human dignity and thriving relationships, with specific criteria, virtues and practices to guide our actions. We recognize that peace requires justice and justice requires peacemaking.

Living Gospel Nonviolence and Just Peace

In that spirit we commit ourselves to furthering Catholic understanding and practice of active nonviolence on the road to just peace. As would-be disciples of Jesus, challenged and inspired by stories of hope and courage in these days, we call on the Church we love to:

• continue developing Catholic social teaching on nonviolence. In particular, we call on Pope Francis to share with the world an encyclical on nonviolence and Just Peace;

• integrate Gospel nonviolence explicitly into the life, including the sacramental life, and work of the Church through dioceses, parishes, agencies, schools, universities, seminaries, religious orders, voluntary associations, and others;

• promote nonviolent practices and strategies (e.g., nonviolent resistance, restorative justice, trauma healing, unarmed civilian protection, conflict transformation, and peacebuilding strategies);

• initiate a global conversation on nonviolence within the Church, with people of other faiths, and with the larger world to respond to the monumental crises of our time with the vision and strategies of nonviolence and Just Peace;

• no longer use or teach "just war theory"; continue advocating for the abolition of war and nuclear weapons;

• lift up the prophetic voice of the church to challenge unjust world powers and to support and defend those nonviolent activists whose work for peace and justice put their lives at risk.

In every age, the Holy Spirit graces the Church with the wisdom to respond to the challenges of its time. In response to what is a global epidemic of violence, which Pope Francis has labeled a "world war in installments", we are being called to invoke, pray over, teach and take decisive action. With our communities and organizations, we look forward to continue collaborating with the Holy See and the global Church to advance Gospel nonviolence.

Appendix 2

Nonviolence nurtures hope, can renew the Church

The following statement was affirmed by most of the participants at the 2019 Path of Nonviolence: Towards a culture of peace workshop, sponsored by Pax Christi International and held at the Dicastery for Promoting Integral Human Development.

As Christians committed to faithfully following in the footsteps of Jesus, we are called to take a clear stand for active nonviolence and against all forms of violence. In this spirit, people from many nations gathered for *Path of Nonviolence: Towards a Culture of Peace*, a consultation held at the Holy See's Dicastery for Promoting Integral Human Development on April 4-5, 2019 in Rome. This was an important follow-up to the Nonviolence and Just Peace conference held in Rome in April 2016 co-sponsored by the then-Pontifical Council for Justice and Peace and Pax Christi International.

Our recent gathering of people of God from Africa, Asia, the Middle East, Oceania, Europe and the Americas included lay people, theologians, members of religious congregations, priests, bishops and cardinals. Many of us live in communities experiencing violence and oppression. All of us are practitioners of justice and peace.

We are grateful for the special focus that Pope Francis has placed on the spiritual and practical power of active nonviolence to promote integral human development and cultures of peace, including through the 2017 World Day of Peace message on "Nonviolence: A Style of Politics for Peace," where he proclaimed: "To be true followers of Jesus today...includes embracing his teaching about nonviolence." We know that Jesus consistently practiced nonviolence in a context that was extremely violent, but "nonviolence was not just a response to particular situations in the life of Jesus – it was the whole life of Jesus" (Cardinal Peter Turkson, University of San Diego, October 7, 2017).

Signs of the times in the light of faith

The Second Vatican Council taught us to see and respond to "the signs of the times" so that the Church can discern how we are called to live the way of Jesus in our lives and our world today. Our recent two-day gathering in Rome urgently called our attention to two critical "signs of the times:" the global crisis of violence with the unspeakable suffering it unleashes and, by the grace of God, the spread of active and powerful nonviolence. Violence, which includes killing, is not in accord with human dignity. Rejecting the legitimation, reasoning, and actualization of violence and war, we need a new path – a paradigm shift to full-spectrum nonviolence – to take us into the future.

Just peace is the goal, nonviolence is the way. A sustainable culture of peace can only be established by nonviolence that absolutely respects human dignity. Rooted in the interconnectedness of God's creation, it also opens the way to an "integral ecology," as expressed by Pope Francis in *Laudato Si'*. Violence undermines this interconnectedness. Nonviolence sustains it. Nonviolence teaches us to say "no" to an inhuman social order and "yes" to the fullness of life.

This is a spiritual reality, but also a practical truth. Over the past century nonviolent practice has increasingly been applied successfully inside and outside the Church to transform lives and to create change. We rejoice in the rich concrete experiences of people engaged in work for just peace around the world, many of whose stories we heard during this gathering. They illuminate the creativity and power of nonviolent practices in many different situations of potential or actual violent conflict. Moreover, credible empirical research into nonviolent and violent conflict in the twentieth century has confirmed that major nonviolent resistance campaigns were found to be twice as effective as violent (or armed) campaigns. And even when they fail, the consequences of their failure are not as disastrous as the consequences of violent approaches.

For the Church, alleviating human suffering is not a pretext, but a moral duty. As Christians we must not "stand idly by the blood of a neighbor" (Leviticus 19:16). We have a duty to protect the life of our neighbor with every tool of nonviolence available to us. In the same way, we have a duty to prevent violence, preserve just peace, and promote reconciliation.

Actively embracing the nonviolent way in the Church and the world

We encourage the Church as institution and people of God to a deeper understanding of and commitment to active nonviolence – following Jesus, embodiment of the nonviolent God, crucified and risen, who taught us to love our enemies (Matthew 5: 44), to put down our sword (Matthew 26: 52), to offer no violent resistance to the one who does evil (Matthew 5: 39), and to not kill. This commitment to nonviolence is formed of compassion and nourished by Eucharist, enabling a nonviolent encounter with the broken heart of God. Through him we discover and apply concrete ways to embrace nonviolence as a core teaching of our faith; to resist violence without violence; to put the power of love into action; and to develop the virtue of nonviolent peacemaking.

In this kairos moment, we strongly urge the Church to bring nonviolence from the periphery of Catholic thought on war and peace to the center - to mainstream nonviolence as a spirituality, lifestyle, a program of societal action, and a universal ethic.

As we recommit ourselves to furthering Catholic understanding and practice of active nonviolence on the road to just peace, and challenged again by stories of hope and courage in these days together, we call on the Church we love:

- to recognize that the Church – ordinary people, saints and martyrs – have done much to promote peace and nonviolence, while confessing the past and present complicity of our Church with cultural, structural and direct violence; to restructure relationships in the Church to just partnerships; and to embrace an ethic of nonviolence as the pathway to genuine and enduring reconciliation, in fidelity to the consistent call of Christ in every situation of conflict;

- to root our conversion to nonviolence in the intense experiences of those most affected by violence – women, youth, migrants and the earth itself – and to recognize that their sufferings are an urgent call to that conversion process;

- to integrate Gospel nonviolence at every level of the Church – dioceses, parishes, families and the "domestic Church," religious orders, seminaries, universities, and schools – through formation, preaching, pastoral life, advocacy, research, and education, with particular attention to developing nonviolence and peace studies programs in all Catholic universities;

- to commit to a nonviolent just peace ethic for Catholic teaching on sustainable peace and conflict, violence and war; to include in the Catechism of the Catholic Church a definition of nonviolence, key nonviolent practices, and the norms of a just peace ethic;

- to advocate for increased public and private, intellectual and financial investment in education for nonviolence and in key nonviolent practices such as restorative justice, nonviolent communication, unarmed civilian protection, trauma-healing, nonviolent resistance, and nonviolent civilian-based defense;

- to consider poor and suffering people, especially those in violent conflicts, as the first persons to be protected by nonviolence and a theology of peace, even as we will seek to protect all people;

- to promote integral disarmament for humanitarian purposes – eliminating weapons already banned and nuclear weapons, continuously reducing all arms and weapons, and ending the development and production of new weapons systems;

- to consider nonviolence as a necessary condition of integral human development, as well as an ecological and social way of mutual relationship and mutual hospitality;

- to initiate a global conversation on nonviolence within the Church, with people of other faiths, and with the larger world to respond to the crises of our time with the vision and methodology of nonviolence;

- to contribute to an ecumenical theology of peace, promoting dialogue between believers and all people working for a peaceful world.

In every age, the Holy Spirit graces the Church with the wisdom to respond to the challenges of its time. In response to what is a global epidemic of violence, we are being called again and again to invoke, pray over, teach, and take decisive action in the spirit of Jesus's nonviolence. Nonviolence is at the heart of the Gospel. It is the calling of the Church. It is not passive or naïve. It is a way of faith and action. It is an effective alternative. It is a constructive force to protect all people and our common home. It includes a broad spectrum of approaches and activities. It is the core of a new moral framework. It is essential to integral human development and at the heart of a culture of peace. It is at the core of the witness and action of Jesus and many who have come after him, including Saints Francis and Clare of Assisi, Mohandas Gandhi, Martin Luther King Jr, Dorothy Day, Beatus Franz Jägerstätter, Saint Oscar Romero, Berta Caceres, Lanza del Vasto, Wangari Muta Maathai, and the many people involved in nonviolent social movements.

In a violent world, nonviolence nurtures hope. Actively embracing the way of nonviolence can renew the Church and invite the entire world to discover the powerful hope of creative nonviolent solutions to the monumental challenges of our time.

Appendix 3

Ten elements of nonviolence

Many understandings of nonviolence have been put forward. Nonviolence is the love that does justice (Martin Luther King, Jr.); it transforms power (Alternatives to Violence); it is co-operative power (Jonathan Schell); and it is love in action (Dorothy Day). It is a force for transformation, justice and the well-being of all that is neither violent nor passive (*Pace e Bene*). It is a stand against violence without violence (Stellan Vinthagen). It is an active form of resistance to systems of privilege and domination, a philosophy for liberation, an approach to movement building, a method of non-co-operation and a practice we can employ to transform the world (War Resisters League).

Each of these can be crystallised in the following basic definition: Nonviolence is a constructive force, an active method and a powerful way of life that challenges violence without using violence, transforms and resolves conflict, fosters just and peaceful alternatives and seeks the well-being of all.

While this description of nonviolence can stand on its own, it can also be seen as embedded in a comprehensive framework that illuminates the depth and breadth of this term. This framework includes the following 10 elements.

- Nonviolence in its most encompassing sense denotes a paradigm of the fullness of life that challenges systemic violence — including all forms of injustice — and actively works for the well-being of all.

- Nonviolent change is possible because it is the human default, not the exception. As Prof. Michael Nagler has written, echoing Gandhi, "Nonviolence is the law of our species," which means that, even deeper than our tendencies towards violence and the scripts that reinforce it, we have a profound unity from which flows our capacity for co-operation, collaboration, and well-being for all.

- Nonviolence is a core capacity that integrates humanity's immense longing for justice with its deep capacity for love. Though it has often been dormant, suppressed or undervalued, nonviolence has always been a core power, potential and practice of the human species to challenge violence, including the violence of injustice, and to create constructive options.

- Nonviolence combines non-co-operation with violence with steadfast regard for the opponent as a human being. It is the process of mobilising the unifying power of empathy, mercy, humility, forgiveness, inclusiveness, creativity, relentless persistence and indomitable courage, and stands in contrast to the destructive power of violence in all its dimensions — direct, cultural and structural — that threatens, dominates, defeats, destroys and separates.

- Nonviolence is a third way beyond fight (action-reaction) or flight (silent submission) when confronting violence, oppression and repression. As Joan Morera Perich, SJ writes, "This third way is a path that requires great lucidity, creativity, faith, and constancy." (*Dismantling the Hells. Practicing the Nonviolence of Jesus Today*, Christianity and Justice Study Center).

- Nonviolence is the power of creative love in action in contrast to the power of fear, hatred and greed. Nonviolence is an orientation, a set of principles, methods, and specific approaches that put this power of love into practice. Love, in this context, is the process of acknowledging, safeguarding and engaging with the humanness, woundedness and sacredness of others, while creatively challenging their violence and injustice. Nonviolence challenges the power of and belief in violence and its destructiveness geared towards threatening, dominating or defeating others. Nonviolence, by contrast, is a form of unifying power: connecting, compassionate, communicative and creative.

- Nonviolence has increasingly been unleashed to create powerful social change. As Gandhi said, "Nonviolence is as old as the hills." Humanity has been exercising this power from its beginning, and has therefore survived and transformed the destructiveness of escalating and retaliatory violence. Beginning in the 20th century, this momentum accelerated with Gandhi's application of nonviolence to win Indian independence and with the use of disciplined nonviolence by the U.S. civil rights movement. These and other pioneering campaigns have inspired countless nonviolent struggles. Some examples include successful pro-democracy movements in Spain and Portugal (1970s), the Philippines (1986), Chile (1980s), Argentina (1980s), Soviet bloc states including the Velvet Revolution in Czechoslovakia, Poland, East Germany, etc. (1989); the thwarted coup in the USSR (1991); South Africa (1980s-1990s); Indonesia (1998); East Timor (2000); Serbia (2000); Georgia (2003); Ukraine (2004); Liberia (2005); and Tunisia and Egypt (2011). These are not isolated cases. The Global Nonviolent Action Database has documented over 1,000 nonviolent campaigns, with many of them successfully achieving their objectives.

- But nonviolence is not limited to civil resistance or large-scale social change. It is a transformative process applicable to all dimensions of life. It is personal, interpersonal and social-structural. It mobilises nonviolent approaches, nonviolent resistance and nonviolent action for social change — but also the everyday techniques and practices of nonviolence, including nonviolent communication, compassionate listening, restorative justice peace circles, peaceful parenting, trauma healing, anti-racism training, diplomacy and nonviolent community-building for personal and interpersonal transformation. It is a method that can be used to change policies and conditions, to protect the vulnerable and to respond to the crises of one's time. It is a virtue and force for good that, for many, is a way of life and a spiritual journey.

- Nonviolence is the process of building the infrastructure for nonviolent lives, relationships, communities, cultures and world. It includes education and training; violence prevention and intervention; restorative and distributive justice; just peace and just peace approaches, including nonviolent peacemaking, peacebuilding, unarmed civilian protection and civilian-based defence; nonviolent action and social movement-building; and the long-term process of fostering just civil societies and cultures of peace and nonviolence. Nonviolence mobilises these dimensions, seeking to end injustice and foster reconciliation, to resist war and build peace, to safeguard the infinite worth of all human persons and to care for the earth and its teeming inhabitants.

- Nonviolence is a process of growth and transformation. Nonviolence calls us to acknowledge our violence and to grapple with it; to grow beyond our belief in violence; to break the cycles of retaliatory violence; to pursue nonviolent options and justice for all with humility, compassion, openness and determination; and to put our nonviolent power and potential into practice in our lives and our world here and now, and going forward.

BS - #0007 - 210621 - C0 - 210/148/18 - PB - 9781784567163 - Gloss Lamination